The Knight's Tale

Dr Charles Moseley was educated at Queens' College, Cambridge. He has been by turns a printer, publisher and schoolmaster and is now lecturer in English at Magdalene College, Cambridge, where he attempts to cajole undergraduates into taking the Middle Ages seriously. He has published (apart from school editions of several of Shakespeare's plays) a number of articles on medieval and Renaissance topics which are mostly buried in journals of august obscurity. He has also edited *The Travels of Sir John Mandeville* for Penguin Classics and commentaries on *The Pardoner's Tale* and Shakespeare's history plays for the Masterstudies series.

Penguin Masterstudies
Joint Advisory Editors:
Stephen Coote and Bryan Loughrey

Chaucer

The Knight's Tale

C. W. R. D. Moseley

Penguin Books

Penguin Books Ltd, Harmondsworth, Middlesex, England
Viking Penguin Inc., 40 West 23rd Street, New York, New York 10010, U.S.A.
Penguin Books Australia Ltd, Ringwood, Victoria, Australia
Penguin Books Canada Limited, 2801 John Street, Markham, Ontario, Canada L3R 1B4
Penguin Books (N.Z.) Ltd, 182–190 Wairau Road, Auckland 10, New Zealand

First published 1987

The text of *The Knight's Tale* used here is that
published in 1940 by J. M. Manly and E. Rickert,
and is reproduced by permission of the
University of Chicago Press

Made and printed in Great Britain by
Richard Clay (The Chaucer Press) Ltd, Bungay, Suffolk
Filmset in Monophoto Times by
Northumberland Press Ltd, Gateshead, Tyne and Wear

Contents

Preface

Reading a poem some six hundred years old is not a simple task. The language presents an immediate difficulty which has to be overcome by sheer hard labour – for if we do not understand what the words mean we shall understand very little else. This job is so taxing that when it has been done we might be tempted to think that our difficulties are over: yet they have only just begun. Any great work of art of any period is not only something which is composed for all subsequent time; it is based on assumptions about man, his art, the universe he lives in, his language and the values which the author and his contemporary audience share. Though a work of art may well modify those assumptions, the fact remains that they will never exactly coincide with our own, and we need to know what they were as precisely as we can. Behind the obvious problem of what the words mean, then, lies a second and much more radical problem of what concepts and values those words represented and how these interrelated both in the artist's mind and in the minds of his audience. So far as we are able – if we are honestly interested in what an ancient author said rather than in making him parrot our own preoccupations – we have to take the trouble to learn his language and to understand the way he thought. As Pope put it in the *Essay on Criticism*:

> Know well each ANCIENT'S proper character,
> His Fable, Subject, scope in ev'ry page,
> Religion, Country, genius of his Age:
> Without all these at once before your eyes,
> Cavil you may, but never criticise.

We shall to a greater or lesser degree get much of this wrong, of course, for we can't simply un-live the centuries that have made us what we are, and, in addition, our knowledge of what it was like to be a fourteenth-century man or woman must necessarily be incomplete. Nevertheless, if the effort is made we shall find that we gain a deeper knowledge of what it is to be human, of the nature of this puzzle of existence; the old values and ideas will test our own. We may well decide that our current assumptions must be provisional, and we may even be forced to realize that we hold some of them for no better reason than that we have grown up with them. We must assume – and there is good evidence for this – that our ancestors were at least as intelligent and capable of sophisticated discussion and thought as we are. Ideas and values cannot be dismissed simply because they are old: frequently (and unconsciously) we patronize the past through a chronological snobbery of just this sort. (Ironically, Chaucer's own generation would have made the opposite assumption, though he is somewhat quizzical about this: that the past was wiser than the present.) We ourselves are living in a historical period that will soon be misinterpreted, and it is not self-evident that the twentieth century has got it right where the fourteenth or earlier centuries got it wrong. The easiest way of reaching a balanced view is to realize that, as L. P. Hartley said, 'the past is another country: they do things differently there'. Medieval art is not like modern art, yet the central issues that human beings face – love, suffering, death, and what it all means – remain common to all peoples and all times. Art, theology and philosophy face these central enigmas and each of us, as an individual, experiences them. News from another land may influence the way we cultivate our own.

The Knight's Tale is a major poem in its own right, as well as being part of another major poem, *The Canterbury Tales*. As such, it needs a fairly wide-ranging discussion before we examine it closely. It is also, in all probability, the first poem of Chaucer's that readers of this present work will have encountered; it may well be the last. No apology is needed, therefore, for attempting to provide a context for it in some detail.

Magdalene College, Cambridge　　　　　　　　　　　　　C.W.R.D.M.
Maundy Thursday, 1985

Acknowledgements

Any editor's debts to his predecessors' work must of course be huge, and it is impossible to catalogue them all. In the preparation of this edition I owe special thanks to Richard Verity and Rupert Preston-Bell, who suffered an early version of the Introduction; and Krishnan Venkatesh's acute criticism of the manuscript drew my attention to several areas of weakness. Stephen Siddall, the head of the English Department of The Leys School, Cambridge, made many helpful comments. My thanks are due also to my son, who helped to reduce paternal ramblings to a coherent text. I am also particularly indebted to Dr Stephen Coote for the constant encouragement he gave me while the manuscript was being turned into a book. Errors that remain are, of course, my own.

Note: References to works of Chaucer apart from *The Knight's Tale* are to *The Works of Geoffrey Chaucer*, ed. F. N. Robinson (second edition, Oxford, 1957), the most generally available complete modern edition.

The passage from Langland's *The Vision of Piers Plowman* (B text) is quoted from the edition published by J. M. Dent in their Everyman's University Library, edited by A. V. C. Schmidt, and is reprinted by permission.

Introduction

This introduction makes no pretence to settle all the issues in *The Knight's Tale*. That would be folly. Men have argued and talked and written about the poem for several centuries and show no signs of stopping. What I propose to do here is to provide some basic contexts against which the work may be read, suggest some lines of approach that must be tested against each person's reading of it, and explore all these in the Commentary. Describing these contexts means starting some way from the Tale, and from *The Canterbury Tales* as a whole.

1. Chaucer: Brief Life

No one has yet written a satisfactory biography of Geoffrey Chaucer, and I doubt whether one will ever appear. The fact is that we know enough of him to be tantalized into suppositions about his character and career, but not enough to be sure we are not making up a portrait of him that is a reflection of ourselves. Much of our idea of him comes from his works, giving flesh to the scanty facts of the documentary evidence, but the inferences we draw must be used with great caution. The 'Geffrey' or the 'I' who often appears in the poems is just as much a creation – and just as distant from the author – as Arcite, Troilus, or Robin the Miller, and any relation of this figure to the real Chaucer is oblique.

Before we go further, we ought anyway to ask whether a picture of him – or any artist – as a person is necessary to appreciation of his poetry. For most serious artists before the nineteenth century, a poem is an artefact, like a kettle or teapot, which must stand on its own feet independently of our knowledge of its author. If we have to appeal to the detailed character of the author to explain or justify the poem, it is probably not much good – though it may still be interesting. Chaucer designed his poems as serious games, whose totality comprises their meaning, to be enjoyed and to be studied; if we use them to hunt the 'real Chaucer' or assume any one aspect represents what 'he' thought or did, we shall not only fail in our search but make the poem do what it was never designed to do. To use the poems as a way of charting his psyche is to belittle their integrity as constructed wholes. Knowledge of the author's (and therefore the poems') context, on the other hand, is absolutely central.

The biographical facts, however, point to the intellectual and social context. As far as can be ascertained, Geoffrey Chaucer was born about 1340 or just after, the son of a prosperous London vintner with minor

Court employment. The family may have originated in Ipswich. It has been suggested that he attended the school attached to St Paul's Cathedral; certainly in his early years he acquired a facility in French and Latin, and caught the taste for reading that the Eagle in *The House of Fame* (655ff.) makes fun of. Whatever happened later, his basic education would have consisted of a grounding in grammar – that is, in the literal understanding of languages followed by a careful and systematic interpretative study of major Latin authors. It would also have included rhetoric – the art of speaking and composition, which was, like grammar, carefully systematized, and developed an understanding of the structures into which words can be put and of the purpose of those structures. Finally there was dialectic – the art of discussion and the beginnings of logic. If Chaucer did start in this way, a bright boy of his station might well have followed an academic career and eventually taken orders. He might even have become a prelate of importance, as Wolsey, son of an Ipswich butcher, was to do later. His poems certainly indicate an interest in matters theological and political. Or he could equally well have become a don at Cambridge or Oxford. Why he did not, we do not know. (There is an old and respectable tradition that for a time he was a law student at one of the Inns of Court, possibly in the 1360s.) In fact, Chaucer is a representative of a new phenomenon in medieval society: the literate layman who is neither cleric nor lawyer. This class grew considerably in the next century, to include merchants, craftsmen and yeomen. From such people a new type of audience and market for literature grew – a group that could read as well as listen, and to cater for which, perhaps, the first secular English lending library was set up in the early fifteenth century.

We next hear of Chaucer in 1357 as a page in the household of the Countess of Ulster, wife of Edward III's third son, Lionel of Clarence. This introduction to Court life set the pattern for Chaucer's future, and it is an interesting example of the considerable social mobility of the fourteenth century. He grew to be a useful and trusted courtier and, when taken prisoner near Reims in 1360 on one of the campaigns of what was to become the Hundred Years War, he was valuable enough for the king himself to contribute the large sum of £16 towards his ransom. Soon after, he acted as a diplomatic courier during the negotiations leading up to the Peace of Bretigny (1360). Seven years later we find him in the king's service and being described, in a grant of a life pension, as 'our beloved servant' (*dilectus vallectus noster*): kings were liberal then with their endearments. The next ten years seem to have been spent in diplomatic business of one sort or another. He made at least two journeys to Italy. The first, of crucial importance to his intellectual and poetic development, was to Genoa and

Florence in 1373. The second was to Milan in 1378, to negotiate with Bernabo Visconti and Sir John Hawkwood. (He may also have been there ten years earlier, just after Lionel's brief second marriage to the daughter of Gian Galeazzo Visconti.) A Spanish journey has been suggested in connection with the marriage of Edward's fourth son, John of Gaunt, to the heiress of Castile. Chaucer certainly went to Flanders and Paris. It is clear that he was being employed on more and more diplomatic business of a delicate nature, such as royal marriages and the conducting of the king's campaigns. He had also been holding, since 1374, the Controllership of Customs and Subsidy of Wools, Skins and Hides in the Port of London, a lucrative civil service job he performed through a deputy from 1377. A picture thus emerges of a young man of affairs rapidly rising in the governmental machine of the time, a man whose services were appreciated and who won his contemporaries' respect, and sometimes, perhaps, their jealousy. There are some indications that during the long minority of Richard II, from 1377 to 1389, Chaucer's rise was blocked by the faction controlled by Thomas of Gloucester, another of Edward's seven sons, who, with his surviving brothers Edmund of York and John of Gaunt, was running the kingdom – and not very harmoniously at that. It may have been Gloucester's influence that ensured that Chaucer, by now living in Kent, was Member of Parliament for that county for only a single year (1386). It could also explain why Chaucer ceased to be Controller of Customs in that year. Only when Richard assumed control in 1389 did Chaucer begin to receive new preferments. He was then given the job – which he held for nearly two years – of looking after building and repair works in the king's palaces. He thus became a sort of one-man Department of the Environment. On leaving (or losing) this job, another royal appointment followed: the deputy forestership of North Petherton in Somerset. How much of his time this took up is not known; it did not stop him from being active in Kent and being often at Court. Royal favour continued right up to the moment of Richard's deposition by the son of John of Gaunt, Henry IV, in 1399. And the new king continued his predecessors' favour to Chaucer, who moved to a house in the garden of Westminster Abbey. He lived there for less than a year before his death in October 1400.

This summary reads blandly, and fails to satisfy our curiosity. We see a successful public man, a hard enough operator to be given tough jobs, but these records tell us nothing of Chaucer the poet. We find him involved in legal wrangles and cases, including (in 1380) the problematical action brought by an unknown Cecily Chaumpaigne for *raptus*. That this means actual physical rape is unlikely; it is far more probable that it means abduction in order to force an heiress into a marriage profitable to one of the abductors. We don't know. Nor do we know much about the private life of Chaucer and his family. He married, possibly as early as 1366, Philippa de Roet, daughter of a Flemish knight. Her sister Katherine, after being left a widow on the death of Sir Hugh Swynford, became John of Gaunt's mistress and eventually his third wife. From her descended the Beauforts, through whom Henry Tudor derived what Plantagenet blood he had. It has been suggested that John was on very intimate terms with Philippa, but the only evidence for this is suppositious and is based on odd payments of money by John to Philippa and her husband. Princes – even highly-sexed ones – ought to be allowed at times to be merely benevolent. However, this marriage with a member of the important Flemish presence at Court (Edward's queen was Flemish) can't have done Chaucer any political harm; nor can the association with John of Gaunt, who eventually became Chaucer's patron and, it seems, his friend. We don't know whether the marriage was happy or not – the joking references in *The House of Fame*, *The Book of the Duchess* and elsewhere to himself as a henpecked husband are not necessarily to be taken as reliable, any more than modern mother-in-law jokes are evidence that all mothers-in-law are like Giles's Grandma. If it were true that Philippa was a scold the whole Court would have known it, given the lack of privacy in living conditions, and Chaucer's jokes would have fallen pretty flat. It is almost certain that there were children, and that the Thomas Chaucer who in 1413 took on the forestership of North Petherton was the poet's son. Chaucer's granddaughter, Alice, married first the Earl of Salisbury and later the Duke of Suffolk.

All we can say is that here is a man on familiar terms with the great in a society that, despite its hierarchical structure, was in many ways much more intimate and socially mobile than our own – it was certainly much smaller. Chaucer's acquaintance with its values and customs is everywhere apparent, and it is evident that he perceived it (as we do our own) through its own conventions. Chaucer was clearly in a position where he would probably have known everybody who was anybody in a number of different fields. His literary acquaintance certainly extended beyond England and included the important French poet Eustache Deschamps (who speaks of him with respect), and probably Guillaume de Machault. His Italian journeys may well have led to meetings with Petrarch and Boccaccio; there is no evidence one way or the other. He certainly read their books, as he did those of Dante. The inevitability of personal, literary, political and social contact in this sort of career should alert us to the probability that in the poetry there will be a vein of often complex allusiveness essential to its proper understanding.

Chaucer's greatness as a poet was recognized by his contemporaries, if the testimony of Occleve and Deschamps is anything to go by. His influence was huge in the next century, and references to him are common. Yet there is something odd about many of these references; they praise him for none of the things we find so admirable in him – his wit, his capacity for formal construction, his humanity, his profundity, and so on. Rather they concentrate, almost with a note of awed gratitude, on him as a master practitioner of the admired art of rhetoric (see p. 18f.), and even more as the creator of a poetic language for English-speaking men. This oddity, when we pursue it, leads us into a fuller understanding of the magnitude of Chaucer's achievement.

2. Linguistic and Literary Context

When Chaucer was very young, English culture (which is not to say it should be distinguished from an international culture centred on the Courts of European nobles and princes) employed three languages. Latin, with the enormous prestige of a direct link back to the great works of the Classical past (giants on whose shoulders modern dwarfs rode, so it was said), was the language of scholarship, learning and the Church. Still a spoken and living language of vast resource, it had about it an aura of permanence and solidity. French was the everyday language of English polite society, though it was a French that Parisians regarded as barbarous, descending as it did from the Norman French introduced by the Conquest in 1066. It was just as artificial as the French used in polite society in nineteenth-century Russia. After the first generation of Normans, French was never a cradle language; English wives and nurses spoke to their infants in what was to become English. When in 1285 Walter of Bibbesworth wrote a French primer for the three daughers of an earl, he assumed English was their natural language. The language was acquired because it was necessary if one was not to be excluded from the society of people who mattered in public and private life. Law proceedings were in French (some of our legal terms, such as 'tort', still are), and French was the language of high culture. Like Latin, French continued to be an international language – literally a *lingua franca* – and a man from the north of England who might speak Anglo-Norman could travel to Spain or southern France and still make himself understood and in his turn, find himself able to understand – very useful at a period when the kings of England had large domains, and even larger claims, on the continent. French literature, too, was the most adventurous in Europe, and expressed the ideals of a highly cultured and much imitated Court society. English, finally, was the everyday workhorse: indispensable, and spoken from infancy. Nevertheless, its development had been profoundly affected by the specialized use of Latin and French. Quite a lot of good English poetry dates from before Chaucer's time (and there is evidence of much that has been lost), but the resources of the language and its forms do not stand comparison with those of contemporary French writing. Only in one area was literary English developed as a fine and precise tool of utterance: in the prose sermon, and in religious writing for a heterogeneous audience. These are highly specialized forms whose conventions and tones are so instantly recognizable (even today, when we listen to very few sermons) that they can't be used for other purposes without awkwardness. Even the raciness of some of the *exempla* (stories which prove a moral point) in the sermons is a specifically applied technique.

This state of affairs had gone on for two hundred and fifty years or more, and certain consequences naturally followed. Languages grow and change with use and time. Syntactical structures are not immutable, and new words are created to cope with new ideas; but if for over two hundred years a culture has been carrying out all its literary experimentation in French, and has been coping in French with new experiences and ideas, it follows that English will, in the end, be nothing like as versatile a tool as French. And this is precisely what happened. There were simply areas of experience and concern an Englishman of the early fourteenth century could not discuss in English, particularly in a written English prose whose range and resources were severely limited. Moreover, men recognized that certain things were appropriate to each language, and kept them separate. For example, when in 1356 Henry of Lancaster, John of Gaunt's father-in-law, came to write his little book of devotions, the *Livre de Seyntz Medecines*, he felt he had to write it in French, even though, not being a literary sort of man, he had little experience of writing in the language. The choice of language thus indicated the kind of audience you were aiming at, as the use of French, Latin and English in the three huge poems of Chaucer's friend, John Gower, implied.

Chaucer was of the last generation to enjoy this trilingual resource. The status of French was extremely vulnerable, since it was a taught language. Remove the teachers, and farewell to French. Furthermore, in 1348 came the Black Death. Over Europe as a whole, up to a third of the population died; in some areas, more. But that average hides an uncomfortable anomaly. There is evidence that the clergy, for example, were hit disproportionately hard – possibly because of their pastoral duties, often performed with exemplary courage, possibly because many of them lived a communal life in schools, colleges and monasteries, thus making life easier for the less athletic fleas. And it was the clergy who were the teachers. In 1315 Ranulf Higden, the historian, wrote that in England boys learnt Latin through French; in 1384 John of Trevisa, translating Higden into English, comments on this passage: 'before the first outbreak of the Black Death this was so, but nowadays children know no more French than the heel of their left shoe'. The decline in French was rapid. It virtually died out as a common medium in a single generation. In 1362 Parliament was for the first time opened by a Speech from the Throne delivered in English. In the same year, again for the first time, law court proceedings were allowed in English. By 1400 French as a common language was a memory.

This change had disastrous effects. Englishmen were cut off from the polite culture not only of Europe but also of their own land. They were faced with the problem of coping with a society that had been shaped and explained by the concepts, thoughts and language of the past two hundred years without any language in which they could discuss it. Imagine the problems a modern man might face if he had to live in today's world without using a single word, concept, expression or sentence structure that was not in use in the time of Defoe, Swift and Pope.

The problem was obvious, and the solution presented another one. The solution was, of course, the wholesale translation of French works into English, and in terms of quantity the major literary activity of the latter half of the fourteenth century in England was simply translation. But translation, even if we understand that term to include (as did the medievals) a free re-working of the original, raises the awesome problem that there simply were not enough words or structures in the English language. One therefore sees in the work of the translators an extensive adoption and naturalization of French words, phrases and structures – the creation, in fact, of a versatile literary English. It is against this background that the praise of Chaucer by his successors as 'grand translateur' must be seen; and it makes very good sense. As a master of the art of rhetoric, thoroughly conversant with the best Italian and French poetry, he vastly extended the range of what could be said in English. Almost certainly he knew Dante's *De Volgari Eloquentia*, and the theoretical arguments in it for a highly developed literary vernacular which could stand comparison with Latin. Chaucer provided, in effect, a poetic language on which many writers in the next century and a half could build. He also wrote poetry that could challenge comparison with the best that had been written in French up to that date. Finally, as well as giving

England a distinct and viable poetic language, he kept its culture firmly in touch with the Court culture of the continent.

No man could take on such a task without a pretty confident view of his own powers and performance. As we shall see in *The Knight's Tale*, Chaucer frequently suggests to us that we might watch not only what he is doing but how he is doing it – he is inviting us to watch the process of literary composition. He often deliberately breaks his illusion to suggest that we should think about how it is being created, and what our (and his) relationship to it is. Throughout his career he maintains this interest in the problematical nature of our response to fiction and its relation to truth.

3. The Relationship to the Audience:
Rhetoric and the Narrator

Obviously this sophistication of approach on Chaucer's part presupposes that his audience will be able to match it with an equally sophisticated response. He presumes an audience that knows something about poetry and art, and his relationship with that audience is crucial. Many of his first audiences would have known Chaucer personally, and how he presents himself as a narrator is therefore important. There is no doubt that much medieval poetry was 'performed' – that is, it was read aloud to the assembled company by the poet as an entertainment. Two implications follow from this. In the first place, the way in which you tell a story when your audience can only take it in by ear will be very different from the way in which you tell it to a single reader. The latter can put the book down, go and get a drink, turn back a few pages to check something, and generally absorb it at his own speed. The listener cannot, and the poet must make absolutely sure that all key points are firmly and unambiguously conveyed. He must signpost his narrative clearly so that people do not grasp the wrong end of the stick, and he must repeat crucial ideas to fix them firmly in the minds of an audience of very mixed and uneven intellectual attainment. The medieval and Classical art of rhetoric is composed precisely of techniques designed to achieve these ends in the most efficient and pleasing way. Ancient writers – Cicero, for example – had defined the purpose of rhetoric as to please, to instruct and to persuade or move. These aims are of equal importance: without pleasure you get nowhere, but you need somewhere to go. The practice of specialized arts of rhetoric was still continuing in Chaucer's day. His friend Eustache Deschamps wrote a very clever *Art de Dictier* which indicates just how sophisticated poet and audience were expected to be. Rhetorical devices and figures were not purely ornamental but severely practical, as can be seen throughout the work of Chaucer and his contemporaries. He clearly indicates the major divisions of his narrative; he tells you when he is leaving one topic and turning to another; he repeats himself in all sorts of different and entertaining ways, and he amplifies his narrative wittily and resourcefully to ensure that the listener can follow it. Often, as we see in *The Knight's Tale*, he deliberately builds important sections into easily remembered structures (often symbolic) which in retrospect provide a key to the narrative's form and meaning.*

Many technical devices designed for these ends are described in the arts of rhetoric. We shall deal in detail with these figures in the Commentary below; the key compositional idea is expressed in a phrase of Geoffroi de Vinsauf, whose *Poetria Nova* Chaucer tells us he knew: *varius sis et semper idem* – roughly translated, 'keep saying the same thing in different ways'. Now this sounds to us like an infallible recipe for tedium, and indeed it can be in the work of a poor poet. The art lies in amplifying in such a way that the repetition not only fixes the basic idea but modifies our first view of it. Of this Chaucer is a master. One of the key differences between medieval and modern fiction rests here, in the way the audience is envisaged, and in the loose and discursive narrative structure devised to meet its requirements. Generally speaking – and *The Knight's Tale* is no exception to this – medieval narrative is designed serially and paratactically: that is, as a series of narrative blocks, often complex in structure, linked together by the voice of a narrator.

But there is a further dimension to this issue. In the manuscript of *Troilus and Criseyde* in Corpus Christi College, Cambridge, there is an illumination of Chaucer reading his poem from a sort of pulpit to an assembly of courtiers, and it has been assumed that this represents an invariable practice. This may be misleading, and it is hard to see how even Chaucer would have had the stamina to read the whole of *Troilus and Criseyde* aloud. It is clear that reading to an audience did not preclude private reading by an individual; quite apart from evidence elsewhere, there are numerous instances where Chaucer not only tells us that he reads privately (and obsessively, in poor light) but also clearly envisages his own poem as being read by single readers – for example, in *Troilus and Criseyde*, V. 270. Now it is obvious that a listener's experience of a poem will not necessarily coincide with that of a reader – the way it is taken in affects what it is. It is also obvious that a listener may read a poem he has already heard, and because he has had an earlier experience of it he will not

* He can also joke about these skills, as at the end of *The Squire's Tale*, or in *The Franklin's Prologue* – a joke that in fact uses the very techniques it affects to send up.

respond to it in the same way. I would suggest that Chaucer was very well aware of this. He was aware that his poems when read would modify his poems when heard, and he directs our attention to the problem of how we perceive them. Thus, in addition to the narrative devices demanded by a delivery that in theory at least was oral, we shall find in *The Knight's Tale* other signposts that could only be appreciated by a reader with the text in front of him. One of the things Chaucer was interested in throughout his career was the way in which language and form modify what we call fact, how our knowledge – of nature, of ourselves, of the past – is rarely objective but is modified by the way we see it and the language in which it has been presented to us.

A fine example of this occurs in *The House of Fame*. There Chaucer summarizes accurately the tragic story of Dido and Aeneas from Virgil's *Aeneid*. Virgil's description is grand and moving; Chaucer, by simply shifting its rhetorical register, putting it into an inappropriately light-weight form (the octosyllabic couplet) and using trivial language makes it ludicrously sentimental and fit only for the pages of a teenage romance magazine. Though the story-line is identical, the stories themselves could not be more different. In *The Knight's Tale* Chaucer has built in clues that will make us, on reading or reflection, modify our first understanding of the story and, I would suggest, impose on it a perspective that seriously alters what we thought was its meaning. Yet both our first understanding (as we read the Tale sequentially) and our second (as we look back on it as a whole) are 'true'. The clash of our second view with our first forces us to think about the reliability of our perception ... the problem is delectable.

The second implication of Chaucer's relationship with his audience is also important. These people had reason to know that the man standing in front of them was anything but a nincompoop. Yet the picture Chaucer gives of himself in much of his verse is of a comic figure, a clumsy lover, a coward, a moral idiot. He puts himself in all sorts of ludicrous positions – as when the Eagle in *The House of Fame* carries him off, squeaking like a rabbit, in his talons, or when he makes unflattering comparisons for himself. He even has his own creation, the Host of *The Canterbury Tales*, patronize the comic distortion of himself he writes into his own story. Why? There is clearly no possibility that the audience would take this seriously. The probable explanation is complex. Firstly, the arts of rhetoric advocated that to win an audience's sympathy and attention one should employ the device of *diminutio* – that is, a conventional modesty, like the phrase 'unaccustomed as I am to public speaking' when it is employed by a practised and fluent debater. Chaucer's presentation of himself is to some degree a development of this *diminutio*. Secondly, it is a good joke for an audience that knows the real Chaucer and knows that *he* knows he isn't the clot he makes himself out to be. Chaucer goes even further. In *The Legend of Good Women* (F416) the poet who, in his own poem, makes his creation say he is a poor poet is deliberately expecting the audience to recognize the irony, and is thereby drawing attention to the very real artistry of the work. Thirdly, the egregious incongruence between the clever poet who wrote the poem and the presentation of himself as a comic figure within it (as in *The Canterbury Tales*) forces the audience to recognize that they cannot take at face value anything put into the mouth of the comic character. So when this comic mask (the Latin word is *persona*) tells you that he said he agreed with the Monk's scandalous views in the *General Prologue*, you are forced by that agreement to look at those views for yourself.* And you will not agree with the persona. The most radical effect of this narratorial persona is to give Chaucer a device for the moral placing of what he is saying, a means of making us think and value for ourselves. He shuts off the options he does not want to take up by making them ridiculous, or by putting them into the mouth of an individual who lacks sense and taste.

The narrator of *The Knight's Tale* is not developed to this extremely subtle extent. Nevertheless his conventional modesty, which appears, for example, at the beginning of the Tale (27ff.), and his frequent interventions, remind us that we are dealing with an artificial structure that cannot be taken simply at its face value. The manipulation of the narrator into tasteless or inappropriate remarks forces the audience to rely on their own judgement.

4. Expectations of Poetry, Theories of Fiction

The audience sitting down to hear (or to read) a poem in Chaucer's day had certain expectations and assumptions about poetry and art. They would, for instance, have a great reverence for the literature and thought of the past. 'Auctoritee', a word Chaucer frequently uses, means more than just 'authority'. It extends that concept to cover moral worth, rightness and value. A new author was at pains to link his present work with the thought and letters of the past from which it was widely agreed the present had so evidently declined. Originality, in our sense of saying something new, would have completely mystified them. For them, originality consisted not in inventing a plot, but in redirecting and re-using

* Since the Monk did not exist, such agreement is in any case logically impossible – *The Canterbury Tales* is not journalism.

an old one. New knowledge and wisdom grew out of old. As Christians, they believed that all human history was in the providence of God, whose wisdom, only dimly and partially perceptible by man, was eternal. It thus followed that old wisdom was part of the same seamless web as new, and vice versa. Chaucer underlines how the new grows out of the old in *The Parliament of Fowls*:

> For out of olde feldes, as men seyth,
> Cometh all this newe corne fro yer to yere,
> And out of olde bokes, in good feyth,
> Cometh al this newe science that men lere. (22–5)

Here the remark is specifically applied to the relevance of Macrobius's Commentary on Cicero's *Somnium Scipionis* – works that were already centuries old – to modern problems and perplexities. It thereby makes the claim that the present poem also has to be taken seriously. *The Knight's Tale* actually uses an old story, originally from Statius's *Thebaid* and more recently handled by Boccaccio, which would certainly have been familiar to many in Chaucer's audience. The *Thebaid* is now hardly read, but it was one of the late Classical epics admired in the Middle Ages. In *The Knight's Tale* and elsewhere, the treatment of the source is what is interesting. The use an author makes of his material shows where his concerns lie; hence the emphasis placed on treatment of literary material both in the theoretical critical work of medieval literary scholars and in the self-referential remarks of medieval poets.

Though one can certainly assume that Chaucer's audience was one of culture and taste, who had acquired a good deal of sophisticated knowledge through the actual experience of literature, it would be foolish to pretend that it was composed of professional literary critics. It has only recently been recognized that there was a fully developed critical idiom for the discussion of literature in the Middle Ages, but this is not what we are concerned with at the moment. What does matter is that any serious artist would have been aware, as would his audience, of certain key ideas about the status and value of fiction. These ideas would have affected not only writing but also reception. The problem with fiction, as theologians never tired of pointing out, was that it was not true, and what business had a Christian society with untruth when it had the truth of Scripture before it? Yet fiction could be hugely enjoyable. For our immediate purpose the most significant answer to this serious charge is given by Dante, the greatest poet of the Middle Ages, whom Chaucer (not uncritically) admired. Dante points out in the *Convivio* that while fiction is literally a lie, its beauty (which must be, if it is beautiful, a part of that eternal beauty whose source is God) can reveal a truth that can be grasped in no other way. Thus the lie can teach a truth. The beauty of fiction is like a veil draped over the truth, and the business of the reader is so to train himself that he can, by logic, knowledge and intuition, remove that veil and perceive the truth. And the poet's activity in making this fiction is analogous to the creative activity of God in the world, though on a much lower level. Yet the poet is himself a creature, and therefore his poem is a part of God's creation. If the wisdom and mind of God can be seen in his creation, as St Paul said (Romans I.20), by the man who earnestly deploys the tools of knowledge, understanding and logic to aid his perception, the poem, though fictional, may to the inquiring mind reveal wisdom and truths hidden below the surface.

Boccaccio, whom Chaucer may have met and who provided a major source for *The Knight's Tale*, makes the fourteenth-century attitude to fiction even clearer for us. In *De Genealogia Deorum* ('On the Genealogy of the Gods') he takes the Classical myths of the various gods and shows how, to the Christian mind, they reveal a 'mythic' truth: thus Cronos eating his children is a symbolic story of how time destroys all. Classical religion and myth, though mistaken, were nevertheless reckoned to contain truths reconcilable with Christianity (see p. 219). The poets, says Boccaccio, were the first theologians. Moreover, in the *Difesa della Poesia* he repeats Dante's arguments, and adds that all serious art is polysemous – that is, it contains several levels of meaning recoverable in different ways. He then gives us a classification of four types of fable: the highest, the 'Virgilian' fable, is long, employs a high or dignified style, and has, besides its literal meaning, three other levels.*

The next classification, the 'Ovidian' fable, was so called after the Roman poet Ovid, whose poetry was much admired and imitated in the

---

*There is an obvious link here (and it is daring of Boccaccio to state it so bluntly) with the way Scripture was usually read. From the time of the Rabbinical scholars of the first centuries B.C., Scripture had been held to reveal God's truth in several ways, and by the time of St Augustine (at the end of the fourth century) the 'fourfold method' of reading was commonly established – as said Alain de Lille, whose work Chaucer knew:

> Litera gesta refert, quid credas allegoria
> Moralis quid agas, quid speres anagogia.

('The literal level tells what happened, the allegorical what one should believe, the moral what one should do, and the anagogical what one may hope for.')

This method was occasionally applied to great pagan poems like Virgil's *Aeneid*. (Virgil, on the evidence of the *Fourth Eclogue* which seemed to predict the Virgin Birth of Christ (though it did no such thing), was a 'virtuous pagan', a state often held to be a sort of honorary Christian. This is why he is made Dante's guide in Hell and Purgatory.)

Middle Ages and Renaissance, and whose greatest work is the *Metamorphoses*, a series of linked stories of the doings of the gods with men in nature. It had, beside its literal level, two other levels of meaning, and was smaller in scale than the Virgilian type of fable. The third classification is represented by the 'Aesopic' fable – the short moral beast-fable with which we are all familiar, where the literal level is accompanied by one other. Finally, says Boccaccio, we come to the last class of stories, those that have only a literal meaning. These he considers to be beneath the notice of a serious poet or audience, fit only for the gossip of old women.

Now what is striking here is that Boccaccio, who as a don is telling us (as dons often do) what everyone else is thinking, is taking it for granted, as beyond argument, that any serious poetry will have levels of meaning which are not apparent on the surface. A poem which proclaims itself as serious, as *The Knight's Tale* does, in its very first lines as well as by its sheer length and dignity, is therefore to be read on several levels, and its audience would approach it with this expectation. The end of man is to know God and enjoy Him for ever, and he can begin to know God through an understanding of nature – this is the purpose of science. Similarly, the poem, as a sub-creation in nature, will be another road by which the discerning mind can begin to know truth.

5. Cues for the Audience: Topos, Iconography, Style, Genre

But all this is much easier said than done. How would a medieval scholar (or reader) begin to analyse a work of art? He would start from the proposition that all wisdom, even human, is a facet of divine wisdom. Solomon, a wise king, says in the Wisdom of Solomon in the Apocrypha (XI.21) that Eternal Wisdom made all things by number, proportion and weight. A first clue, then, would be to look at the shape or form of a poem . or a building, of a painting or a piece of music. A reader or viewer might then go on to recognize certain symbols employed by the artist; for example, in Raphael's Sistine Madonna, the Blessed Virgin has a cloak billowing out behind her as if in a stiff breeze. When we understand that Raphael knew that his audience recognized this as one of the conventional attributes of pagan depictions of Juno, we see that it is done to emphasize Mary's status as Queen of Heaven. She has taken over all the powers once posited of Juno. Medieval and Renaissance art employs a great deal of 'picture language' or iconography (which can also be adapted to verbal expression) as a shorthand of meaning.* Animals and birds can also represent or

*Some helpful books on this topic are listed in the 'Iconography and Symbol' section of Further Reading (p. 229).

suggest key ideas, and are particularly important for the purposes of comparison. We moderns, who do not automatically share this means of communication, need to watch out for it. There are examples of it in *The Knight's Tale* and they are discussed in the Commentary.

Next, as a result of the heavy dependence on older works of art that I mentioned earlier, there is the extensive use in art and poetry (and not only that of this period) of what are called 'topoi' – the Greek word *topos* means 'place', or 'commonplace'. An example will make this clear. If a poet or painter had a garden to describe (as he not infrequently had in medieval art), almost the last thing he would do would be to go and look at one. He would draw on earlier examples of the garden in art, and thus all garden descriptions tend to have a family resemblance. This may seem stultifying, but in fact it can be the opposite. It relates all special instances of gardens, in this poem or that painting, to an archetype in the audience's mind – the archetypal garden of unfallen man in Eden, or the garden state of the Classical Age of Gold when Saturn reigned. This automatically introduces a value into the description. Because the elements in the description tend to be pretty fixed, addition or omission is immediately noticed and will therefore be significant. In fact the topos is an economical tool that releases the artist to modify at will a pre-existing set of expectations in the minds of his audience. There is an interesting use of this topos, linked with another, the May morning, in *The Knight's Tale*, when Emelye is first seen. We visualize her against the remembered background of the Garden of Love in the season of love in innumerable poems, and values and ideas are suggested which relate, without overt statement, to the issues of the poem. The point is that in iconography and topos the artist can make use of a second language which, far from restricting him, allows him to admit some ideas, exclude others, and play, if he wishes, with what his audience anticipates.

Similarly with the tools of rhetoric: a poet has three basic levels of style to choose from – high, middle or low. If he chooses the high, certain assumptions about the nature of his story will be present in the minds of his audience from the very first line. If he suddenly switches to the low, he is either incompetent or he may deliberately be making some sort of moral and aesthetic point. (For example in the predominantly middle-style *Miller's Tale*, when Absolon, a ludicrous character, suddenly serenades Alisoun in a high style, the effect is deliciously comic – the more so as Chaucer deliberately endowed this fashion-conscious young man with what we would call 'provincial' speech; it also suggests a way in which we should look at both Absolon and Alisoun, who is so inappropriately addressed.) A poet also has, in the arts of rhetoric, a selection of stylistic structures which will be appropriate or, to use a word we shall meet again, 'decorous', for some cases and contexts and for some purposes, but not for others; match or mismatch make the point.

Finally, there is the question of mode and genre. When Chaucer begins *The Knight's Tale* with the word 'Whilom' he is giving a signal to his audience, as we might start a story with 'Once upon a time ...'. He is indicating the broad genre. By that signal he is excluding other genres, and thus both restricting the range of references the audience should apply and pointing his audience in the right direction. In the same way, today, we would not expect a sonnet to do the same job as a letter to a newspaper. Or, to take a better example, the Western film, as a genre, has certain conventional elements we expect to find, and deals with areas of experience and interest closed to other types of film.

One of the remarkable things about *The Canterbury Tales* is that in them Chaucer has employed all the small forms or genres of the time, each carrying its own signals and assumptions – the sermon of *The Pardoner's Tale*, the comic parody of popular romance in *The Tale of Sir Thopas*, the saint's life of *The Second Nun's Tale*, the high romance of *The Knight's Tale*, a range of bawdily comic tales, and so on. Chaucer carefully and elaborately introduces *The Miller's Tale* as a 'cherles tale' to determine one way it might be listened to. What it all boils down to is that medieval writing relies heavily on what can be summed up in the word 'convention'. To us, this is often a word of disapproval (and that disapproval is itself a convention). But 'convention' simply means an area of agreement between author and audience where one does not need to go into the whole background. It is thus a great force for economy; and of course convention can be either confirmed or denied, used negatively or positively.

In sum, the medieval artist was in a dynamic relationship with the society of which he was a part. He shared with other members of that society a language of convention, topos, genre and symbol; he shared with them an assumption about how to read literature, a certainty that it set a problem which had to be teased out and discussed after the expression of the poem was over (notice how Chaucer ironically touches his hat to this at the end of Book I of *The Knight's Tale*); and he confidently expects that we will penetrate the surface.

6. The Date of *The Knight's Tale*

The Knight's Tale is the longest of the verse stories in *The Canterbury Tales*. The *Tales* itself is a collection of stories within another story – that of the story-telling contest on the fictional pilgrimage – and it engaged Chaucer for the last decade and more of his life. But Chaucer was a frugal poet, and it is clear that he re-used in *The Canterbury Tales* some stories that were written long before he had conceived the idea of a fictional pilgrimage. Though there is evidence of later revision to make it fit its teller in the framework of *The Canterbury Tales*, *The Knight's Tale* was not originally written for that book. I shall, therefore, first discuss the poem without relating it to the rest of the *Tales* or to the Knight himself. Those issues come later.

A version of the story of Palamon and Arcite, which clearly bears some important relation to *The Knight's Tale* and may even be the Tale itself, is mentioned by Chaucer in the Prologue to *The Legend of Good Women* (F420; G408), which is usually dated in the early to middle 1380s. How long before this the Palamon and Arcite story was written we do not know; the list of books with which it is linked may be governed by the phrase inserted in the G version of the Prologue (G400): 'while he was yong'. Internal evidence in *The Knight's Tale* of the heavy dependence on Boethius's *The Consolation of Philosophy*, which Chaucer translated, would suggest a date later than that translation, which is usually put at just after 1380. If we suggest a date after 1380 and before 1384 for the first version of *The Knight's Tale* we shall probably be fairly safe. This would be when Chaucer was about forty, and reaching the height of his powers.

7. Romance and Chivalry

The mode of the story is that of chivalric romance. By being simply that, certain types of story and treatment are automatically excluded, and others, from which Chaucer could choose, are automatically on offer. Moreover, by signalling in the first few lines what sort of story he is telling, Chaucer has already prepared the audience for one kind of response and not for another. The audience are not going to be given a salacious comic story, and they are not going to expect a sermon – though there are circumstances in which an author might find it profitable and necessary to up-end their expectations. What they can expect is a narrative that will deal with serious issues in a civilized, profound and entertaining way; with the noble life, as it was then understood.

'Romance' is a very wide term indeed, and it certainly does not mean only what goes under that label in modern fiction. Originally the word merely signified the language in which something was written, 'romanz' being an overall term for the vernaculars of Italy, Spain, France, England (the Norman French), and Provence, rather than the dignified Latin.

Then, through the concept of what was decorous to Latin or the vernacular, the word gradually comes to mean 'that type of story which you don't write in full-dress Latin, and which is lighter in tone and less comprehensive and political (though not necessarily less serious) than the epic for which you would use Latin'. But sorting out a definition runs into great difficulties, for there are so many kinds of romance that further precision is impossible. There are romances that have magical happenings in every nook in the wood, and romances that have none; those that take the hero off to the land of faerye, and others that seem never to have heard of the place; those that are comic and those that are serious; large and small romances, written in one type of verse (or prose) or another, and set in the present, the past, or nowhere – the list is infinitely expandable. If one had to look tentatively for one common narrative denominator, it might lie in the word 'adventure'. This does not quite mean what is understood by the word 'adventure' nowadays, for *aventure* in both Middle English and French suggests a chance occurrence that happens to someone. The romance seems to focus its interest on how people are affected by *aventure*. On the negative side, romance as term excludes the considerations that typify other genres of medieval narrative. The edificatory, moral and theological interest of the saint's life (of which there are so many examples) is not a central concern, the great historical issues of the epic or *chanson de geste* are only peripheral, and the comic pratfalls of the *fabliau* are largely absent. It doesn't require a great deal of insight to see that if Chaucer was searching for a story that he could decorously give to the Knight he had created, none of these last would do, but a romance would.

The romance usually (though not exclusively) has as its central characters people of noble birth. Their moral nobility (not always the same thing as nobility of birth, as Chaucer points out in his ballade *Gentilesse*, or in *The Wife of Bath's Tale*, D1109ff.) is often put to the test. Naturally, therefore, the social values prized by high medieval society are often major issues. Christian morality, of course, makes equally imperative claims on all, of whatever rank, and about its values there is little secular argument (though there may be about their application). Where the moral perplexities arise is in the two great moral codes parallel, as it were, to Christian morality: chivalry, and what is commonly called courtly love. Both of these are fundamental to *The Knight's Tale* and need extended discussion.

Chivalry, or *chevalerie*, was the code of ethics and behaviour deemed to be appropriate to members of the class that fought on horseback rather than, like commoners, on foot. The knights and nobles came to feel that power, rank and privilege entailed restraints and responsibilities, and although it is true that some knights behaved like thugs, the ideal was that they should not. War, however ritualized, is basically an organized way of killing one's fellow humans, often in rather nasty ways; but it is a fact that as long as the chivalric ideal retained any force at all, the horrors of war were to some degree diminished. We must beware of taking too cynical a view of our fathers' ideals, and also of letting our own quite proper horror of war blind us to the historical fact that for much of human history the participants at least saw it as glorious and noble, and as a high activity of mankind – 'the pomp and circumstance of glorious war', as Othello puts it. It shakes us a little to realize that Christ himself, the Prince of Peace, is in the medieval centuries often pictured as a knight – *Christus miles* – doing lethal battle and engaging in a knightly quest to rescue man from the Devil. This is exactly how He is depicted in the splendid Passus XVIII of *Piers Plowman*, a long religious poem contemporary with Chaucer's later work. It is not merely a cheap rhetorical flourish to say that many thought that if Christ was knightly, knights should be Christlike. The ideal knight, as we see in Chaucer's description below (p. 69), was not only brave and a good fighter; he was generous, merciful, a succour to those in distress and a loyal friend. He scorned to fight against his inferiors or those weaker than himself, he was tireless in his defence of the right and the good, he was honourable and self-controlled.*

In his picture of the Knight in the *General Prologue* (see p. 69), Chaucer summarizes the values: 'trouthe' – integrity, fidelity; 'honour'; 'fredom' – liberality; and 'curteisie'. 'Curteisie' is literally the behaviour expected of members of a Court. It extends from cleanliness of person to considerateness, tact, humility, gentleness and mercifulness; from having good table-manners to social and artistic accomplishments like singing, composing poetry and dancing. If one had to sum it up in a phrase, the emphasis is on the civilized self-control of power. These are not undesirable qualities, and, even if men fell short of the ideal, the very existence of an ideal may have saved many from a relapse into barbarism. Chivalric romance often centres round such qualities and puts the hero (or heroine) in situations where these are tested, or where apparently harmonious virtues are brought into an agonizing clash. For example, does loyalty to one's lady take precedence over loyalty to one's friend? (an issue aired in *The Knight's Tale*). It will be seen that this complex of values suggests there will be a strong moral interest in any fiction that deals with them.

The connection of these issues with the pagan figures of Arcite, Palamon and Theseus is already obvious. But there is a public as well as a private

---

*Honour could be almost quixotic; King John II of France, taken prisoner at Poitiers in 1356 and released for a ransom under the treaty of Calais in 1360, returned voluntarily to his prison when one of the guarantors for his ransom escaped in 1364. He died in captivity.

dimension to knighthood, which affects how we view Theseus. The knight's public duty was to support the king in the just rule of his kingdom,* and to extend Christendom in order to save droves of benighted pagan souls from going to Hell for want of a true doctrine. The Crusades show that practice fell short of the latter part of this ideal, but the ideal itself is not ignoble and probably did some good. In the case of conflict between Christian states, too, the issues were not as simple as their presentation in fiction might suggest. Despite the elaborate devices for containing a conflict and imposing a truce, the Middle Ages are not the least bloodstained in European history. War between Christian peoples ought, of course, to be impossible, and it was a perennial complaint of preachers and writers that Christendom was tearing itself apart when its military forces ought to be united against the infidel at the gates.

In the *General Prologue*, Chaucer juxtaposes (without open comment – we have to supply that, and the juxtaposition is itself comment) two pictures of noble fighting men. The Knight's moral excellence we have already outlined; he is tireless in his activity, but has fought only in Crusades against the infidel; he is as self-effacing as a young girl in his behaviour, and dresses soberly. His religion is so central to him that he has set out on his pilgrimage without going home to scour the rust off his hauberk.†

His son, the Squire, is a very different figure. He dresses in the latest fashion, rather flashily; he ostentatiously parades his musical talents; he is an accomplished socialite. His battles have all been against fellow Christians, and his chief concern in fighting has not been, like the Knight's, 'for oure feith' but in hope of winning his lady's favour. I do not think it is fanciful to see Chaucer as here presenting us with an ideal of chivalry and an example of what it means in normal practice. And the point is made sharper by the lack of comment; if we find the Knight admirable but forbidding and the Squire the more immediately attractive, that tells us quite a lot about ourselves and our own values and practice.‡

* The task of the ruler, seen as God's vicar on earth, was to provide, as far as possible in a fallen and corrupt world, a framework of justice and order in which each individual could seek his own ultimate good and in which crime would be punished and quarrels between individuals reconciled. These are key political ideas from the period of St Augustine's *City of God* in around 400 A.D., through the time of Dante's *De Monarchia* in the early 1300s, and then down to the Renaissance. They impinge significantly on the way Chaucer has presented Theseus in *The Knight's Tale.*

† The argument propounded by some that the Knight is merely a mercenary is now largely discounted. Chaucer's portrait of the Knight is discussed fully below (p. 69).

‡ Later in *The Canterbury Tales*, the Franklin comments on the attractiveness of the Squire. The comment is double-edged and tells us quite a lot about the values of the Franklin as well.

There are two other places where Chaucer deals with the issue of chivalry. In *Troilus and Criseyde*, close in date to *The Knight's Tale* and handling a lot of the same concerns, we are given a glimpse of one of the Nine Worthies, Hector of Troy, who alone surpasses in knighthood his brother Troilus, the hero of the story. Hector has the same high seriousness as the Knight and he is tireless in the defence of his city against the Greeks; therein lie his chief values. Troilus at the beginning of the poem is in the same sort of league, but when he falls in love with Criseyde his chief thought ceases to be of Troy – indeed, he is quite prepared at one point to abandon the city – and his attention is concentrated on Criseyde herself. Yet we are made to explore the paradox that love for a mortal woman, a lesser moral claim than love for his city, makes him a better fighter and increases in him qualities of generosity and mercifulness. He becomes significantly more attractive. But the fact is that he is now in the service of an ideal which, we know, will ultimately betray him. The irony is that, as with the Squire, the lesser ideal may have the more immediately attractive effects, but we are being asked to look at the final cause of those effects in their evaluation. It is clear that Chaucer thought the issue of chivalry to be far from simple, and full of paradoxes. Merely looking around him would confirm that human beings and their ideals are puzzles. The same Black Prince who fought nobly and brilliantly at Crécy (1346) and Poitiers (1356), who was a model of domestic courtesy and chivalry, was the man who perpetrated the horrendous sack of one of his own towns, Limoges.

The third place where the problem of chivalry is glanced at is, of course, in *The Knight's Tale* itself. Theseus is a key figure who will be discussed more fully later (pp. 50–51), and the poem – significantly – opens and closes with him. Here is the just ruler, using his might to punish wrong, listening to the afflicted and succouring the widows, providing a framework for the settlement through trial by battle of the quarrel between the two young knights Arcite and Palamon. Valour in defence of their city has got them where they are at the beginning of the poem. They are linked in a friendship apparently as indissoluble as that of other warrior-companions in literature, such as Aeneas and Achates, Roland and Oliver, and Amis and Amiloun – or, indeed, Theseus and Peirithous. Their basic similarity, and indeed their virtually identical natures, are stressed.

The basic ideas and insights about chivalry are thus the same in all three places, though of course Chaucer is making a point in the *General Prologue* and probably in *Troilus and Criseyde* that he is not in *The Knight's Tale*. The latter does explore, however, what noble conduct – for a ruler, a lady or a mere knight – is about, and it plays to its audience's expert taste with a painstaking and gorgeous description of the ceremonies of public chivalric life: the great tournament and its preparations, and the funeral of Arcite. It also airs the difficulty of the ruler in administering justice where both parties have right on their side. It takes the ideals seriously, but is not blind to the paradoxes and problems contained in them. It also raises the issue of friendship, companionship in arms, deliberately drawing a parallel between the friendship of Arcite and Palamon and the brief appearance of that of Parotheus and Theseus. A component of the ideal of chivalry is selfless devotion to one's friend and to his ultimate good. Yet, as we see in *The Knight's Tale*, that devotion may well be challenged by another imperative claim, that of love.

8. Love

Much has been written about 'courtly love' – the phrase is modern – that is frankly misleading. Recent studies* have tended to suggest that an idea of it as a rigid code of almost invariably adulterous or extramarital passion is a serious impediment to the understanding of medieval texts. There are not a few major medieval poems in which love, as fine as any, ends in happy marriage. Equally, there are those in which love is adulterous. There is no adultery in *The Knight's Tale*, and the poem closes with an image of order and harmony in the marriage of Palamon and Emelye. (Ironically, though there is no doubt that Palamon is glad enough to have Venus's promise to him fulfilled, the marriage is a political one arranged by Theseus (see p. 30) and is not a direct result of his own feelings.) The *Confessio Amantis* of Chaucer's friend Gower offers through its many stories an ideal of *fin amour* that is again intimately connected with Christian marriage. It is easy to be misled into untenable generalizations on the subject by witty and cynical books like Andreas Capellanus's *De Arte Honesti Amandi*. Andreas's book is frankly scandalous if we take it at face value, a textbook on adultery, a manual of seduction, a guide to behaviour decorous in all sorts of combinations of relationship (a noble with a bourgeois woman, a clerk with a peasant, and so on), even to the extent of providing a phrase-book of pre-pillow talk. But of course we should not take it seriously. It was written to entertain through sheer outrageousness a highly sophisticated and rather fast Court – that of Champagne – where one amusement was the discussion of 'love problems'. And it is very funny. It is more useful to start from the other end, as it

*For example, A. I. Denomy, *The Myth of Courtly Love* (New York, 1948) and F. X. Newman, *The Meaning of Courtly Love* (New York, 1972).

were, and look at the descriptions of love in particular fiction and only to generalize tentatively.

The earliest (and one of the finest) poems to explore *fin amour* or courtly love at length is the *Roman de la Rose*, first begun about the middle of the thirteenth century by Guillaume de Lorris, who wrote 4,000 lines, and finished with a further 18,000 lines written by the much coarser-grained (but also very funny) Jean de Meung some forty years later. The first part is an elaborate and delightful allegory of a young man's falling in love. Allegory is an unfashionable mode nowadays, though it can be used successfully; after all, we all know George Orwell's *Animal Farm*, and have no difficulty in recognizing that it is not an everyday story of country folk but a shrewd attack on what was happening in Soviet Russia, and could happen in England. If one were pressed to give a definition, it might be that an allegory is a narrative which has one coherent meaning on the surface and another entirely independent meaning on another level. Medieval men did not exactly invent allegory – it had been used as a tool of interpretation of Scripture for centuries – but they delighted to use it in their art. It appealed to precisely that philosophical view we have already glanced at: that everything had a meaning below as well as on the surface, that the world was a vast encyclopedia of significance. As the twelfth-century poet and theologian Alain de Lille put it:

> Omnis mundi creatura,
> Quasi liber et pictura,
>   Nobis est, et speculum.
> Nostrae vitae, nostrae mortis
> Nostri status, nostrae sortis
>   Fidele signaculum.

('All the created things in the world are like a book or picture or a mirror for us. They are a faithful symbol of our life, our death, our state and our fate.')

Moreover, the employment of this artificial type of narrative allowed the discussion of often very private feelings and concerns which would be embarrassing and painful if not distanced. De Lorris's *Roman de la Rose*, for example, is on the surface a story of a young man who desires to enter a walled garden. He is let in by a young lady, who is a sort of gatekeeper, and meets various other ladies therein. As he wanders about he finds a spring, and gazes down, like Narcissus, into its cool, translucent depths. He sees a rose bush, protected by obstacles and hedges, and desires to pluck the rose that grows on it. As he reaches out to do so, a hideous figure appears and drives him off. Now, the allegorical reading goes thus:

the young man is let into the beautiful spring garden (which is like a memory of Eden before the fall of man) by the porter, Idleness. In other words, only those who have leisure can cultivate the finer feelings of love. The spring garden, in which the birds are singing to their mates, is the Garden of Love, where one tastes fleetingly a memory of man's first bliss. The young man meets figures like Wealth – that is, to be a proper lover, one must have the rank and fortune to pursue refined behaviour, and good manners to go with it. He then looks into the fountain which waters the garden: he has for the first time looked into the clear eyes of the Lady who will be his beloved, and from her all blessings flow. (The echo of Narcissus introduces a delicate irony.) He then meets Fair Welcome – in other words, his lady is friendly towards him. At times he is racked by self-doubt, aware of his difficulties and unworthiness, and seeks counsel from Frend; the friend is both external – a person to whom he can talk – and the Lady's own well-disposed regard for him. Finally, and to cut a long story short, the lover tries to pluck the rose from the bush; here he is attempting either to kiss the Lady or actually to possess her, and in modesty and fright she draws back, sending him off with harsh words. The Giant Daunger is her anger and refusal to be his lover.

This artificial story enjoys its own witty artifice. It delights in elaboration of the nuances of being in love, and the refinements of the lover's feelings and emotions. It delights in the sumptuous descriptions of the garden, the fountain and the rose, where every phrase helps to focus in our minds an idea of perfect beauty and suggests an approachable correlative to the indescribable beauty of the Lady and the unquantifiable subtleties of human feeling. The poem actually seems to delight in the panache that allows it to overcome the real difficulties of the extended psychological allegorical narrative. But above all the work presents us with a detailed analysis of love as a serious art, a crafting of the whole mind and personality, almost a perfecting of the self so that in the symbolic, paradisal Garden of Love it may reach back to the ideal of man's perfection before the Fall. The *Roman de la Rose* was a vastly influential poem (it is also a very good one), and Chaucer himself made an English translation of at least part of it. It had an effect on the way refined men saw themselves and on their sexual consciousness every bit as profound as the effect later produced by *Clarissa*, or *Jane Eyre*, or *Women in Love*.

The basic quality of *fin amour* is idealization of the beloved, and the feeling of the lover that he can do nothing to deserve her or even to be worthy of her. This is not so far from what we all feel when we are in love. It should be remembered that for those in love it is a deadly serious matter, while for the observer it may well be comic. The beloved becomes (at least in the lover's eyes) the fount of all virtue, the abode of all graces, the arbiter of one's living or dying. The lover as yet unsatisfied goes off his food, writes poetry (very often dreadful poetry), becomes absent-minded, weeps readily at sentimental stories and generally goes through hell while providing sport for those who do not share his temporary affliction. He tries to attract his lady's attention by feats of skill, daring and nobility, all the while in the hopeless realization that he can do nothing to win her love; she must give it freely if he is to get it at all. The majority of medieval poems (though not all of them) tell us very little of what the lady feels. She is literally the object of the man's affections, remote and unobtainable, and her actions and reactions have the distant impersonality of those of a goddess. She may grant him (the phrase is significant for what it reveals of the way in which women's sexuality was regarded) her love sooner or later; or she may be cruel and enjoy her power over him, sending him off to do impossible tasks for her sake. When Chaucer wrote his fine elegy, *The Book of the Duchess*, for Blanche, wife of John of Gaunt, he played wittily and movingly with this topos. He makes the figure who represents John in the poem describe his courtship in these hopeless terms (and he includes the bad poem*), and the fact that we find him slightly funny in his serious love-pain makes it the more poignant. Then he passes to a description of Blanche, where the real flesh-and-blood woman whom the audience could recognize – they did, after all, know her – is subsumed into an ideal of womanhood straight out of the love-romances. This not only suggests something of the way a lover's consciousness works, but also generalizes a very private emotion and makes it accessible to all of us. Yet at the end he makes this paragon flout the literary stereotype of the lady of romance. She does not send her lover off on ridiculous quests all over the known and unknown world, 'hoodles to the Drye Se/And come hom by the Carrenar'; she does not descend to such 'knakkes smale'. The literary joke suddenly brings Blanche alive. Again, in *The Franklin's Tale* Dorigen devises an emphatic way of saying 'no' to the squire Aurelius, who irresponsibly loves her *à folie*; she tells him to remove all the rocks round the coast of Brittany, a task she knows to be impossible. Aurelius understands that she means 'no'; yet in his unwisdom he decides to assume she is setting him a 'romance' task and sets out to trick her into having to keep her own terrible bargain.

Of course, *fin amour* or courtly love is a convention which impinges on only one area of experience. Many medieval writings, particularly the *fabliau* and the sermon, show knowledge of a much more earthly type of

---

* Which is excellent in context because it *is* so bad – one of the paradoxes of his art Chaucer loved to play with.

love, and also great awareness of feminine sexuality and passion. (There is one notable poet, Christine de Pisan, a near contemporary of Chaucer's, who explores feminine reactions in love with a rare delicacy.) But it is a fact that much of the best work of the period is governed by the conventions of *fin amour*, though it is not always without humour and irony. Gower's unhappy lover in the *Confessio Amantis* is entirely believable (and very interesting) in his torment; but when at the end he is seen to be an old man whose 'green grass has become withered hay', he suddenly becomes pathetic and foolish – he is a *senex amans* (another topos), the aged lover who ought to know better and deserves to be laughed at. In *The Merchant's Tale* the same topos is used in the ludicrous attempts (selfish through and through, while true love is selfless) of the aged January to be a 'jolly thriving wooer' to May. The way in which May is described, as if she were the ideal of a lady, both suggests how she is regarded by the self-deceiving January and highlights her obvious animality that finds itself satisfied athletically in the boughs of a pear tree.

   Troilus and Criseyde is a serious and profound poem whose whole dynamic is provided by the adoration of Criseyde by Troilus; yet when he is lying sick in bed through unsatisfied love, when he ceases to be capable of rational thought or action, he becomes comic to us even while we recognize how serious the matter is for him. (Aurelius and Arcite also become comic to us in a similar but less extended way.) Yet the paradox is that being comic in this manner is open only to a highly refined nature. Palamon and Arcite go through the same sequence of feelings: our distance from them, maintained by the narrator, ensures that we do not see them without irony. Both young men love the same woman; yet each has a picture of her that is irreconcilable with the other's, and not necessarily a reflection of the real Emelye (who is deliberately left undeveloped and undescribed, except in so far as she appears to other people). Moreover, the comedy is pointed sharply by Theseus when he finds Palamon and Arcite fighting in the wood. He acknowledges the power and seriousness of love, which has mortals at its mercy. But he also sees the ludicrousness of any death which could result from Palamon and Arcite's deadly strife:

> 'But this is yet the beste game of alle,
> That she, for whom they have this jolitee
> Kan hem therfore as muche thank as me.
> She woot namoore of all this hoote fare,
> By god, than woot a cokkow o[r] an hare!'

> (948–52)

Fin amour, then, can be both serious and comic, chaste and unchaste, licit and illicit. As a poetic convention it has its roots in human feeling and social behaviour, which are themselves affected by poetry and poetic convention. (Often we take from art and illusion the models from which we interpret unfamiliar experience.) Each poetic handling of the idea of human sexual love in this period must take up some sort of stance towards the ideas and practice of *fin amour*; and a poem of any merit will take a unique stance. Like all conventions, it is, properly used, capable of infinite variation and elaboration of matter and treatment.

A final point needs to be made about *fin amour*. The devotion of the lover and the exaltation of his mistress have formal analogies, if not material ones, with the worship the human mind addresses to God. 'Adore', 'devotion' and 'worship' are words which work equally well in both contexts. The concept of the lover never deserving love – and only getting it by the lady's grace, freely given – is analogous to the impossibility of the sinner being justified by his works and only receiving salvation by the free grace of God. The common vocabulary forces a parallel between the two types of devotion, and the parallel is often extensively exploited. Religious devotion is frequently described in terms of sexual love. (The theologians and commentators found, it seems, a good biblical precedent for this in the superb collection of love-songs known in our Authorized Version as the Song of Solomon.) Christ as lover of the soul, the soul searching for union with Him, are discussed in these terms from the twelfth century to at least the seventeenth century, as Herbert or Donne show us. Similarly, the beloved is often addressed in religious terms, and human love borrows the terminology of religion and theology – even, in art, some of its practices. There are cases where the love-poem employs a witty blasphemy as a major mode of statement. The irony, however, of this 'parallel theology' is never totally forgotten. Occasionally one finds the two integrated: Dante in *La Vita Nuova*, for example, writes a series of love-poems which are clearly addressed to a mortal woman, and then in his commentary shows that they point beyond that mortal woman to the eternal beauty and love of God, of which a small spark has been glimpsed in her. Or, in the *Divine Comedy*, his *fin amour* for the mortal Beatrice is transfigured when she becomes, because they love each other selflessly, his guide and mentor in the ways of divine love. *Fin amour* can thus be an important metaphor for a yet deeper level of experience.

But of course, as we all know, love (even if refined) can be utterly selfish rather than self-giving and self-forgetful. The irony is that the symptoms of both types, and the vocabulary we use to talk about them, are often nearly indistinguishable. The language used by the ludicrous and self-absorbed Absolon to serenade the self-absorbed Alisoun in *The Miller's Tale* is taken from the Song of Solomon, which was seen as the great expression of selfless divine love. A fundamental strand in medieval moral and theological thought concerns just this area: the distinction between self-giving love, *caritas*, and selfish desire, *cupiditas*. That one may grow from the other is possible; that they are in opposition despite the coincidence of vocabulary is usual. The text of the sermon Chaucer wrote for his fictitious Pardoner is a theological truism: *Radix malorum est cupiditas* ('The root of all evils is selfish desire' – not, as often mistranslated, the desire for money, though the sermon glances ironically at that interpretation). By this sin the rebel angels fell. True love (*caritas* or *agape*) is automatically virtuous, automatically wise, automatically good: the key virtue. St Paul (I Corinthians XIII) underlines this in a famous passage that many of us know even today; and St Augustine summed up the whole issue in a striking phrase: 'Love – then do what you want'. The *cupiditas/caritas* distinction is basic to much medieval art and thought, and a major idea in Chaucer's work. It is certainly important in *Troilus and Criseyde*, and some people argue that it is a major concern in *The Canterbury Tales* as a whole. As we shall see (pp. 63–4), there are four characters in the *General Prologue* who are selfless in their particular avocations; all the others are full of cupidity of one sort or another.

These issues have a bearing on the use of the love-motif in *The Knight's Tale*. It is the love Palamon and Arcite conceive for Emelye that is, after all, the chief dynamic in the central plot. When Arcite and Palamon fall in love, Arcite loves a mortal woman – he is in no doubt about that. Palamon, however, sees her at first not as a mortal woman but as a goddess, and speaks of her in those terms. While both desire her, one desires possession and the other desires her love, as their prayers show. However hyperbolical Palamon's speech may be, it admits an important distinction between the type of love each holds. I do not want just yet to go into the symbolic structure of *The Knight's Tale* but there is good reason for regarding the prison from which Palamon and Arcite see her as a metaphor for life on this earth. Both, therefore, could be said to display not only different types of love but also different relations to this world and the next. It does not seem to me to be an accident that it is the lover who sees through Emelye to a cosmic principle of love and harmony who eventually marries her. And the marriage takes place at the end of a poem which began with the marriage of the Martial principle of Theseus with the Venusian principle of Ypolita – a symbol of cosmic harmony and concord. Love, as theologians explained tirelessly and as Chaucer underlined in *Troilus and Criseyde* (III. 1–49), is the ultimate law, the ultimate principle in the universe. Human love, comic or serious, tragic or happy, is a facet of it and ultimately, properly understood and managed, a note in the great harmony of the universe. The climax of the poem is Theseus's great speech on divine love at its end.

9. Sources and Setting

Why is a study of sources important, when surely what matters is the work of art as we have it? The question is a fair one. In the first place, looking at the sources themselves provides a background and a context for the work before us. We can see the materials the artist had to work with. Secondly, when we are trying to get to grips with a work of art several centuries old we have a problem in grasping the way in which it was conceived and received, as we have seen. By examining the sources we can obtain some sort of check on the inferences we draw from the text: if the way the sources have been handled and adapted (or not) confirms what we think from a reading of his poem the poet is doing, all well and good; if not, we ought perhaps to reconsider. Finally, a close look at the detailed handling of a source may actually allow us to overhear, as it were, the artist's mind working. For example, when in *The Parliament of Fowls* Chaucer uses a passage from Boccaccio's *Teseida* describing a Garden of Love (cf. above, p. 25) and a temple of Venus, he translates it word for word except that he alters the order of the stanzas. When we compare the two passages we can see exactly where Chaucer's attention was concentrated. He was happy with the matter Boccaccio provided, but he wanted it to be seen in his poem in a different way and with a different climax. The second-hand bricks build a new house. When we look, however briefly, at Chaucer's handling of the *Teseida* in *The Knight's Tale*, we can see that he is not just paraphrasing an admirable Italian original; he is making something quite different out of it, in the full confidence that his powers are up to the job.

The two main sources for *The Knight's Tale* seem to be the *Teseida* and Statius's *Thebaid*. The epic poem in twelve books of the Roman poet Publius Papinius Statius deals with the expedition of the Seven against Thebes in the fratricidal strife between the sons of Oedipus, Eteocles and Polyneices. The poem is not without its fine moments, and it fathered a twelfth-century vernacular adaptation, the *Roman de Thebes*. Statius enjoyed considerable prestige in the Middle Ages, for it was believed that he had been converted to Christianity – an event to which Dante refers in *Purgatorio*, XXII.89. Thus the authority of a distinguished Classical author of almost the best period is married to a comfortable feeling that in his work one finds glimmers of the truths revealed in the Bible. *The Knight's Tale* certainly draws on the *Thebaid*. The epigraph (which appears in all the best manuscripts) is from XII.519ff., and the first fifty lines more or less summarize Book I. There is no doubt that Chaucer had read the poem and admired its poet (cf. *Troilus and Criseyde*, V.1792). He also had direct recourse to him elsewhere in *The Knight's Tale*, and probably to the *Roman de Thebes* as well. But Chaucer's main source, which he does not cite, was Boccaccio's *Teseida*. This long poem of nearly ten thousand lines in twelve books has distinct pretensions to the large scale of epic. It relies extensively on Statius and probably the *Roman de Thebes* also, but the central plot of the rival lovers is in neither source. Whether Boccaccio invented it or drew it from an undiscovered source is not known. It might be said, however, that the story of the rival lovers belongs to a type not altogether uncommon in medieval romance. But Chaucer is very far from slavishly following Boccaccio; his is a very free handling indeed. In the first place it is only about a quarter the length of its original and only about a third of it corresponds to anything in the Italian text. Thus, in addition to the wholesale excisions, abbreviations and summary of the Italian source, Chaucer had plenty of room for substantial additions and alterations of his own. For example, the descriptions of the temples of the gods and the philosophical reflections are to all intents and purposes Chaucer's own additions to the story. And even when he did use Boccaccio he often altered his text significantly, as when he transfers to Egeus the trite moralizing of Boccaccio's Theseus, and then gives Theseus his own addition, a long speech on divine love (see below, p. 51). Again, the whole of Boccaccio's first book, on the campaigns of Theseus against the Amazons, is condensed into twelve brief lines at the beginning of Book I. Moreover, he deliberately adapts the setting and action, as he adapted those of Boccaccio's *Il Filostrato* in *Troilus and Criseyde*. Where Boccaccio tries to capture some of the details and feeling of a Classical poem and makes a real attempt at *romanitas*, Chaucer alters so that the action focusses sharply on Arcite and Palamon's love-conflict as the catalyst for the discussion of key moral and philosophical concerns of his own day. He alters the detail of the setting, mainly by omission but also by significant addition, so that although the fourteenth-century audience knew (and are reminded) that the events all took place a very long time ago indeed, they would see in the poem a society whose moral problems were indistinguishable from their own. More examples of these parallels and alterations will be found in the Commentary.

It would be very unlikely that many among his audience would have known the *Teseida*. Many, however, would at least have known of the

Thebaid, and all would have an idea of the Classical past in which it was written. After all, for a fourteenth-century audience there was a lot less history to know. The three great Matters of Romance – Arthur of Britain, Charlemagne of France, and the Matter of Antiquity (comprising the stories of Troy, Rome and Thebes) – made up, with the history of the Jews and of the Crusades, pretty well all the important events in world history. The references to the story of Thebes in *The Knight's Tale*, therefore, immediately signal that this poem is claiming a connection with the high seriousness and authority of the Classics, and is itself to be taken seriously. It also introduces an important symbol. The fall of Thebes, like the fall of Troy, is often in medieval romance a symbol of the fate of the cities of this world, all of which must fall. For us, no more than for Arcite and Palamon, 'here is no abiding city'.

Although Chaucer 'medievalized' Boccaccio's story, it is still, like *Troilus and Criseyde*, set in a Classical past which, as Chaucer carefully emphasizes, is significantly different from his own. In the Tale he frequently includes phrases like 'as was tho the gyse' that remind us of the 'otherness' of this imagined world, and in the funeral rites, for example, he deliberately imitates the pagan funeral rituals he had read of in Classical epics. The small detail of 1556ff., where Arcite dedicates his long hair to Mars, is another use of what Chaucer knew was a custom of antiquity. Now in *Troilus and Criseyde* Chaucer is careful to emphasize that the pagan society he is constructing has not had the joyful revelation of Christianity; it lacks the keys to the understanding of man's destiny and predicament provided by the revelation of God in Jesus. Any virtue it possesses, then (and the theologians admitted that the ancient world did possess virtue), was arrived at by a process of deduction from experience and not by revelation. It is wonderful that the people that walked in darkness saw as much light as they did. But the key point that Chaucer is using is that options which are open to a pagan, and which, by God's mercy, may lead to salvation, are not open to a Christian society such as his own. Conversely, if a pagan society could get so far, what excuse is there for a Christian society if it fails to go further? Chaucer is thus by his setting forcing the audience to distance itself from the society described in the poem and to use its distance as a means of almost choric ironic understanding; to use the depiction of that society as a means for self-examination.

The Knight's Tale does not take this point as far as it is taken in *Troilus and Criseyde*, but it is surely present: the Tale deals on a smaller scale with many of the issues raised. Both poems have qualities which fully entitle Chaucer to the title 'noble philosophical poet' given to him by Thomas

Usk (d.1388), in that in both there is a serious attempt to get to grips with the place of suffering in human life and with the nature of the universe we live in. It is just these issues that dominate Theseus's last speech (see below, p. 51). On both poems the influence of Boethius is huge, and to explain this last point we must now turn to Boethius himself.

Anicius Manlius Severinus Boethius (?470–525) is one of the most important figures in the development of Western culture. Though we may not realize it, we are all in his debt today. He had a busy political life, being a member of one of the great aristocratic families at the end of the Empire, and was consul in 510. For a long period he was confidant and counsellor of Theodoric, King of the Ostrogoths, but was judicially murdered (probably as a by-product of some political and ecclesiastical horse-trading with the Eastern Empire) by having a cord gradually tightened round his temples. His writings on music and arithmetic provided the basic texts for academic study of those subjects down to the Renaissance, and he is the sole conduit through which flows to the Middle Ages much of the learning and scholarly method of late Antiquity. His finest work by far is *The Consolation of Philosophy*, the argument of which is given in a brutally condensed summary in Appendix 3 (pp. 223–7). It is a very beautiful and moving book, which grows out of Boethius's own experience in the prison where he wrote it while awaiting what he knew would be a cruel death. It addresses itself to the perennial problems of the human condition, and is as relevant today as it has ever been. This book was universal reading for anyone presuming to call themselves educated from the sixth to the eighteenth century. Gibbon, with a sly irony which tells us much about Gibbon himself, calls it 'a golden book, not unworthy of the leisure of a Tully [Cicero]'. It was translated into English by King Alfred, by Queen Elizabeth and by Chaucer, and by numerous others, and it has never lacked readers until today. (Happily, there is a good Penguin translation in print.) Yet an age like our own, so similar in many ways to late Antiquity in its moral and religious perplexity, beset by a sense of the precariousness of existence, and living, so it might seem, in a meaningless universe, has grave need of its clear-eyed wisdom.

Boethius was a Christian, but in the *Consolation* he deliberately set himself the task of discussing the meaning of good, of free will, of fortune, chance, destiny and providence, without using any Christian premises.* Indeed, only at one point (III, prose 12) in the entire book does he allude to the Bible, and even there one can miss the allusion unless one is very alert. He is proceeding entirely on terms that his Stoic or neo-Platonist

---

*One might be tempted to connect with this Chaucer's use of a pagan setting in *Troilus and Criseyde* and *The Knight's Tale*.

friends would have accepted, and gradually bringing them by logic to the point where their view of the universe is entirely consistent with a Christian one. The book reconciles our experience of what seems to be the amoral randomness of the universe with the idea of an eternal wisdom that is just. It shows how time relates to the concept of eternity; it shows that evil is not an entity in itself; and it shows that, paradoxically, all fortune is good fortune. Fortune, the blind goddess on whose wheel men are bound to rise and fall whatever their deserts, is but a tool or servant of an ultimate purpose; she is constant only in her inconstancy. The wise man will see behind accident to, as Dante put it, 'the love that moves the sun and other stars'. The use of the academic philosophical premises and procedures of late Antiquity gives us a way of looking at the universe which is independent of Christian doctrine but which can be seen to need that doctrine for its fulfilment. Chaucer must have encountered this book early in his life, as it was a staple of the curriculum in education. But his translation of it around 1380 seems to have altered radically the way he wrote and the subjects he was interested in. Boethius was both a source for and influence on *The Knight's Tale* and *Troilus and Criseyde*. That is, the book profoundly affected the way Chaucer handed the stories he found in Boccaccio, and also gave him much of the material he actually used in the poems. For example, the vast majority of the philosophical references in *The Knight's Tale* are adaptations from Boethius; and the most impressive of all, Theseus's closing speech, is a free paraphrase of a crucial section of the *Consolation* (see pp. 51, 203, 226). (In Appendix 3 I have included a list of passages in *The Knight's Tale* seriously indebted to in Boethius.) The important point is that Chaucer's use of Boccaccio's story is so affected by his reading of Boethius that the major themes it handles are fundamentally different from those of Boccaccio. Love is certainly still a theme common to both, but in Chaucer human affective love is clearly put in a much more complex perspective. It is seen not only as immensely valuable in itself – as indeed Boethius saw it; it is also one of the routes by which the human mind rises to the perception and reciprocation of divine or cosmic love. Again, accident, chance, fortune, providence and suffering bulk large not only in the ideas of the persons in the Tale but also in the narratorial comment, so much so that it must be said that the heart of the Tale lies not in the story but in what the story symbolizes.

There are further parallels. Both *The Knight's Tale* and *The Consolation of Philosophy* are 'dramatic' – that is, they are cast in the form of a fictional narrative and handle their philosophical concerns through dialogue and speech. There is a similarity between the situation and experience of 'Boethius' (i.e. as a character, even if the real Boethius was actually in prison) in the *Consolation* and that of Arcite and Palamon. 'Boethius' lying in prison awaiting death and mourning his fate, sees a vision of a beautiful lady. This is Philosophia (Love of Wisdom), and in the course of the *Consolation* she teaches 'Boethius' what true happiness is and reconciles him to his condition. The prison becomes a metaphor for the world beyond which the human mind so rarely looks. The similarity with Arcite and Palamon is close enough to be suggestive; they, also in prison, have a vision of beauty which changes their lives – Arcite's reaction to Palamon's cry of pain immediately invokes metaphysical ideas which are developed later in the poem. Love of Emelye in the course of the Tale is the mainspring of the plot which brings both knights to a fuller understanding of their human predicament. We, watching their reactions and that of Theseus, are brought to consider deeply the issues of happiness, human love and the nature of the universe, as 'Boethius' is by Philosophia. We are also made aware that just as the power of Theseus that keeps them in prison seems to them arbitrary and irrational, but is not, so the apparent irrationality of the world may be nothing of the kind. We are given a glimpse of the gods working on a level beyond that on which Theseus deliberates and judges. *The Knight's Tale* raises important philosophical issues, and Boethius not only isolated these issues in the first place but provided the terminology for their discussion.

The Knight's Tale is full of the influence of the *Consolation*, especially apparent in the conception of chance, destiny and fortune (see p. 225). There are three places where use of the *Consolation* is particularly concentrated – each, significantly, a speech by a person within the prison of the Tale seeking to understand his predicament. The speeches of Arcite at 393–414, of Palamon at 445–75, and of Theseus at 2129–83 are all on a related theme: the way in which providence stands in relation to man's happiness. Arcite is sure that God's providence does all for the best, but cannot understand it; he sees himself as an example of a man stumbling around blindly seeking what turns out to be false happiness – exactly the sort of confusion Philosophia describes in the *Consolation* (III, prose 2). The balanced contrasting speech of Palamon, however, shows no such perspective; he takes the position 'Boethius' did at the beginning of the *Consolation* (cf. I, metrum 5) and cries out against the cruel gods who allow the innocent to suffer. But Theseus blames neither God nor himself. By looking carefully at the divine plan and the principle in the universe whereby the perfect and stable God modulates his purposes through agents who, as they get further removed from his perfection, become less and less stable and perfect, he shows that there is an established order which men must obey and which does turn all to good. This is exactly what Philosophia does in I V, prose 6 and metrum 6. Clearly the common interest in these speeches means we have to look at them as reflecting on each other; Palamon's and Arcite's are rhetorically and structurally contrasted and obviously present irreconcilable opposites – and the irony that in earthly terms it is the one who complains about the cruelty of the gods who eventually wins the lady. (One wonders whether there is a further irony, in that, however symbolic of harmony the marriage may be, the happiness of marriage is a false felicity in Boethius's analysis.) At the end, however, it is Theseus's view, which shows the limitations of those of Arcite and Palamon, that we are left with; and its nobility is much enhanced by the contrast.

10. Convention and the Persons of the Tale

There are great differences between the depiction of people in medieval and in modern art. These differences are symptomatic of something much deeper: a difference in the concept of the self and the personality. It is of course true that modern concepts of both are at least in part – quite a large part – the fruit of developments both made by and reflected in art and literature, and that it is possible to look at, say, a Shakespeare play and approach the characters in it using common modern assumptions and concepts to analyse them without feeling any particular unease (though perhaps we should feel some unease). But the fact remains that our fathers did not think of the individual human personality as we do, and this is reflected in their art, literature and architecture if we read the signs right. Character in medieval literature is not like character in modern. A just understanding of *The Knight's Tale* must take these differences into account.

Role is of great importance. Even as late as Shakespeare's time, we have characters in his drama referring to themselves seriously, in an idiom we still use ironically, as 'playing a part' in a drama whose stage is the world; Marvell, in 'An Horatian Ode upon Cromwell's Return from Ireland', implies exactly the same of Charles I going to his execution – the king was conscious of being cast in a particular role, and played perfectly (and consciously) to the expectations of it. We find the same sort of thing in medieval literature and life. The Black Prince, according to the Chandos Herald, deliberately adopted the appropriate (almost literary) mode of behaviour when greeted by his wife Joan at the entrance to Bordeaux, despite his having just taken part in a gruelling military campaign. We see this sort of behaviour again in the love of symbolic pageantry in real politics, where the actors were not representing but actually doing; we see

45

it in art, and in ceremonial entertainment, for instance in the elaborate pageants the French King Charles V put on for the Emperor Charles I V on his visit to Paris in 1378. This particular view of human life, the self-judgement and self-projection against a role stereotype, only really began to set with the death of the Sun King, Louis XIV. While there was certainly an interest in personal morality and personal emotion in medieval art, theology and moral philosophy, the interest tends to be in classifying and generalizing; the individual is a special instance of a general type, and the personal moral perplexity, sin, guilt or whatever, can be understood by reference to the type to which it belongs. Lovers always feel they are unique, but in medieval literature lovers are always plotted in by reference to a type. The type brings with it certain assumptions, expectations and values. The recent work of the structural anthropologists, with their study of kinship systems and social roles, has perhaps made it easier for us to accept this notion than it would have been fifty years ago. Ironically, it makes the medieval notion of character look fashionably modern.

It follows, then, that in looking at character in literature we have first of all to look at what class of person the figure belongs to and what role he is playing. On those baselines the author works; and he can choose either decorum (the Knight of the *General Prologue* is decorous in the way he fulfils the role-model), or indecorum (the Monk, from the perspective of what the role-model should be, stands utterly condemned despite the surface energy and vigour of the speech and views and life invented for him). In *The Knight's Tale*, Theseus's role-models are two overlapping concepts: the knight, and the just ruler. Get the audience to recognize those two, and half the work is done. Chaucer is then free to do as he likes. As it happens, he confirms both; Theseus has power, uses it in the interests of justice in punishing Creon, is merciful when appealed to by the ladies, and out of an insoluble impasse proposes a way that ultimately coincides with the design of Heaven. And, like the wise ruler, he is fully aware of the meaning of what he is doing. The order imposed by him, the ritualizing of the personal conflict, is the local and special manifestation of the cosmic order imposed on chaos of which he talks in his last speech. Similarly, Arcite and Palamon are knights – one set of values; lovers – another set; and they are young. For even youth and age, as the *senex amans* ('aged lover') topos underlines, have their forms of appropriate speech, their ideas, qualities and behaviour.

It is clear that this emphasis on the public face of personality and on role will exclude concentration on the internal, personal and psychological aspects, as we employ those terms today. The critical assumptions and tools of our own time will not, therefore, be the best we could use for the problem – in any craft success depends on choosing the right tool for the job; you don't do marquetry with an axe. We can get some sort of idea what tools might be useful by looking at the rhetorical manuals and the *artes poeticae*. Chaucer had mastered these and knew that his audience had an informed enjoyment of the use of their techniques.*

The representation of human beings in fiction is discussed in most of the *artes poeticae*, and they drew their precepts from two sources: the precedent of Classical literature, and the contemporary academic and scientific habit of systematic classification and analysis. The good poet, being *varius et semper idem*, will delight and inform his audience by the way he 'amplifies' (i.e. elaborates) his work (*amplificatio*), and *descriptio* is one of the means of amplification. Geoffroi de Vinsauf's *Poetria Nova* (Chaucer's – with some irony? – 'deere maister soverayn'), and Matthieu de Vendôme's *Ars Versificatoria* both handle the problem of description. Matthieu de Vendôme says the aim of the artist is to create a picture that is credible: three eyes simply will not do. He then has to choose between an external description, where he will show only the appearance of a person, or an internal, where he will outline the possession (or not) of such characteristics as *ratio* (reason), *fides* (faith) *patientia* and *honestas*. The distinctive quality of a person consists of ten attributes: name, nature, fortune, social condition, occupation, disposition, judgement, situation, action and speech. (Look how this confirms all we have said above.) Finally, the author must decide his attitude to a character and choose the details he will use for his description accordingly. Matthieu de Vendôme is here concentrating on what there is to be said. In section III of his book, Geoffroi gives examples of how the picture might be completed through the device known as *effictio*, a convention specifically applied to literary portraiture, particularly of women. One should begin at the top of the head and work down, feature by feature, employing appropriate metaphor and simile and word-play, until 'her leg is graceful in its length, and her tiny foot joyfully dances at its own littleness'. There is no *chiaroscuro* (variations of light and shade) in the description; it is all vivid, sharp, evenly lit, like the figures in a medieval illuminated manuscript. Moreover, it is all objective; the metaphors and similes, even, relate the perfections of the person to external referents such as snow, ivory, jewels, gold, the sun, stars, and so on. It is in exactly this way that we are given

---

*Sometimes he plays games: one of their recommendations is the decorous matching of speech to speaker's role and status, and matching of speech to audience. Look how in the introduction to *The Miller's Tale* he pretends to be acutely embarrassed by the indecorum of the story he must, decorously, tell. (The ultimate joke is his pretence that what we all know to be fiction is in fact reportage.)

our first glimpse of Emelye. The id or ego of the person (had such concepts been invented) could hardly have been handled by such a method. The concept of literary character, then, tends to externalize what we would internalize. (It is perhaps easier now to see why allegory was so popular a mode.)

It is also quite clear that behind such character-drawing lie some important assumptions about its place in the economy of narrative. First, the poet's control of his material is absolute and he shapes it to his own design, to which he often explicitly alludes; second, the persons are merely one element in the total conception, and will subserve the interests of the whole. They can never become or even seem to be independent, and the action of the poem puts them under inescapable constraints. Third, naturalistic description is not really a goal – though vividness may be. Thus it is the meaning of the whole work to which ultimately our attention will be directed, rather than to a narrow appreciation of character for its own sake.

There is no reason to believe that Chaucer ever seriously disagreed with these basic assumptions even though he treats the rhetorical manuals with confident freedom – as any good poet would. In his entire work, Chaucer gives us only a few *effictiones* – for example, the comic one of Alisoun in *The Miller's Tale*, where the comparisons all link her with animals and food, and the serious one of Blanche in *The Book of the Duchess*. Elements of the *effictio* stress the inappropriately attractive femininity of the Prioress in the *General Prologue*. Elsewhere Chaucer uses *descriptio* and *effictio* very loosely indeed. One would expect the *General Prologue*, by its nature, to have been a gallery of descriptions according to the model. Instead, we get a treatment cavalier in the extreme – external mixed with internal, characteristics in no sort of order, ideas of quite unequal weight and seriousness rudely juxtaposed. Why did Chaucer so boldly work against his audience's knowledge of the normal type? The reason is that he had cast the *General Prologue* and the Canterbury frame in the mould of a first-person narrative, and he is therefore by this disorder conveying something about the narrator's perception, moral ineptitude and control of material which is important when he wants to use him as a control on our response. The norm is as useful and important when it is *not* followed as when it is.

In *The Knight's Tale* we have two longish personal *descriptiones*, balancing one another in method, form and length, in the portraits of the two kings, Emetreus and Lygurge, in Book III. These are objective, heraldic and symbolic, rather than personal; the colours and animal similes prepare us for the violent tournament in which they are to take part. We do not, however, have any formal portrait of Theseus: we see him only in action, action which is prejudged for us by the epithets 'noble' and 'gentle' prefixed to his name, and the categories 'duc' and 'conquerour'. Arcite and Palamon completely lack any detailed physical presence we can visualize; as in Theseus's case, we see them by their roles, simply as young knights and lovers, and at the beginning they are indistinguishable either by syntax or coat armour:

> Two yonge knyghtes liggynge by and by,
> Bothe in oon armes, wroght ful richely ...
> (153–4)

It is evident that while we can – and should – visualize the two kings in order to be able to grasp the splendour and seriousness of the set-piece tournament, in the characters that really matter in the Tale Chaucer is deliberately making us look at their roles and actions rather than at extraneous personal details. Similarly with Emelye; we might expect a full-scale *effictio*, but instead the only objective information we receive about her in the twenty lines of her first appearance (177–97) is that she was an early riser, had yellow hair in a long braid right down her back, and was gathering flowers to make a garland. The rest of these lines concentrate on subjective responses – 'fairer than the lily', 'fresher than May', 'singing in a heavenly way like an angel'. The precision of the correlative leaves Emelye deliberately vague, yet the similes show how people – the audience – would react to her if they saw her. We learn nothing at all about Emelye herself at this point. It is through the action, then, rather than description that Chaucer explores the roles and values in which he is really interested.

The lack of naturalism extends further than simply the description of persons. As in many poems, Chaucer gives them long and elaborate speeches, often at significant points in the narrative, which are quite unlike anything that could be spoken under stress or on the spur of the moment. Frequently they have an elaborate rhetorical articulation, their range of reference deliberately reflects on and deepens our view of the narrative, and no distinctive style is developed for each speaker. The artificiality is obvious to us, and may cause difficulties in our appreciation. But an analogy with opera may help; people don't sing like angels if they are dying of tuberculosis, they don't naturally cast their thoughts in rondo form if they think they have been cuckolded, and action and consequence certainly don't stop while they get it off their chest. But we accept the unrealistic convention of the aria in opera with no trouble, and the speeches in many medieval poems work in an exactly similar way. The action – often in a very abbreviated form – brings us to a crucial point in its development, at which either the narrator or one of the characters he is controlling may take off into an elaborate *tour de force* of eloquence which discusses and 'places' his situation and the story so far. Momentarily the action halts. This technique is very noticeable in *The Knight's Tale*.

Theseus

Theseus is first a knight, and second a conqueror and ruler. The first category places him firmly beside the Knight of the *General Prologue*: both 'love chivalrye', both are 'wis'. He is a 'trewe knight' in defending the cause of widows, as the Knight of the Tale is true in defending the faith against the infidel (see the notes on these abstract terms, p. 71f.). Theseus, again like the Knight, carefully observes the laws of arms and of justice. Chaucer found no precedent in Boccaccio for Theseus's shock at finding the informal duel between Arcite and Palamon 'withouten juge or oother officere'; equally Theseus is pleased when he can set up a formal trial by combat, and promises to be a just judge. The linking of a tale in which Theseus is a main character with the Knight in the *General Prologue* could not be more decorous.

On this basis Chaucer has built an impressive figure. In many of his speeches there is a wisdom, a humour and a sanity – and a seriousness – that we do not find in Boccaccio's Teseo, who is quite incapable of the profundity of Theseus's last speech. Theseus is quickly moved to pity, and readily postpones his long-awaited homecoming to avenge wrong (the similarity of this action to that of the great emperor Trajan, who in both Langland and Dante got to Heaven, is discussed in the Commentary). Easily moved to anger though he is, he is yet capable of reflection, and a knowledge of his own mistakes which allows him to show mercy. He is deliberately linked, in his championing of justice, with the Divine Ruler. (And, indeed, his action, in the way it limits the freedom of Arcite and Palamon's behaviour, is parallel on the human level with the divine control of human parameters in general.) Chaucer seems to have deliberately adapted Teseo into something like the ideal ruler. In Theseus's behaviour we have a picture of what true gentility, nobility, chivalry and rule ought to be like. Theseus's last speech (2128–31) provides the climax and denouement of the Tale and shows him in judgement; it needs some discussion and summary here.

The build-up to it, and its position at the climax of the most 'epic' and 'heroic' of the four books of the Tale, clearly indicates that Chaucer intended it to be given very close attention (see below, p. 203). It replaces that originally given to Teseo by Boccaccio, which Chaucer transfers to Egeus. (The first thirty lines at least are heavily dependent on Boethius: see Appendix 3, p. 223.) A narratorial intervention, to suggest an overview or interpretation of the Tale, would be nowhere near as effective as giving the speech to one of the persons within the imagined pagan world, who has to make sense of the events on what are believably his terms. This allows the audience, who, simply by living in a world with a different set of assumptions, do not share those terms, to look with detachment at the argument and at the narrative of which it is a part. Moreover, it is not just a philosophical discussion, but is set in a political context and so is part of a public political action. Theseus has been built up throughout the Tale in a way that emphasizes his knowledge, wisdom, power and mercy – as a human analogue of the divine all-seeing wisdom, as all rulers ought to be – and there is nothing in this speech which is inconsistent with the type of figure he is or the type of utterance he has been given so far; rather, it is a natural conclusion to it. Highlighted by Egeus's facile emphasis on change, it immeasurably deepens the issues and attempts to see behind mere vicissitude, which the events could (and for Egeus, do) exemplify, to a notion of causality and purpose.

The structure of the speech reflects its narrative context, in a parliament where political action has to be taken. (Criticism of it for not keeping on a consistent theoretical level is, therefore, beside the point.) It moves from an argument about general ideas, through exemplification, to a series of general conclusions. It then quite properly turns to the local and special applications of these ideas; philosophy must in the end take account of the everyday problems of living in this 'wrecched world' (see Commentary on 2129ff.). Theseus may see further and wield more authority than anyone else in the Tale, but he is still human, still limited – as are we all – in knowledge. He is still, in fact, in the prison of this world, and his wisdom is perhaps the best that can be gained without the revelation of God in Christ that is – in terms of this poem and its rhetorical decorum – not open to him. The audience, however, by having this revelation, can perhaps see a little further. They will certainly notice the irony that, despite the neat conclusion to the story of Arcite and Palamon, the married couple have lost at least eight years of their lives which no Theseus can give back, and the road to this conclusion has been paved with suffering. The human condition, even for the man who seeks wisdom, like Theseus, is still subject to time and loss. The only alternative to an Egeus-like resignation (or despair) is Theseus's faith in the ultimate incomprehensible goodness and purpose of the universe.

Arcite and Palamon

The handling of Arcite and Palamon again shows how free Chaucer was with his source material. Boccaccio does not distinguish them much in person and character, and at the beginning Chaucer suppresses even the little information Boccaccio gives. But at the sight of Emelye, where, having emphasized their similarity, Boccaccio makes them both see Emelye as Venus on earth, Chaucer introduces an interesting differentiation: Arcite is quite clear that he sees a woman, and only Palamon sees her in religious terms. Each is given the appropriate stylistic register for his speech in reaction to the first sight of her. Palamon uses the religious terminology of some forms of *fin amour*, while Arcite, since affective love is competitive, speaks in a lower register with a certain blunt self-interest: 'Ech man for himself, there is noon oother'. Their differing reactions highlight the collision of the claims of love for Emelye and of sworn brotherhood – both admirable in themselves and both absolute. This leads to the irony – comic and grim and painful at the same time – where the chivalry out of which that sworn brotherhood grew makes each help the other to arm, 'as frendly as he were his owene brother', for a combat over Emelye in which each tries his best to kill his beloved foe. In that combat, and in the tournament it prefigures, all the value references are to ferocious animals, creatures of uncontrolled appetite. Their situation is further made ironic and problematical by the fact that, as Theseus points out, Emelye does not know of their existence, and when she does, she cannot have both and really wants neither. Yet any divergences do not affect their basic similarity in nobility and refinement. Each goes through the refining process of love through a long-term fidelity (Chaucer emphasizes that it is seven years long), each suffers from the maladies of love: Arcite from the lover's 'hereos' (see Commentary, 516 n.), Palamon from another sort of madness in love. Ironically, in Book II each envies the other, and each does what he expects the other to do. Each rallies exactly balanced forces for the final combat, and each is supported by a god. Both of them at the end think generously and affectionately of each other, and both of them – another Chaucerian addition – ponder the meaning of their lives and suffering, reminding us that the plot of the story has a symbolic and moral dimension we must extract from it.

By deliberately stressing their similarity and underlining that their differences are those of situation and accident rather than of nature, Chaucer forces our attention on to the issue of what so much energy, passion and suffering might mean, and what sort of universe it expresses.

And here the key point is that all Arcite's and Palamon's behaviour in Books I and II results from an incomplete and partial perception of the world of the poem as we, the audience, can see it actually to be. The irony provided by our fuller knowledge is thus crucial, and figures not only the fuller knowledge and political control of Theseus, but also, perhaps, the providential overview to which Theseus seems to be referring in his last speech. By a consummate irony – for he doesn't understand the resonances of what Chaucer has given him to say – Arcite also refers to it (393 ff.).

Emelye

The differences between Boccaccio and Chaucer in the presentation of Emelye are striking. Boccaccio's Emilia is a very self-assured young lady indeed. She sees Arcita leave prison, is attracted to him, and later penetrates his disguise. She enjoys seeing the knights look at her from the window; she finds them fighting in the wood; and she has a blend of conscious shyness and cleverness which is quite unlike Emelye. Chaucer, as we have seen, deliberately makes her a flat character, important in the reactions she arouses in others. Only at one moment do we glimpse a point of view for her and that is when she prays to Diana that she may remain a maid, or, if that is not possible, have him as her husband who loves her best. Yet even this we can misinterpret; Chaucer is giving Emelye a prayer that a young maiden of breeding and chastity in the refined world of romance might decorously offer. It is, in fact, a confirmation of the Emelye we have first glimpsed through the knights' eyes on that first May morning: her role is that of the Lady to be loved, and the love of the lovers and its effects is the key concern. Her grief – which we are told about rather than observe closely – at Arcite's funeral is conventionally hyperbolic. At the proposal of cementing a political alliance with Thebes by her marriage to Palamon, she is enjoined to react as a noble lady who is beloved ought to; by showing 'pitee'. Moreover, she is symbolically linked with the gift of fortune in two important places – see the syntactical sleight-of-hand at 1002–3, and her prayer to Diana in the temple.

11. Plot, Narrative Structure and Fable

Most medieval art is serial and paratactic in structure: that is, it is composed of a number of discrete elements, each with its own internal organization, linked together in a structure which brings them both into a significant context and into significant relationship with each other. An analogy from architecture will make this clearer.*

In a medieval cathedral, the totality is a unit itself designed as an act of worship which exists as a dynamic setting for the drama of the liturgy. The stone frame, significant and symbolic as it is, contains numerous stained-glass windows. Each of these is coherent, complete in itself, and can be so appreciated, as on a postcard. Each of them is a focus for the memory, being often based on a biblical narrative, and through them the 'Light by which we see light' streams into our mind. Yet each is drawn into a meaningful sequence and relationship with other windows, which modify and extend its meaning without destroying its unique quality. Further, all the windows are drawn into additional perspective of meaning by the symbolic form and function of the whole building. The aesthetic principle behind such a structure is aggregative: the repetition of the pattern (the bay or arch, with a strong emphasis on the means of joining them – the stonework), and the adding of separate unit to separate unit to make the whole. We shall need to keep this analogy in mind when we look at the relation of *The Knight's Tale* to *The Canterbury Tales* as a whole. It is also helpful in considering the Tale itself.

It follows from this that the concept of plot in romance is not what we expect of plot today. While we think of a good plot as one in which events are linked by a chain of probability and consequence, and expect narrative to generate a tension, an illusion, and a commitment in us which is only resolved at the end, medieval writers and audiences saw it as a series of events interrupted by chance or coincidence. (This is not necessarily 'unrealistic'.) Understanding this series is impossible from within, as it were. Understanding can only come from a standpoint outside it. (The goldfish in its bowl can never see the real nature of its problem, but its owner can.) As a result, medieval narrative is usually composed of a series of carefully designed blocks, linked together by bridging passages of less complexity (though not without their own complexity), rather like beads on a chain. One sees here how the demands of possible oral delivery, of aesthetic theory, and of philosophical understanding of the texture of life may well coincide in this narrative form. Some of the blocks are designed to dominate our memories of the narrative – in the case of *The Knight's Tale* the prison, the two kings, the temples, for example – and provide a guide for our interpretation and understanding of the narrative's

---

* We can use such an analogy because the Middle Ages were fond of pointing out the closeness of the arts of poetry, architecture and painting in the way they were constructed, the way they worked and the symbols they used. Chaucer shows (*Troilus and Criseyde*, I. 1065) that he is fully aware of Geoffroi de Vinsauf's analogy between the poet and the builder.

significance. Frequently we find the narrative and illusion being interrupted abruptly – just at the point where we would expect a crescendo building to a climax – in order to change direction, or to alter the way we have been looking at the text. *The Knight's Tale* is clearly composed on these lines. The individual narrative blocks, framed by the narratorial voice, are built into the larger units of the four separate books. We shall need later to look at the way in which the books, as well as the blocks, relate to each other. The narrative is carefully patterned by similarities of event, style, structure or description to invite our comparison of like with like. Its meaning can also be altered by a shift of perspective.

Structure is an important factor in conveying meaning, and we need first to look at the balanced structure of the Tale. This balance is clearly exemplified in the two speeches of Arcite and Palamon at the end of Book I. The germ from which the entire poem grows is the love of two knights for Emelye. Already we have an ironic situation because, while both may be worthy, only one can have her. This must lead to a conflict which shatters their sworn brotherhood. Chaucer emphasizes first their similarity. Then, keeping within the type of the knightly lover, he gives them speeches of considerable rhetorical dissimilarity in order to explore different emphases in their love. Their first reactions to the sight of Emelye are strongly contrasted, and both are given in detail. Each reaction is decorous in accordance with the speaker's perception of her. Arcite's style is lower, brusquer, much less complex, more martial, as is appropriate in one whose patron later will be Mars. He has no doubt that his love is earthly, 'par amour' (297), and that its aim is his own satisfaction: it is certainly *eros*, and may well be *cupiditas*. Palamon, however, sees Emelye as Venus, a goddess to be worshipped, and for whose love he would gladly die. There are certain elements here of *caritas* and *agape*, and, as the Commentary points out, the rhetorical formulation of the speech is close to devotional language and style. Their quarrel which follows is not naturalistic, vigorous though the speech-rhythms are. Their long speeches are formally balanced and contrasted. When Arcite is released and Palamon is kept in prison, each envies the other, and each is given a long speech bewailing his lot. These two passages of the Tale (365–416; 423–75) are exactly the same length; the rhetorical procedure is the same; both start with 'Allas'. Their opening sentences and ideas are mirror-images of one another. Each knight then proceeds to a comparison of his rival's opportunities and then emphasizes the speaker's sorry state. Next they move on to a consideration of fortune (Arcite) and the gods (Palamon) *vis à vis* man's position and their own. The irony of human wishes and ignorance is the next theme; and both close with an anticipation of the speaker's death. The comic irony of each envying, quite wrongly, the other's lot is pointed sharply by juxtaposition and close rhetorical parallels, but the similarity also points out the differences between their attitudes to fate and fortune. Palamon personalizes the gods and their operation as 'cruel', while Arcite concentrates far more on human ignorance and incertitude. (It must be said that their respective attitudes could equally well be reversed.) Thus, as well as opening up the love-situation, the speeches highlight two different possible views of man's lot and make a serious contribution to clarification of the issues at the heart of the poem.

There is a similar example of closely juxtaposed, identically structured set-pieces in Book III – the Temples of Venus and Mars (1060–1108; 1117–92). Palamon's and Arcite's patrons are strongly contrasted, just as physically they are placed at opposite ends of the theatre (itself an important image of the enclosed world we inhabit). Structurally they are very similar, and technically they belong to a rhetorical genre of description called *ecphrasis*. Both begin with the same word, and then proceed to describe the wall-paintings in an exactly similar manner. These passages illustrate, with examples historical, mythological and allegorical, the effects (both good and bad) of the influence of these gods. The predominant effect is unpleasant and concentrates on their power over mortal suffering. Each description closes with almost identically executed portraits (1097–1108: 1183–92) of the statues of the gods, in the iconographic panoply familiar to us from Renaissance painting. The quarrel of Arcite and Palamon has now been lifted to a plane where the conflict is between two cosmic principles, each terrible and uncontrollable. One of the big philosophical issues of the late Middle Ages and Renaissance was the question of how one can reconcile love and strife – how, as Hippolyta says in *A Midsummer Night's Dream*, we can find the 'concord of this discord'. (Botticelli's neo-Platonic 'Venus and Mars' in the National Gallery, London, deals with the same issue, the interdependence of love and strife.) Set against these two balanced pictures is a third, that of Diana, whose temple is midway between the other two, on the northern boundary of the theatre. Again, an identical plan is followed in the description: the wall decoration, the myths of Diana's vengeance and the miracles of her pity. Then follow eleven lines (1217–28) on her statue, described in exactly the same mode – symbolic and iconographic – as those of Venus and Mars. Here is the cosmic principle to which the human Emelye relates. We now see that the conflict of human desires and emotions is part of something very much bigger. These descriptions generalize and isolate the limited and confused standpoints of Arcite, Palamon and Emelye. Though the temples are made with hands (art) and thus reflect a human understanding, which may be partial or fallacious, of the principles in life, nevertheless they suggest that human action is intimately involved with the forces of the universe. Yet it is not at this point that Chaucer wants us to move finally on to this level of thought; and so by a brilliant bathos he lifts us right back from this gorgeously ornate scene to our humdrum, gumbooted world where we will apply the lessons of the poem: he tells us how much the paint cost (1229–30)!

The large-scale oppositions epitomized in art (within art) in the temples are seen once more on a human level in the opposing amplified descriptions of Lygurge and Emetreus (1270–96; 1297–1329). These two passages are of about the same length, and follow the same order: the king, his features, his device (bearskin or garland), the animals which accompanied him and his company. Imagery of size, violence and power dominates. Raised up to this level we now see the exactly equal claims of Palamon and Arcite on Emelye. The love-debate between them admits of no solution within its own terms, and merely widens the circle of conflict as long as it continues. Behind the gorgeousness of the descriptions and set-pieces the audience would enjoy, and hidden in the violence of the animals which accompany the kings, lies a sinister hint of the suffering involved. It is not only the two knights who are concerned now, but – however chivalrous the motives may be – two armies. The use of animal imagery, here and elsewhere, in the opposition of Palamon and Arcite underlines the danger of passion, the 'animal' impulses in man.

These oppositions of balanced blocks are intimately related to the original balanced opposition of Palamon's and Arcite's speeches and open up the issues there raised. In turn, that balance extends the original differing reactions to the knights' first view of Emelye. The formal parallels of the poem, therefore, are not just decorative or ironic. The form is actually exploring something, mirroring something, in the central moral and philosophical concerns of the poem. And the process continues when Emelye and the lovers make their sacrifices and offer their prayers.

Arcite's prayer and Palamon's are again closely similar in form; both are followed by portents which seem to ensure that their apparently irreconcilable requests will be granted. But Chaucer here has altered the order we would expect from the order of the temples. Instead of Arcite, then Palamon, then a lighter touch on Emelye, we have Arcite and Palamon balanced around a centrally placed Emelye, whose sacrifice is more elaborately described. Emelye is praying to Diana, and Diana, as well as being the goddess of Chastity, is also goddess of the Moon (cf. 1219), identified with *Fortuna Imperatrix Mundi* (Fortune, Empress of the World, as she was often called), whose sphere encloses all that is changeable and corruptible. Emelye's prayer is answered by a theophany of Diana Venetrix, who tells her she must abide by eternal decree. Emelye accepts her fate. Clearly Chaucer is here continuing to expand the significance of the human conflict and at this point introduces – although we cannot yet see how it will work – an element which informs us that the impossible dialectic of the love-quarrel will be resolved.

These narrative and amplificatory blocks are closely juxtaposed. From time to time the forward movement of the narrative is deliberately slowed down, as if a frame in a film were held for a few seconds, and it is easy to see that the blocks must be played against each other. There are, however, other structural blocks whose positioning is important but which do not work in the same way.

In *Troilus and Criseyde* Chaucer makes Pandarus, with unconscious irony (for the remark refers to the whole poem as well as to Pandarus' speech to Criseyde), repeat the proverb 'Th' ende is every tales strengthe' (II. 260). *The Knight's Tale* is broken into four episodes in four books, and these mark important divisions of the narrative; each book is a narrative unit with a beginning, a middle and an end. It is worth looking at how the intermediate 'ends' relate to one another and to the whole. In Book I the narrator leaves Palamon and Arcite desperate, each envying those precise elements in the other's lot which make him unhappy. Their expectations and desires are mutually exclusive. Chaucer suddenly and without warning addresses the audience, and suggests they are to see the story so far as a love-debate of a type quite familiar in this and later periods: which lover is in the worse case? This question suggests an overview of the story which reduces the suggestive complexity of the Tale so far to something relatively trite, but it does focus sharply on the paradoxical situation and the issue of subjective and objective happiness. At the end of Book II Theseus, having pardoned Arcite and Palamon, takes control, and offers the possibility of a physical resolution of the triangular problem. The book closes with both knights happy, yet it is a happiness as paradoxical as their unhappiness at the end of Book I. Both books close with a focus on human affective love. At the end of this book, too, Theseus is given a speech in which the terms 'destinee' and 'fortune' appear, and he sees himself as setting up a situation where destiny can be worked out. We can see that the way into the poem offered to us at the end of Book I was shallow and self-limiting, because we had not allowed for the effect of time and circumstance. At the end of Book III the prayers are answered, but they are answered in another apparent contradiction and conflict of the gods which on first reading we may not see through. Emelye, we know, will marry one of the knights; yet Arcite has been promised victory in a battle to win Emelye, while Palamon has been promised Emelye herself. These promises seem mutually exclusive, even to the gods (except to Saturn, the god of Age). But this ending develops strongly in a major key what in Book I we have only heard in a minor: the supernatural machinery which in Book I Palamon saw as cruel (445) and Arcite as benevolent (393ff.). Moreover, Theseus's reliance on destiny at the end of Book II is now supported by a mechanism of causality and destiny, as yet inscrutable. Perhaps the supernatural beings *do* intervene in human life, and perhaps their intervention *is* in its own terms comprehensible and rational. Justice, the truth of the gods' word, and causality suddenly become central to an understanding of human life, and the key interest of Book IV. It is noticeable that Chaucer moves very quickly out of Book III, throwing an enormous weight on the word 'effect' ('how this worked out in practice').

The end of Book IV is also the end of the poem. The paradox of the whole Tale is resolved by time (as the paradox of Book I was partly resolved in Book II), and by death. Theseus's long speech centres round the ideas of purpose behind accident, love behind apparent cruelty and indifference, wisdom behind naked power. This speech occurs at exactly the same point in Book IV as his earlier long speech did in Book II; they demand comparison. Where in Book II Theseus was working within fortune and destiny, in Book IV he is now handling those ideas again from the outside, as it were, in an attempt to provide an overview of the whole Tale and of his own actions (including those in Book II). The speech faces squarely, as we all must, the issues of pain, suffering and loss in human life, and his acceptance of them as part of a loving purpose is not facile. Chaucer has made Theseus understand that while he sees further than anyone else – beyond his own father Egeus's view of the world as mere 'transmutation' – he does not yet see all: he is still human. We feel that he is seeking the wisdom sought by Solomon. The consequence of the recognition of his limited knowledge is patience and acceptance – ironically echoing Arcite's facile counsel while in prison (226ff.). In Book II, Theseus reflected on the power of appetitive love in mortal affairs, with humour and irony; now in Book IV love is at last seen not just as a human appetite, but as a cosmic principle. The gods kept their word, and Arcite was given the best of all deaths, one at the summit of his powers and ambitions. The quarrel of Arcite and Palamon over a wordly good – human love – which dominated the first book is now resolved by time and what looks to them like accident (but which we see is no such thing) into a restoration of their first magnanimity and generosity. The poem closes, as it opened, with conflict resolved in marriage – Venus disarming Mars.

The cosmic, the political and the private are linked in a final synthesis – for it is a fine irony that the marriage of Palamon and Emelye is the result of a political decision by Theseus to cement the alliance of two states. The endings of the books have progressively shifted our vision of the story from the ethical and situational to the philosophical and cosmic.

If we express this diagrammatically, it will make clearer how the endings of the books relate to, contrast with, and highlight each other. It also clarifies how they fit into the poem.

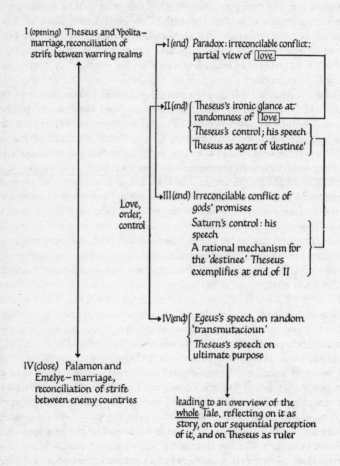

I (opening) Theseus and Ypolita – marriage, reconciliation of strife between warring realms

I (end) Paradox: irreconcilable conflict: partial view of love

II (end) Theseus's ironic glance at randomness of love
Theseus's control; his speech
Theseus as agent of 'destinee'

Love, order, control

III (end) Irreconcilable conflict of gods' promises
Saturn's control: his speech
A rational mechanism for the 'destinee' Theseus exemplifies at end of II

IV (end) Egeus's speech on random 'transmutacioun'
Theseus's speech on ultimate purpose

IV (close) Palamon and Emelye – marriage, reconciliation of strife between enemy countries

leading to an overview of the whole Tale, reflecting on it as story, on our sequential perception of it, and on Theseus as ruler

Comparison of like with like, or position with position, then, can lead us a good way into an understanding of the issues Chaucer has set out in the Tale. It is clear that the story of Arcite and Palamon, which looks at first so run-of-the-mill, is being deliberately developed into something mythic – that is, expressing through fable an intuition about an eternal moral truth. The narrative alters its meaning as our vision is modified by each succeeding book. Since we must be aware of the way in which our view is shifting, our responses to the story become part of the subject of the whole poem. At first we focus sympathetically on Palamon and Arcite and their pathetic (not tragic) story of impossibilities and a cruel fate. This level is then distanced by the figure of Theseus. First, he is the just ruler executing a proper revenge on the unjust ruler, Creon: Palamon and Arcite therefore suffer justly for the sins of their earthly city. (Note the irony of Palamon's complaint that they are in prison because of 'tirannye' (253). He means the tyranny of Theseus, but the real tyranny is that of his kinsman Creon, rightly punished by the just Theseus.) Second, Theseus on the human level stands to them as a sort of Providence, inscrutable and all-powerful, controlling the prison, the lady, the tournament, and so on. His perception of their quarrel in the wood as comic marks a level of understanding beyond anything Palamon and Arcite could yet reach, but we can share it. Once we have grasped Theseus's viewpoint, we can no longer identify with those of Arcite and Palamon. Next, we see the struggle in the beginnings of a cosmic perspective – a struggle between the planetary gods. Only Saturn's influence (time) can save the honour of Venus and Mars and resolve each planetary god's partial, apparently contradictory, knowledge into a just synthesis (cf. 1805ff.). Saturn, on the planetary level, seems momentarily to parallel Theseus's control on the human plane (cf. 2177n.), but the ultimate view, suggested to us by Theseus's wisdom, is of a providential love which is wise and just, above even the just ruler and the planetary gods – rather like the poet behind the poem (cf. above, p. 23). But because we are imprisoned (by the body, our cognition, the world), this power often seems to us unjust and irrational.

As in another poem, there is 'no cause for lamentation now'. Arcite, 'of chivalrie the flour', died with honour, and Theseus is right to reprove those who wept so readily for his death. At the end we must look back on our reactions to the poem while it was incomplete and see the fallibility of our judgement of fiction. Manipulated by the poet we have passed through successive levels of causality to a glimpse of the first cause on which all depends. Can we be sure our judgement of reality is any less partial than our interim judgements of the poem? Our vision must be cleared if we are to be wise. The clearing of that vision is part of the purpose of the poem, and a large part of its subject.

12. *The Canterbury Tales*, the Knight and *The Knight's Tale*

The Canterbury Tales is unfinished, and there is good evidence that Chaucer changed his mind about its final extent and the number of tales to be included as he was compiling it from both new material and older poems which he revised to a greater or lesser degree. He seems also never to have decided the exact order of the tales. They have come down to us in a series of fragments, and some of those told as the pilgrims near Canterbury clearly precede ones told earlier on the journey. Despite this unfinished state, we can still form some idea of the outline of Chaucer's intention.

The 'frame' of the pilgrimage is, of course, itself a story which moves a group of people through space and time. The 'plot' of this story is provided partly by the tales the pilgrims agree to tell, partly by their reactions to them and to each other, and partly by the nature of the pilgrimage they are making. The fictional nature of the frame needs stressing, for it means that the pilgrimage must be approached with the same assumptions about story as any of the individual tales; it also means that while any tale will work on its own, detached from its setting, it will also gain in significance when seen within the frame. The levels of meaning conveyed by the frame will affect and extend – and may even provide an ironic perspective on – the meaning in the story. Inorganic form, as described above (p. 53f.), here achieves a triumphant subtlety.

The frame story is based on the chance assembly of a group of pilgrims at the Tabard Inn in Southwark. The fact that this inn and an innkeeper called Harry Baillif actually existed should not make us class the poem as journalism; the persona is plainly not the real Geoffrey Chaucer, and tells us things only an omniscient poet could know (like the debts and illegal currency speculations of the Merchant), and the pilgrimage and the pilgrims themselves clearly have a symbolic dimension. In the first place, the pilgrimage without exception in medieval literature (and in life!) is seen as analogous to the life of man on earth and on his journey to the heavenly Jerusalem. This point is emphasized when Chaucer makes the Parson, who is given the tale immediately preceding the arrival of the pilgrims at Canterbury, specifically draw the parallel:

> And Jhesu, for his grace, wit me sende
> To shewe yow the wey, in this viage,
> Of thilke parfit glorious pilgrimage
> That highte Jerusalem celestial.
>
> (X. 48–51)

(The Parson refuses to tell a tale – the fictional character rejects fiction – and instead preaches a not inappropriate academic sermon on the Seven Deadly Sins of pride, anger, lust, envy, gluttony, avarice and sloth.)

Secondly, a pilgrimage, like the Muslim *hajj*, was something that most members of society would perform at some time or other in their lives; despite the Church's ambivalent attitude towards pilgrimages, they were very well organized, with recognized routes, inns and places of assembly. The pilgrimage was almost the only institution in medieval society where people of different rank could mix and talk on nearly equal terms. Chaucer is therefore able credibly to draw into his story representatives of all classes, giving each a tale decorous to his or her position and circumstances.*

Thirdly, it was well known that while some went on a pilgrimage purely out of motives of devotion (as do the Knight, the Parson, the Clerke and the Plowman), many saw the pilgrimage as the medieval equivalent of the package holiday to Mallorca: an opportunity for a wild time, no questions asked when you got home and the chance to commit sins which would be forgiven on arrival at the shrine. The Wyf of Bath is clearly in this class; she must have been frightfully wicked to have had to go to Jerusalem thrice, to Rome, to Santiago da Compostela and to Cologne. Chaucer's delicious remark 'She coude muchel of wandringe by the weye' (*General Prologue*, A467) clearly means more than one sort of exploration. The pilgrimage motif therefore provides not only a metaphor; it is also an elegant, inclusive evaluating frame.

Behind the apparently random assembly of these pilgrims lies another clever valuing device. There are only four characters whose excellence is fully endorsed: the Knight, the Plowman, the Clerke and the Parson. When we realize that, conventionally, medieval society was seen as divided into three mutually interdependent estates, those who work (the Plowman), those who fight (the Knight), and those who pray (the active Parson and the contemplative Clerke), the significance is clear. Chaucer is providing us, in those characters who fulfil the decorous obligations of their role, with moral yardsticks by which to judge all the others who must, by definition, fit into one of the three estates. And the narrator's

* For comparison, Boccaccio's frame in the *Decameron* automatically limits the speakers he can use to the gilded youth of the aristocracy.

apparent sympathy – as in the case of the Monk, or the Prioress – is a warning that something is very badly wrong not only with what that character represents but also with the way society, represented by the naive narrator, tolerates them.

The *General Prologue*, then, is not just a gallery of vivid characters, on the model of the Classical writer Theophrastus, but a moral analysis of a society. It could be argued that the tales themselves take that analysis further.

The pilgrims assembled, the Host elects himself master of this pilgrimage (a sort of Master of the Caravan).* By rank this job ought to have fallen to the Knight, and it is not fanciful to see the Host as a sort of Lord of Misrule whose authority was absolute for the short period convention allowed it to last. It is he who proposes (to the distinct increase of his custom!) the tale-telling contest, and it is he who devises the choosing of the first teller by lot – by chance. With consummate irony, chance confirms the hierarchy: decorously, the Knight begins the story-telling, just as the Knight was the first in the catalogue of pilgrims. The interest in chance and order which we see in *The Knight's Tale* is present also in the frame story, and the noble Knight accepts the order imposed by the Host, while the ignoble and disordered Miller reduces even this temporary order to chaotic quarrelling and personal abuse. (It is noteworthy that it is the Knight who intervenes to stop an incipient brawl between the Pardoner and the Host (VI.(C)962).) The values attached to the figure of the Knight have already been discussed in some detail. He is meant to be a typical figure (just as all the others in some ways relate to a type), yet he is also firmly linked, by details we are given about him, to Chaucer's own day and society. Not a few Englishmen had fought in the very campaigns mentioned, and thus the type figure is almost a real brother-in-arms; those who had not fought would nevertheless have known about the campaigns of Peter I of Lusignan, King of Cyprus, against the Saracens; they would have known about the Crusades in southern Spain and North Africa, and many had served with the Teutonic Knights against the pagan tribes along the Baltic. But the contemporary focus simply sharpens the ideal type. In the context of *The Canterbury Tales*, when read as a whole, all other examples of knighthood are valued.

As a fictional character, the Knight could not of course 'write' *The Knight's Tale* any more than the other characters could write their stories, and it is pointless to see the Tale as an extension of his own personality.

---

*The problem of safety while travelling meant that people would wait in the inns until a largish group had assembled, and then set out in company under a leader who knew the way – like the caravans of the Near East.

It is concerned with far more important issues than that, and, of course, it existed before he did. The link between the Tale and its supposed teller is here, as in other cases, merely decorum; the tale is the sort of story that might be told by a noble in whom virtue reigns. And when the Tale begins, we are in a world quite different from that of the road to Canterbury; the figure of the Knight ceases to have importance for us and the narrator clearly cannot be identified with him.*

But though the story did once exist in a vacuum and can still (and, for a time, should) be so read, Chaucer drew it into the Canterbury frame and gave it an important position. It is significant that the plan of *The Canterbury Tales*, as we deduce it from what is left to us, starts with *The Knight's Tale* and deals first with man's passions and the loving Providence which governs the world he lives in, and that it closes with *The Parson's Tale* which provides a detailed diagnosis of what is wrong with man and an assurance of the forgiveness of a loving God. The high moral seriousness of these two tales, in such different forms, suggests that they set out for us the parameters within which to analyse the stories they enclose, each of which represents some aspect or view of human life. Thus the tales as individual visions of human life are structured in a way similar to the catalogue of pilgrims: the ideal characters value the rest of their company, and the stories they tell† help to provide values for the rest of the tales. Clearly we are meant to understand each tale in the collection on its own, and then to set tale against tale, and then the tales against the even larger account of the whole pilgrimage.‡

* There is evidence elsewhere, in Chaucer's lack of revision, of this decorous yet inorganic linking of tale to teller. The Second Nun speaks of herself as an 'unworthy son of Eve', and *The Shipman's Tale* presupposes a female narrator. But both tales are the sort of thing such tellers might tell.

† The Plowman has no tale.

‡ The first tale and the last enclose a remarkably diverse collection, which includes examples of all the small forms of narrative in Chaucer's day. We have the lives of the saints, like *The Prioresse's Tale* and *The Second Nun's Tale*, and the legend of high virtue in *The Clerke's Tale*, all told in an appropriately high register of language and ornate form, the 'rime royale'. We have the 'confessions', paralleled in other works of the day, of *The Wyf of Bath's Prologue*, *The Pardoner's Prologue* and *The Canon's Yeoman's Prologue*. There is the ironic verse sermon of the Pardoner and the academic prose sermon of the Parson. We have the parody of popular tail-rhyme romance in the brilliant *Tale of Sir Thopas*. There are examples of romance of 'faerye', folk-tale, *fabliau*, beast-fable and Breton lay. The social inclusiveness of the pilgrimage device allows an unparalleled inclusiveness of literary form. All these forms had been developed to do a specific job and carry with them accepted expectations and values, which Chaucer exploits.

For example, *The Clerke's Tale* presents us, in Griselda's history, with a story which explores unrelentingly just what is involved in the concept of the 'good wife' in the Book of Proverbs. Its form is deliberately that of the legend of a saint. It is openly set against the racy and vigorous self-exposure of the Wyf of Bath, who, by a clever irony, thinks she is justifying herself when all she is doing is confirming in exact detail all that the sermon-writers, drawing on the Book of Proverbs and other sources, said of the 'bad wife'. The imagery of alchemy in the dignified and polished rime royale tale of St Cecilia (*The Second Nun's Tale*) forces comparison with the alchemy in the racy confession of the charlatan Canon's Yeoman; one alchemy is the transformation of men into saints, the other is mere fraudulent greed. The similar situations of the Franklin's and the Merchant's tales force us to compare both their values and the attitudes to marriage they offer; and it is not an easy comparison, for neither is sound. Perhaps *The Clerke's Tale* is relevant again? The noble romance of *The Knight's Tale*, which uplifts and educates, needs a nobleness of mind in order to be appreciated; if romance gets into hands which cannot manage it, the result is the (delicious) irresponsible triviality Chaucer gave the figure who represents himself in *The Tale of Sir Thopas*. One can extend this considerably, but for our present purpose the important thing is to see how *The Knight's Tale* works when juxtaposed with *The Miller's Tale*.

The Miller is made to lose control of himself (it seems) in his drunkenness – though it is an odd sort of drunkenness – and breaks the order imposed by the Host even before it is properly established. (Notice that the Knight, a pillar of order telling a tale of order, obeys the Host and the Miller does not.) He demands to tell the next tale, to 'quite' *The Knight's Tale*. With that significant introduction, underlining the need for comparison, begins one of Chaucer's cleverest creations.

The Miller's Tale is the one story we can be fairly sure anyone who has heard of Chaucer will know, and so a summary is not needed. It is introduced with great emphasis as a 'cherles tale' and belongs roughly to the class known as *fabliau*. *Fabliau*, with its predominantly comic (usually sexual) plot and humble setting, is almost the flip side of romance; certainly both types of story would be familiar to the same audience. One would expect it to belong to Boccaccio's fourth – useless – class of fable, but with Chaucer anything can happen. *The Miller's Tale* is very funny indeed, but it is also very serious.

The parallels with *The Knight's Tale*, as well as the differences from it, are remarkable. Two men love the same woman in each poem; in each poem an older man is in significant relationship to them. The description of Alisoun has some parallels with that of Emelye. Absolon and Nicholas employ (the word is exact) some of the conventional features of the sorrowing lover. Nicholas, like Arcite lamenting the loneliness of his death (1921), lies 'Allone, withouten any compaignye' (A3204). John, like Theseus, has metaphysical leanings. Both catastrophes employ accident and defeat expectations. It is almost as if *The Miller's Tale* sets out to send up that of the Knight, reducing love to mere animality and appetite (look at the imagery applied to Alisoun), justice to mere getting away with it, and meaning to nonsense. In *The Knight's Tale* we see a remote world of the past which looks accidental, where meaning and purpose are hidden, and gradually we are brought to see that the diagnosis of happening as accident is merely dependent on point of view. Behind all is a loving purpose, exact in its justice. We are given in Theseus a figure of what maturity should be – sober, wise, self-knowing, just, authoritative. In *The Miller's Tale* we are firmly thrust into contemporary England – precise details are given – which we take to be comprehensible and meaningful. Yet ... the cleverness of Nicholas's plot, even if it had gone according to plan, would have ensured that he could never have enjoyed Alisoun on more than one occasion. His intellectual pursuits are a fraud and are used fraudulently. John understands nothing, not even the basic tenets of his religion, and is the *senex amans* to boot. Finally, the least guilty of all, John, gets the worst punishment and the scorn of his neighbours; the most guilty, Alisoun, gets off scot-free. In this picture of an apparently everyday world, so comfortably secure (unlike the precarious past, where cities fall and realms are destroyed), lurk madness, unreason, injustice. It is a symptom of a meaningless and amoral universe.

The Miller's Tale and *The Knight's Tale*, then, I see as setting up a dialectic about the nature of the world man inhabits and the nature of his motivating passions which, with great subtlety and profundity, the rest of the book explores. The *General Prologue* has already hinted as much: it opens with the spring morning topos which usually signals a poem about love, and immediately connects this causally with the metaphor of the pilgrimage. Love of one sort or another, from the terrible picture of *The Reeve's Tale*, where the actions of sexual love are used for hate, from the selfish and deceptive *cupiditas* through to the cosmic love which moves the stars, is a recurrent motif. Chaucer's friend Gower, with complete orthodoxy, saw love as the binding force not only in human society but also in the universe. Chaucer takes the same view. Like Gower, he is tackling the great question first posed by the psalmist, 'What is Man, that Thou art mindful of him?'

13. Note on the Text

For the first hundred years of its existence, Chaucer's work was transmitted and disseminated by copies made from manuscript, and copies of those copies. His original manuscripts have, as far as we know, perished. Inevitably corruption set in early – a poor script, a spelling mistake, an inattentive or bored scribe (or simply lack of understanding) could all make the transmission of a text resemble a game of Chinese Whispers. By the time Chaucer's work came to be printed all his texts were to a greater or lesser degree corrupt, and, while typesetting may have reduced the kind of error that comes from handwriting, it introduces a new breed of error all its own – as a glance at a daily paper will show. The recovery of what Chaucer actually wrote, therefore, has been a major task of scholars for over two hundred years. Manuscripts (there are over ninety of *The Canterbury Tales* alone – not all of equal value) have to be sorted into families of descent and then compared, and usages of words elsewhere must be consulted; every word must be scrutinized. The work is still going on.

The text used here is that published in 1940 by J. M. Manly and E. Rickert, and is reproduced by permission of the University of Chicago Press. For the reader's convenience, punctuation has been added, but no attempt has been made to modernize its spelling apart from the (silent) regularization of 'u' and 'v' as vowel and consonant respectively, and the modification of consonantal 'i' to 'j'. Where the text derived from the manuscript indicates elision of the 'e' of the definite article, or the 'o' of 'to' before a following vowel (e.g., 'theffect', 'tendite'), the modern convention of inserting an apostrophe ('th'effect') has not been followed. A very few small changes have been made in the text, all on good authority; these are indicated by square brackets.

Note on the Knight

Medieval men thought of society as divided into three interdependent estates: those who work, those who fight, and those who pray. No society is ever perfect, medieval no more than any other, and the literature of the period is full of complaints about the failure of members of the three estates to live up to their ideal. The *General Prologue* has a strong connection with what is called Estates Satire – the criticism of abuses in a particular estate, often by using individual representative figures, always with reference to an ideal of social harmony and interdependence. John Gower and William Langland, as well as several anonymous poets, draw on this concept, as Chaucer does; how widespread was the idea of complaint – that is, castigation of abuses – is to be seen from the surviving sermons and manuals for preachers. The ideal for each calling is clearly indicated, as are its typical faults.

The first portrait in the *General Prologue* is of the ideal fighting man in a Christian society. Though attempts have been made to see in Chaucer's portrait of the Knight the lineaments of a real man of his time, they have never been convincing. The contemporary detail is deliberately included so that his audience would recognize the closeness of the issues raised to their own actual experience and knowledge. Many Englishmen did in fact share in these actual campaigns. The number this tireless and selfless figure took part in suggests the unceasing battle against Islam that a worried Europe was waging at this time. The knightly ideal is expressed by using details that had a real contemporary relevance. There is no reason to suspect any reserve on Chaucer's part about the ideal of chivalry, even though we, working from different assumptions, perhaps might find it questionable.

The form of the portrait of the Knight owes something to the *descriptio*, but the details are in no sort of order. The apparent randomness is a useful way of indicating the narrator's flawed judgement and partial understanding of his material. Furthermore, the lack of rhetorical order and the inclusion, here and elsewhere, of oddly peripheral details forces the audience to impose its own valuation. The validity of that valuation becomes, with hindsight, an issue in the poem.

The Text, with Commentary

The Prologue

A KNYGHT there was, and that a worthy man,
That fro the tyme that he first bigan
To riden out, he loved chivalrye,
Trouthe and honour, fredom and curteisye.
Ful worthy was he in his lordes werre,   5
And ther to hadde he riden (no man ferre)
As wel in cristendom as in hethenesse,
And evere honoured for his worthynesse.
  At Alisaundre he was, whan it was wonne.
Ful ofte tyme he hadde the bord bigonne   10
Aboven alle nacions in Pruce.
In Lettow hadde he reysed, and in Ruce,
No cristen man so ofte of his degree.
In Gernade at the seege eek hadde he be
Of Algezir, and riden in Belmarye;   15
At Lyeys was he, and at Satalye,
Whan they were wonne, and in the Grete See
At many a noble armee hadde he be.
At mortal batailles hadde he been fiftene,
And foghten for oure feith at Tramyssene   20
In lystes thries, and ay slayn his foo.
This ilke worthy knyght hadde been also
Som tyme with the lord of Palatye
Agayn another hethen in Turkye.

4   *honour*: as the word is linked with *trouthe* (integrity, loyalty), it is clear that a moral quality, more than just 'fame', is meant – 'honourableness', perhaps. *fredom*: nobleness. On *curteisye* and *chivalrye*, see Introduction, pp. 29ff.

5   *in his lordes werre*: in his king's service.

6   *ferre*: further afield.

8   *worthynesse*: the word occurs five times in this description. See note to line 26.

9   *Alisaundre*: see note to line 16.

10   He had often sat at the head of the table in the place of honour.

11   *nacions in Pruce*: foreign contingents in a Crusade, like foreign students in universities, were organized into 'nations' of compatriots. The point is that the Knight had been recognized as senior of the English 'nation' in the Prussian campaigns of the Order of Teutonic Knights against the heathen Lithuanians and Russians. (The Lithuanians were converted to Christianity in 1368.)

12   *Lettow*: Lithuania. *reysed*: been on military expeditions. *Ruce*: Russia.

14   *Gernade*: the Moorish kingdom of Granada, in Spain. Alfonso XI of Castile campaigned against it for most of his reign, receiving some foreign support, including English. He captured *Algezir* (Algeciras) in 1344.

15   *Belmarye*: roughly the modern Morocco. There were campaigns against the Moors there in the 1340s, 1360s and 1380s.

16   *Satalye*: the ancient Attalia, in what is now southern Turkey. It was captured from the Turks by the remarkable Peter I of Lusignan, King of Cyprus, in 1361. He toured Europe, visiting England in 1362–3 and seeking support for his Crusades. He went on to take Alexandria (*Alisaundre*) in 1365, and Ayas in Armenia (*Lyeys*) in 1367.

17   *Grete See*: the Mediterranean.

18   *armee*: expeditionary force.

20–21   *Tramyssene*: Tlemçen, in Algeria. Note that the Knight fights for the faith against pagans thrice in single combat (*In lystes thries*), while his son merely fights against fellow Christians to win his lady's favour (A85–8); and see Introduction, p. 30.

24   *another hethen* suggests that the Lord of Palatye is also a heathen. The Lord of Balat, the ancient Miletus in Asia Minor, in 1365 was indeed a Moslem, and was in alliance with Peter of Lusignan. This could be what Chaucer is reminding us of.

And evere moore he hadde a sovereyn prys;   25
And though that he were worthy, he was wys,
And of his port as meke as is a mayde.
He nevere yet no vileynye ne sayde
In al his lyf un to no maner wight.
He was a verray parfit gentil knyght.   30
  But for to tellen yow of his array:
Hise hors were goode, but he was nat gay;
Of fustian he wered a gypoun,
Al bismotered with his habergeoun,
For he was late ycome from his viage,   35
And wente for to doon his pilgrymage.

26 *wys*: the exact meaning of 'wisdom' varied according to one's calling. For a knight, it meant 'prudence', which was normally used in opposition to 'boldness'. The Knight tempers his bravery with wisdom. *Worthy* here means 'bravery', the basic quality that enables a knight to discharge his calling.

27 Modesty was an important courtly characteristic.

28 *no vileynye*: he never spoke rudely.

29 *maner wight*: sort of man.

30 *verray parfit*: truly perfect.

33 *fustian*: coarse cloth. *gypoun*: surcoat.

34 *bismotered*: bespattered. *habergeoun*: coat-of-mail. That the knight does not pause after his arrival in England to go home to change before his pilgrimage suggests his sincere devotion.

Heere bigynneth the Knyghtes Tale

BOOK I*

Whilom, as olde stories tellen us,
Ther was a duc that highte Theseus;
Of Atthenes he was lord and governour,
And in his tyme swich a conqueror
That gretter was ther noon under the sonne.   5
Ful many a riche contree hadde he wonne;
What with his wysdom and his chivalrye,
He conquered al the regne of Femenye,
That whilom was ycleped Scithia,
And wedded the queene Ypolita,   10
And broghte hir hoom with hym in his contree
With muchel glorie and greet solempnitee,
And eek hir yonge suster Emelye.
And thus with victorie and with melodye

---

* It was probably copyists who added to several manuscripts an epigraph from Statius,
XII.519ff.:

> I amque domos patrias, Scithice post aspera gentis
> Prelia, laurigero, &c.

('And now, after fierce battle with the Scythian people, in his laurel-decked chariot [Theseus
approaches] his native land . . .')

1 The opening line gives several signals about the type of tale we are to experience. *Whilom* has a force not entirely dissimilar to 'Once upon a time'; the story we are to hear will deal with a remote locale and we are prepared for an extraordinary event. *olde stories*: *storie* is much closer in meaning and overtones to the Latin *historia* than to the modern 'story'; it suggests a considerable measure of one or other type of truth, and a good deal of authority (see Introduction, p. 21ff.). With *olde*, the word combines to suggest the importance of what we are to experience.

The *Thebaid* as well as the *Teseida* is behind the introductory passage; Theseus's night march (112) and the Minotaur (122) are probably drawn from it.

2 *Theseus*: properly King of Athens. Chaucer's anachronistic use of the title 'duke' (copied from Boccaccio) is characteristic of his way of presenting a remote Classical past in a terminology familiar to his audience. (For the myths surrounding the figure of Theseus, see any good Classical dictionary.) Note how he is built up deliberately as the most powerful earthly ruler (*under the sonne*, 5) whose success is due in equal parts to his *wysdom* (7) and *chivalrye* (7).

7 *what with*: by means of.

8 *Femenye*: the land of the Amazons, a realm ruled by warrior women. There are many medieval versions of this Classical legend: see, for example, *The Travels of Sir John Mandeville*, Penguin Books, 1983, Ch. 17, pp. 116–17). Often localized in *Scythia* (9), on the southern borders of what is now Russia. The linking of war and marriage right at the beginning of the Tale is important.

10ff. Note the stress on active verbs, and the structuring of the sentences into a rapid sequence of similar clauses. This is part of Chaucer's technique of *abbreviatio*, used when he wants to move quickly over a series of important points in his source without developing any of them. The audience is warned this is happening by the *repetitio* of 'And' + verb (cf. 23ff.).

14 The zeugma of *victorie* and *melodye* is interesting. Music would indeed form part of a triumph, but Chaucer need not have emphasized it in this striking way. The ideas of harmony and order it lets in may be important

Lete I this noble duc to Atthenes ryde   15
And al his hoost in armes hym bisyde.
    And certes, if it nere to long to heere,
I wolde have toold fully the manere
How wonnen was the regne of Femenye
By Theseus and by his chivalrye;   20
And of the grete bataille for the nones
Bitwixen Atthenes and Amazones;
And how asseged was Ypolita,
The faire hardy queene of Scithia;
And of the feste that was at hir weddynge,   25
And of the tempest at hir hom comynge –
But al that thyng I moot as now forbere.
I have, God woot, a large feeld to ere,
And wayke been the oxen in my plough;
The remenant of the tale is long ynough.   30
I wol nat letten eek noon of this route;
Lat every felawe telle his tale aboute,
And lat se now who shal the soper wynne.
And ther I lefte I wol ayein bigynne.

17ff. The rhetorical figure being used here is *occupatio*, a refusal to describe or narrate. Chaucer uses it a lot; here, though in fact a lot of his source material is cut out (see Introduction, pp. 40ff.), there is a mild irony in that he spends so long in telling us what he is *not* telling us that in fact a good deal of information is conveyed in summary form. Notice again the summarizing use of *anaphora* or *repetitio* (*And how*, *And of*, etc.). The effect of this summary of heroic events is to relate the romance episode of the Tale to a heroic – and therefore highly serious – context.

20 *chivalrye*: either Theseus's personal qualities or the actual body of knights under his command.

22 *Atthenes*: Athenians.

23 *asseged*: Chaucer is almost certainly punning here. The courtship and winning of a woman was often expressed in the imagery of a siege, battle and sack. Chaucer would be familiar with it, if only from the closing lines of the *Roman de la Rose*.

26 *tempest*: occasionally used to mean 'commotion'; it could echo Boccaccio's *tomolto* to describe the welcoming crowd. Neither Boccaccio nor Statius mentions a storm.

28ff. These lines deliberately suggest an awareness of the *dispositio* or structure of the Tale, and are the first hint that invites our attention to it.

The self-deprecating figure (28–9) is *diminutio* (see Introduction, p. 20). The agricultural image is a little unexpected, but Chaucer elsewhere frequently makes a link between the business of writing and reading poetry, the production of bodily food, and the winning of the grain of spiritual and moral sustenance from the chaff of story (see *The Nun's Priest's Tale*, B4633; *The Legend of Good Women*, 1160; and especially *The Parliament of Fowls*, 22–5).

31–4 These lines clearly refer to the pilgrimage, and cannot have been part of the original version of the Tale. This neat glance at the context of *The Knight's Tale* in *The Canterbury Tales* marks the point where Chaucer has completed his basic introduction and will now take off into the story itself (cf. the similar re-entry into the world of *The Canterbury Tales* at line 2250).

The introductory section of the poem, now concluded, has emphasized (a) the problem involved in telling a story, and suggested attention to its form, and (b) that although the story is 'history', it is also fiction – with all that that implies (see Introduction, p. 22).

This duc, of whom I make mencioun,　35
Whan he was comen almost to the toun,
In al his wele and in his mooste pride,
He was war, as he caste his eye aside,
Wher that ther kneled in the hye weye
A compaignye of ladyes tweye and tweye,　40
Ech after oother clad in clothes blake.
But swich a cry and swich a wo they make
That in this world nis creature lyvynge
That herde swich another waymentynge;
And of this cry they nolde nevere stenten　45
Til they the reynes of his brydel henten.

　'What folk been ye, that at myn hom comynge
Perturben so my feste with cryynge?'
Quod Theseus. 'Have ye so greet envye
Of myn honour, that thus compleyne and crye?　50
Or who hath yow mysboden, or offended?
And telleth me if it may been amended,
And why that ye been clothed thus in blak.'

　The eldeste lady of hem alle spak,
Whan she hadde swowned with a deedly cheere,　55
That it was routhe for to seen and here.
She seyde, 'Lord, to whom Fortune hath yeven
Victorie, and as a conquerour to lyven,
Noght greveth us youre glorie and youre honour,
But we biseken mercy and socour.　60

35ff. Note the complexity of this sentence, with its change of focus from the 'I' telling the story (35) to 'he' (Theseus) (38), and finally to the ladies (40): a neat transition from the world where the story is being told to the recreated world of the story proper.

40–41 The mourning ladies present themselves very formally. Their grief need not be seen as the less great for being formally structured. The use of superlatives in medieval fiction is usual; the invented world heightens the normal.

46 A formal gesture of supplication, which any 'gentle' knight must heed.

47–8 The style of Theseus's polite question is formal and balanced. Notice how sorrow and joy are symbolically mingled in this situation, as they are to be in the Tale as a whole.

52 *telleth*: plural imperative.

55 The lady's swoon (faint) and her deathly pale countenance are to be taken seriously, as indicators of extreme grief. Chaucer adds, for poignancy, these details of her swoon; he rarely misses a chance of pathos, however he may frame it.

57ff. The speech as a whole is beautifully structured (it is not in the least 'realistic', for had the lady been as distraught as her swoon suggests the chances of her speaking in so collected a way, with so complex a syntactical organization, are slim). The opening is close in structure to a formal Collect, used in the services of the Church: apostrophe ('Lord') + relative clause + request. After this general introduction, in which fortune and mercy are emphasized (see below), we hear a specific complaint about their misfortunes and the lack of mercy of Creon (the type of the tyrannical ruler in this poem). The appeal closes with the speech of all the ladies in unison as a concluding chorus of petition; again, the themes are their misfortune and Theseus's duty to pity it (92–3). The whole exchange is therefore tightly linked thematically. The style, like Theseus's original reply to them, is in a register appropriately high for those who have so suffered.

57 The stress on fortune reminds us that the triumph is inherently unstable, for Theseus, despite his qualities and despite being the one area of stability in the human world of the poem, is after all human.

Have mercy on oure wo and oure distresse.
Som drope of pitee, thurgh thy gentillesse,
Upon us wrecched wommen lat thow falle.
For certes, lord, ther is noon of us alle
That she ne hath been a duchesse or a queene: 65
Now be we caytyves, as it is wel seene;
Thanked be Fortune and hir false wheel
That noon estaat assureth to be weel!
Now certes, lord, to abiden youre presence,
Here in this temple of the goddesse Clemence   70
We have been waytynge al this fourtenyght;
Now help us, lord, sith it is in thy myght.

   'I, wrecche, which that wepe and waille thus,
Wan whilom wyf to kyng Cappaneus,
That starf at Thebes – cursed be that day!   75
And alle we that been in this array,
And maken al this lamentacioun,
We losten alle oure housbondes at that toun
Whil that the sege ther aboute lay.
And yet now the olde Creon, weylaway!   80

61–62   *mercy ... pitee ... gentillesse*: crucial qualities of the noble mind, particularly when it exercises power. Elsewhere in the Tale (903), in a line he repeats several times in his work, Chaucer emphasizes that *gentillesse* is most ready to pity. It is worth noticing that the ladies' appeal is made precisely because they assume these qualities in the just ruler. The qualities are also given emphasis by their placing in strong positions – before the caesura and at the end of the line.

67   *Fortune*: depicted in art as a queen (often blindfolded), turning a wheel on which human beings were bound to rise and fall. The changing moon is her emblem. The thematic importance of Fortune in this Tale is heavily stressed here, and given concrete expression: the ladies' falls are object-lessons of her power. See also the examples of reversals of fortune at the beginning of Book III (cf. 57n., above).

70   Both Boccaccio and Statius put this temple (*Clemence* = Mercy) inside the city.

71   Might it be significant that a fortnight is exactly half the cycle of the moon, so closely associated with fortune?

73–4   Chaucer is fond of using alliteration, and alliterative tags like *wepe and waille* occur in lines he wants to emphasize. On his use of formal alliterative verse, see below, 1742n.

74ff.   *Cappaneus*: killed by Zeus's (Jupiter's) thunderbolt for boasting, he was one of the Seven who banded with Polyneices, son of Oedipus, to oust Eteocles, Oedipus's other son, from the throne of Thebes. Both brothers died in combat, and their uncle, Creon, ruled harshly after them. It was Creon who had expelled the self-blinded Oedipus from Thebes. Eventually Oedipus found rest and peace with Theseus at Athens – the beginning of the myth of Theseus as the wise ruler, friend of the gods. Creon, in contrast, is the type of the tyrant, and the Thebes he rules over is deservedly punished for its crimes. (It thus becomes, like Troy, a symbol of the city of this world whose end must be disaster.)

That lord is now of Thebes the citee,
Fulfild of ire and of iniquitee,
He, for despit, and for his tyrannye,
To do the dede bodyes vileynye
Of alle oure lordes, whiche that been slawe,   85
Hath alle the bodyes on an heep ydrawe,
And wol nat suffren hem, by noon assent,
Neither to been yburyed, nor ybrent,
But maketh houndes ete hem in despit.'

   And with that word, with outen moore respit,   90
They fillen gruf, and criden pitously,
'Have on us, wrecched wommen, som mercy,
And lat oure sorwe synken in thyn herte!'

   This gentil duc doun from his courser sterte
With herte pitous, whan he herde hem speke.   95
Hym thoughte that his herte wolde breke
Whan he saugh hem, so pitous and so maat,
That whilom weren of so greet estaat.
And in his armes he hem alle up hente,
And hem conforteth in ful good entente;   100
And swoor his ooth, as he was trewe knyght,
He wolde doon so ferforthly his myght
Upon the tiraunt Creon hem to wreke
That al the peple of Grece sholde speke
How Creon was of Theseus yserved,   105
As he that hadde his deeth ful wel deserved.

   And right anoon, with outen moore abood,
His baner he desplayeth, and forth rood
To Thebesward, and al his hoost bisyde;
No neer Atthenes wolde he go ne ryde,   110
Ne take his ese fully half a day,
But onward on his wey that nyght he lay;

82–4   *ire ... iniquitee/ ... despit ... tyrannye/ ... vileynye*: to be strongly contrasted with the qualities of Theseus – *socour ... mercy ... pitee ... gentillesse* (60–62); *gentil ... pitous* (94–5). The words are positioned at emphatic points in similarly structured lines. *Vileynye* is a particularly strong word – the type of behaviour expected of the lowest of all moral types. (One must be careful. The word originally related to the lowest social group, the tied villeins; but Chaucer is quite clear – cf. his ballade *Gentilesse* – that moral behaviour is nothing to do with social rank.) Notice the positioning of the words at emphatic points in similarly structured lines. Much the same pattern is used in the fourfold negatives of lines 87–8, which build up through the rejections of increasingly serious conventions to the vivid picture of the dogs eating the corpses. A fine example of Chaucer's command of rhetoric: the speech progressively intensifies emotionally.

94ff.   Notice Theseus's courtesy in dismounting, and the entirely proper sympathy he feels for them. The speed of his reaction is emphasized by the use of coordinated main verbs (99–101) in a *repetitio*, using the figure too of *parison* or *compar*, where the same construction is repeated.

96   *Hym thoughte*: it seemed to him. The impersonal construction is common, and the verb *thinke* for 'seem' is difficult to distinguish from *thinke(n)*, 'think'.

101   Theseus swears by the integrity and honour that belongs to true knighthood.

102   Theseus's determination to right a great wrong on the supplication of the ladies is very similar to the action of the Emperor Trajan, another of the 'just ruler' figures of the Middle Ages. (Both Dante and Langland regard Trajan's place in Heaven as assured – *Purgatorio*, X.73ff., and *Paradiso*, XX. 100ff.; *Piers Plowman*, BXI.141; XI.281.) Trajan was on his way to an important battle when a widow appealed to him for redress from wrong. Postponing the battle, Trajan sorted things out for her. He then carried on to his delayed victory. He is specifically linked with pity by Gower in *Confessio Amantis* (VIII. 3140ff.). The linking of Theseus with Trajan through similarity of action would be quite consistent with the way Chaucer is building him up as the type of the just ruler.

108   Displaying the standard is the signal for war.

110   *go ne ryde*: more than a metrical fill-up; a traditional antithetical formula, 'walk or ride'. The sense is that he would on no account go nearer to Athens.

112   'He made camp along his route'.

And sente anoon Ypolita the queene,
And Emelye hir yonge suster sheene,
Unto the toun of Atthenes to dwelle   115
And forth he rit; ther is namoore to telle.
   The rede statue of Mars with spere and targe,
So shyneth in his white baner large,
That alle the feeldes gliteren up and doun.
And by his baner born is his penoun,   120
Of gold ful riche in which there was ybete
The Mynotaur which that he wan in Crete.
Thus rit this duc, thus rit this conquerour,
And in his hoost of chivalrye the flour,
Til that he cam to Thebes, and alighte   125
Faire in a feeld, ther as he thoghte to fighte.
   But shortly for to speken of this thyng,
With Creon, which that was of Thebes kyng,
He faught, and slough hym manly as a knyght
In pleyn bataille, and putte the folk to flight.   130
And by assaut he wan the citee after,
And rente adoun bothe wal and sparre and rafter,
And to the ladyes he restored agayn
The bones of hir freendes that were slayn,

113–14 The casual mention of Emelye and Ypolita at the end of this paragraph indicates that our interest is to be firmly fixed on Theseus.

116 *namoore to telle*: well, of course there is; but Chaucer is using an *occupatio* to signal he had reached the end of a narrative block. This downbeat reticence highlights the brief description of the campaign that follows.

117 *rede statue*: the device or picture of Mars, who has always been associated with the colour red. It is interesting that Theseus by his banner is linked with Mars. (See Introduction, p. 38.) Theseus swears by Mars at line 850 and elsewhere (another Chaucerian addition).

119 'So that everywhere the countryside shone with it.' An oddly hyperbolical expression, but paralleled elsewhere, for example in *Anelida and Arcite* (40–41), and in Barbour's *Bruce* (VIII.227–8).

120 *penoun*: his personal ensign as a knight, as distinct from the standard of his realm or army.

121 *ybete* here must mean 'worked' or 'embroidered'. Theseus destroyed the monstrous man-bull, the Minotaur, in Crete. The Minotaur, Theseus and his helper Ariadne appear not infrequently in Christian art (until the Revolution the centre of the maze at Chartres Cathedral had a brass of them). The story was allegorized as man conquering his own evil passions and the Devil, with the help of the Blessed Virgin Mary. The mention of the defeat of the Minotaur may therefore not be insignificant in Chaucer's building-up of Theseus.

129–30 *manly as a knyght/In pleyn bataille*: in single combat during the pitched battle. Another touch in the build-up of Theseus.

130ff. The rapidity of action is achieved once more by the paratactical linking of active verbs, and the frequent use of the coordinating conjunction 'and'. The lines are given a remarkable forward force by the emphatic stresses on the verbs. The *abbreviatio* which this sort of style indicates is capable of a vivid economy which also hints that the key interest of the Tale will not lie here; you do not abbreviate your central issues in the plot. (Notice Chaucer's *shortly* (127) which underlines this point. It is repeated at 142.)

132 A graphic picture of the sack of a city is gained through this tiny detail.

134 *hir freendes: freendes* has overtones of the Middle French *ami* (i.e. lovers); other manuscripts read 'housbondes', others again 'lordys'.

To doon obsequies, as was tho the gyse.   135
  But it were al to long for to devyse
The grete clamour and the waymentynge
That the ladyes made at the brennynge
Of the bodies, and the grete honour
That Theseus the noble conquerour   140
Doth to the ladyes whan they from hym wente;
But shortly for to telle is myn entente.
  Whan that this worthy duc, this Theseus,
Hath Creon slayn, and wonne Thebes thus,
Stille in that feeld he took al nyght his reste,   145
And dide with al that contree as hym leste.
  To ransake in the taas of the bodies dede,
Hem for to strepe of harneys and of wede,
The pilours diden bisynesse and cure,
After the bataille and disconfiture.   150
And so bifel, that in the taas they founde,
Thurgh girt with many a grevous blody wounde,
Two yonge knyghtes liggynge by and by,
Bothe in oon armes, wroght ful richely;
Of whiche two, Arcita highte that oon,   155
And that oother knyght highte Palamon.
Nat fully quyk, ne fully dede, they were,
But by hir cote armures and by hir gere
The heraudes knew hem best in special
As they that weren of the blood roial   160
Of Thebes, and of sustren two yborn.
Out of the taas the pilours han hem torn
And han hem caried softe unto the tente
Of Theseus; and he ful soone hem sente
To Atthenes to dwellen in prisoun   165
Perpetuelly; he nolde no raunsoun.
  And whan this worthy duc hath thus ydoon,
He took his hoost, and hom he ryt anoon,
With laurer crowned as a conquerour;
And ther he lyveth in joye and in honour,   170
Terme of his lyf; what nedeth wordes mo?
And in a tour, in angwissh and in wo,
Dwellen this Palamon and eek Arcite:
For evere moore ther may no gold hem quyte.

135 A reminder of the difference between this imagined world and the contemporary one.

136ff. Another *occupatio*. Chaucer has actually made a significant change in his source material here. Boccaccio has the defenders running off and the Athenians taking the city unopposed. Chaucer has given us a glimpse of a medieval city being taken by storm. He thus emphasizes the power of Theseus's justice, links it with contemporary experience, and suggests the retribution that follows not only tyrants like Creon but also their innocent followers.

146 *as hym leste*: Theseus's absolute power is emphasized by the dismissive 'as it pleased him'.

153–4 'Two young knights lying side by side, both in the same coat-armour.' Chaucer stresses the similarity of Arcite and Palamon right at the beginning by the identity of their armour. The similarity allows Chaucer to use their subsequent divergent lives to explore what fortune means.

157 The balanced contrast is an example of *contentio*, used here to indicate the precariousness of their hold on life.

159 The heralds' place in medieval warfare was important. They were not only privileged emissaries; it was also their task to identify from the arms borne on shield or surcoat the participants in the struggle. At this time they were beginning to have important functions as genealogists and in property law.

165–6 Sending them to live in prison *perpetuelly* has suggestive overtones. Allegorically, Theseus could be seen as adjudging them to a sort of Hell; his absolute power over them, analogous with that of God, is stressed.

Theseus's refusal of ransom (emphasized at 174) is Chaucer's own addition. The point is important, for the prison becomes a dominating image of the poem. Arcite's and Palamon's prison and the knowledge of which they are capable while confined in it suggest the prison of human life, in which even Theseus is caught. No complete knowledge is possible, not even to poets, while the human mind bounds what can be thought.

169–74 The contrast between the Theseus favoured by fortune (cf. 57) and crowned with the conqueror's laurel wreath, and Arcite and Palamon in prison, is pointed by the contrast between *joye and in honour* and in *angwissh and in wo*; but especially by the emphatic time-dimension underlined by a similar stylistic parallel: *terme of his lyf* against *for evere moore*.

This passeth yeer by yeer, and day by day,   175
Til it fil ones, in a morwe of May,
That Emelye, that fairer was to sene
Than is the lilie upon his stalke grene,
And fressher than the May with floures newe
(For with the rose colour stroof hir hewe –   180
I noot which was the fairer of hem two)
Er it were day, as was hir wone to do,

176   *it fil*: it so chanced. The choice of the verb relates to the thematic interest of the Tale in chance and fortune. On the differences between Chaucer's handling of the lovers' first sight of Emelye and Boccaccio's treatment, see Introduction, p. 52. The vivaciousness of their quarrel in Chaucer may owe something to his treatment of a similar rivalry in the noble eagles in *The Parliament of Fowls*.

   morwe of May: a deliberate though very brief invocation of the 'spring morning' topos. We are now given a clue that love is to be an important motif. The season of the year also suggests a new beginning, a development from the static situation at the end of the previous paragraph.

177   *Emelye*: she is presented not as a person but as a type of the beautiful maiden. It is quite important for the emotional balance of the Tale that we do not think of her feelings in any serious or connected way. Chaucer is not showing us what Emelye was like, but how she appeared to the two young men. It is their reactions that matter. The description – which is not a full *effictio* – is much fuller than that of the two knights, though it is still in very generalized terms. Her appearance, as has already been remarked (see Introduction, p. 44), may remind us of the appearance of Philosophia to the imprisoned narrator in Boethius. That appearance led 'Boethius' to an understanding of fortune, love and eternity; this one, through the fable, eventually leads us to the same sort of understanding.

178   *lilie*: a flower associated with purity, whose beauty is the gift of the Creator ('the lilies of the field ... they toil not ...'). The flower suggests both a woman's outward beauty, and what her inner quality should be. Lilies always appear in medieval and Renaissance portrayals of the Annunciation.

180   'Her complexion vied with the colour of the rose.' The rose of medieval gardens may well have been more delicate in coloration than many modern ones, but the comparison is a standard one to indicate surpassing feminine beauty. Roses and lilies are commonly used as comparisons for the female complexion for the next two centuries at least (cf. Campion's 'There is a garden in her face', and Shakespeare's ironic 'My mistress' eyes are nothing like the sun' (Sonnet 130). The rose is also the flower of love.

181   The narrator's intervention, reminding us that this is art, with its own limits, distances the description. The reticence invites us to supply our own details.

She was arisen, and al redy dight.
For May wol have no slogardye anyght;
The sesoun priketh every gentil herte   185
And maketh it out of his sleep to sterte,
And seith, 'Arys, and do thyn observaunce!'
This maketh Emelye have remembraunce
To doon honour to May, and for to ryse.
Yclothed was she fressh, for to devyse: 190
Hir yelow heer was broyded in a tresse
Bihynde hir bak – a yerde long, I gesse.
And in the gardyn, at the sonne upriste,
She walketh up and doun, and as hir liste,
She gadreth floures, party white and rede,   195
To make a subtil gerland for hir hede.
And as an aungel hevenysshly she song.
    The grete tour, that was so thikke and strong,
Which of the castel was the chief dongeoun,
(Ther as the knyghtes weren in prisoun   200
Of which I tolde you, and tellen shal)
Was evene joynant to the gardyn wal
Ther as this Emelye hadde hir pleyynge.
Bright was the sonne, and cleer that morwenynge,
And Palamon, this woful prisoner,   205
As was his wone, by leve of his gayler
Was risen, and romed in a chambre an heigh,
In which he al the noble citee seigh,
And eek the gardyn, ful of braunches grene,
Ther as the fresshe Emelye the shene   210
Was in hir walk, and romed up and doun.
This sorweful prisoner, this Palamoun,
Gooth in the chambre romyng to and fro,
And to hymself compleynyng of his wo;
That he was born, ful ofte he seyde, 'allas!'   215
    And so bifel, by aventure or cas,
That thurgh a wyndow, thikke of many a barre
Of iren greet and square as any sparre,
He caste his eye upon Emelya,
And ther with al he bleynte, and cride, 'A!'   220

184–5   The customs associated with the month of May until the time of the Civil War included early rising and visits to the neighbouring countryside for merrymaking and the gathering of flowers. It is possible that the *double entendre* common in the word *priketh* is reinforced by a similar overtone in the previous line. If so, the creative and regenerative impulses of springtime are being deliberately linked with human sexual desire.

191   The conventional golden hair of the romance heroine is in a long braid down her back – the usual style for unmarried women.

193   *at the sonne upriste*: at sunrise.

195   The flowers she gathers echo the colours associated with her. Her setting in the dawn garden makes her almost a symbol of spring and love. In illustrations and carvings of the 'works' (occupations) of the twelve months, May is sometimes depicted as a woman with a garland.

197   Singing like an angel seems often to have been an accomplishment of romance heroines. But her harmony is still human: the simile, while it emphasizes likeness, states un-identity.

199   *dongeoun*: the keep or donjon of the castle.

200–201   The parenthesis reminds us that this is a story, and reminds the less attentive or intelligent of an important fact they may have missed.

203   'Where Emelye was enjoying herself.'

207, 211, 213   The repetition of the verb *romen* ('stroll', 'roam') suggests the purposelessness of their movement and thus stresses the accidental nature of what happens.

214   *compleynyng*: lamenting – we are meant to imagine something quite formal.

215   'Often he said, Alas, that I was born!'

216   *And so bifel, by aventure or cas*: 'It so happened, by chance or accident . . .' The great emphasis, three times in this line, on randomness draws our attention to the nature of chance, which is one of the subjects the Tale discusses. It is most significant that the line introduces Palamon's crucial sight of Emelye, on which all the subsequent events depend.

217–18   'Barred with many bars of iron, thick as rafters.'

219   Chaucer significantly alters Boccaccio by making Palamon the first to see her (see Introduction, p. 52).

As thogh he stongen were unto the herte.
   And with that cry, Arcite anoon up sterte,
And seide, 'Cosyn myn, what eyleth thee,
That art so pale and deedly on to see?
Why cridestow? Who hath the doon offence? 225
For Goddes love, take al in pacience
Oure prisoun, for it may noon oother be.
Fortune hath yeven us this adversitee.
Som wikke aspect or disposicioun
Of Saturne, by som constellacioun, 230
Hath yeven us this, al thogh we hadde it sworn;
So stood the hevene whan that we were born.
We mote endure it; this is the short and playn.'
   This Palamon answerde, and seide agayn,
'Cosyn, for sothe, of this opinioun 235
Thou hast a veyn ymaginacioun.
This prisoun caused me nat to crye.
But I was hurt right now thurghout myn eye
Into myn herte, that wol my bane be.
The fairnesse of that lady that I se 240
Yond in the gardyn romen to and fro
Is cause of al my cryynge and my wo.
I noot wher she be womman or goddesse –
But Venus is it, soothly, as I gesse.'

223ff.   Arcite's speech is in a familiar middle-register style appropriate to converse between close friends.

225   *Why cridestow?*: Why did you cry out?

226ff.   Arcite's counsel of patience – the readiness to accept suffering, and whatever else comes, with fortitude – is in ironic contrast to his own behaviour later. He accepts that their *adversitee* is unalterable, the decree of Fortune, acting through the conjunction of unfavourable planets (see Appendix 2, p. 220f.); it was their destiny from the moment they were born, and there was nothing they could do to avoid it. He shows some incomplete understanding of the mechanics of the situation; and it should be remembered that we know, as Arcite forgets, that Theseus's action is part of the explanation as well as Saturn's. Again, our attention is being directed beyond the narrative to the understanding of what lies behind the events (cf. 2185ff.).

228   The rapid transition suggests a link between fortune and the planets (see Appendix 2, p. 220f.).

231   *al thogh we hadde it sworn*: even though we had sworn the contrary (i.e. even if we protested as much as possible that this was not the case).

233   *this is the short and playn*: this is the top and bottom of it.

235–6   A deliberate (if momentary) ambiguity: at first it looks as if *veyn ymaginacioun* refers to Arcite's views on fate and human life, rather than to his understanding of Palamon's cry. 'What you've just said (*opinioun*) depends on a false understanding (of what has happened).'

238–9   In conventional love poetry, Cupid's arrows strike through the eyes and lodge in the lover's heart (cf. Chaucer's translation of the *Roman de la Rose*, 1728–30). Palamon is made to use the lover's terminology.

243–4   Translation makes the oddity of these lines clear: 'I do not know whether she be woman or goddess' – the subjunctive leaves the question wide open – 'but truly it is Venus, so I suppose.' The uncertain certainty of 'not knowing'/'truly it is'/'so I suppose' underlines the ambiguity not only of Palamon's apprehension of what Emelye is, but of all knowledge.

And ther with al, on knees doun he fil, 245
And seide, 'Venus, if it be thy wil
Yow in this gardyn thus to transfigure
Bifore me, sorweful wrecched creature,
Out of this prisoun help that we may scape.
And if so be my destynee be shape 250
By eterne word to dyen in prisoun,
Of oure lynage have som compassioun,
That is so lowe ybroght by tirannye.'
   And with that word Arcite gan espye
Wher as this lady romed to and fro. 255
And with that sighte hir beautee hurte hym so
That if that Palamon was wounded soore,
Arcite is hurt as muche as he, or moore.
And with a sigh he seyde pitously,
'The fresshe beautee sleeth me sodeynly 260
Of hire that rometh in the yonder place;
And but I have hir mercy and hir grace,
That I may seen hire at the leeste weye,
I nam but deed; ther nis namoore to seye.'
   This Palamon, whan he tho wordes herde, 265
Despitously he loked, and answerde,
'Wheither seistow this in ernest or in pley?'
   'Nay,' quod Arcite, 'in ernest, by my fey!
God help me, so me list ful yvele pleye!'
   This Palamon gan knytte his browes tweye. 270

245 Palamon's kneeling in prayer indicates clearly the type of love he feels. He exalts the mortal woman (as he soon understands her to be) to the point where he sees through her to divinity (cf. Introduction, pp. 52, 55). The prayer is Chaucer's invention, and may be compared with the other prayer to Venus (1363ff.). Palamon prays to Venus as goddess of Love – as a pagan might decorously be imagined to do – but for the contemporary reader there are also overtones of Venus as planet (as with Saturn, 230). Our view of Palamon here begins to develop an ironic twist that depends on this realization that what he thinks he sees is not what is physically there; Emelye is not Venus.

The prayer is in an appropriately high style, with two parallel conditional constructions. Note that again the issues of destiny and fate are raised.

The speech is placed at the centre of Book I; in medieval and Renaissance art the central place is often given to elements in the composition that have an important bearing on the whole work. Cf. below 759–61n., 1124n., 1320n., 1936n.

247 *transfigure*: make (yourself) manifest or apparent.

253 *tirannye*: we know Theseus is no tyrant, but he might appear so to Palamon. Once again, point of view alters understanding of reality. (See Introduction, p. 61.)

255 *romed*: the repetition of the word again stresses the casualness of Emelye's progress, oblivious of the confusion she is causing, and makes a deliberate parallel between Palamon's first sight of her and Arcite's.

260ff.: Arcite's reaction is strongly contrasted with Palamon's. The style is middle rather than high, and the focus of the thoughts is firmly on human love and its satisfaction, rather than on divine compassion for their fall and imprisonment. Arcite is in no doubt that Emelye is a woman, and his speech is briefer and more direct than Palamon's. (See Introduction, p. 52.)

263 'So that at least I can see her.'

265 *This Palamon*: note how the demonstrative adjective is frequently applied to Palamon and Arcite (for example, in lines 173, 212, 234, 270, 294). In *Troilus and Criseyde* it is also applied to Troilus, but never to Criseyde. The implication there seems to be that Criseyde is beyond ready understanding, that her role and nature defy characterization. Something like that may be happening here. We have already seen that Chaucer is careful to introduce Palamon and Arcite as types – that what is important is the fable in which they play a role; we need to be reminded by this dismissive and summarizing word of the generality of their nature (cf. 673n., below).

269 'God help me, I've little inclination for joking!'

'It were to thee,' quod he, 'no greet honour
For to be fals ne for to be traytour
To me, that am thy cosyn and thy brother
Ysworn ful depe, and ech of us til oother,
That nevere, for to dyen in the peyne,   275
Til that the deeth departe shal us tweyne,
Neither of us in love to hyndre oother –
Ne in noon other caas, my leeve brother.
But that thow sholdest trewely forthre me
In every caas, as I shal forthre thee,   280
This was thyn ooth, and myn also, certeyn.
I woot right wel thou darst it nat withseyn.
Thus artow of my counseil, out of doute;
And now thow woldest falsly been aboute
To love my lady, whom I love and serve,   285
And evere shal, til that myn herte sterve!
Now certes, false Arcite, thow shalt nat so.
I loved hire first, and tolde thee my wo
As to my counseil, and my brother, sworn
To forthre me, as I have told biforn.   290
For which thou art ybounden as a knyght
To helpe me, if it lay in thy myght:
Or elles artow fals, I dar wel seyn.'

    This Arcite ful proudly spak ageyn.
'Thou shalt,' quod he, 'be rather fals than I;   295
But thou art fals, I telle thee outrely.
For par amour I loved hire first er thow.
What wiltow seyen? thow woost nat yet now
Wheither she be a womman or goddesse!
Thyn is affeccioun of holynesse   300
And myn is love, as to a creature;
For which I tolde thee myn aventure
As to my cosyn and my brother sworn.
I pose, that thow lovedest hire biforn:
Wostow nat wel the olde clerkes sawe   305
That, "Who shal yeve a lovere any lawe?"
Love is a gretter lawe, by my pan,
Than may be yeve to any erthely man.
And therfore positif lawe, and swich decree,
Is broke al day for love, in ech degree.   310

274   The oath of brotherhood between friends or relatives was regarded at the time as more binding even than blood ties. Palamon is invoking a very high sanction indeed, but it is not clear why he should claim Arcite's help rather than the other way round (cf. 279–81). There is some comedy here, as well as seriousness.

275   *for to dyen in the peyne*: 'even if we had to suffer death by torture'.

276   *departe*: separate.

284ff.   The seriousness of Palamon's passion can be felt in the rushing speech rhythms and the mixed tenses of the speech; but if we keep our balance it remains ironic. As Arcite points out (316–18), neither of them is in a position to do anything about Emelye.

297   *par amour*: as a lover loves his mistress.

300–301   'Yours is a feeling (*affeccioun*) of religious devotion, while mine is the love of one creature for another.' Arcite is made to underline for the audience the fact that he and Palamon may have seen the same woman but are not loving the same object.

304ff.   Chaucer throughout his career was puzzled by the nature, effects and values of love. He adds a series of ethical arguments at this point to suggest ways in which the lovers' quarrel could be viewed.

305   *olde clerkes sawe*: Boethius. *The Consolation of Philosophy* (III, metrum 12); Orpheus was ordered not to look back at Eurydice until out of Hell, but 'what is he that may yeven a lawe to loverys? Love is a grettere lawe and a strengere to hymself [thanne any lawe that man mai yyven]' (Chaucer's version).

306–11   Note the play on *lovere … lawe … love … lawe … lawe … love … love*, emphasizing the two poles of the argument.

309   *positif lawe*: enacted rather than natural law.

A man moot nedes love, maugree his heed.
He may nat fleen it, thogh he sholde be deed,
Al be she mayde, wydwe or ellis wyf.
And eek, it is nat likly al thy lyf
To stonden in hir grace; namoore shal I,   315
For wel thow woost thy selven, verraily,
That thow and I be dampned to prisoun
Perpetuelly; us gayneth no raunsoun.
We stryve as dide the houndes for the boon –
They foghte al day, and yet hir part was noon;   320
Ther cam a kyte, whil they were so wrothe,
That bar awey the boon bitwixe hem bothe!
And therfore, at the kynges court, my brother
Ech man for hymself – ther is noon oother.
Love, if thee list, for I love and ay shal.   325
And soothly, leve brother, this is al:
Here in this prisoun moote we endure,
And everich of us take his aventure.'
    Greet was the stryf and long bitwixe hem tweye
If that I hadde leyser for to seye;   330
But to theffect: it happed on a day
(To telle it yow as shortly as I may)
A worthy duc that highte Parotheus,
That felawe was unto duc Theseus
Syn thilke day that they were children lite,   335
Was come to Atthenes his felawe to visite
And for to pleye, as he was wont to do,
For in this world he loved no man so;
And he loved hym as tendrely ageyn.
So wel they loved, as olde bookes seyn,   340
That whan that oon was deed, soothly to telle,
His felawe wente and soghte hym doun in helle;
But of that storie list me nat to write.
    Duc Parotheus loved wel Arcite,
And hadde hym knowe at Thebes yeer by yere,   345
And finally, at requeste and prayere
Of Parotheus, with outen any raunsoun,
Duc Theseus hym leet out of prisoun,

311   *maugree his heed*: in spite of all he can do. The emphasis on the absolute power of love over humans ties in with Chaucer's discussion of its power in *Troilus and Criseyde* (III.1–49), and lays some of the foundations for Theseus's speech on love as a cosmic force at the end of the poem.

313   *Al be she*: 'Whether the lady is . . .'

315   *stonden in hir grace*: win her favour. The hopelessness of their situation is restated to underline the ironic comedy of their quarrelling. The similes that follow (319ff.) are belittling too. But there is a further irony in that they are not in prison *perpetuelly* (318): time (and Theseus) will release them.

318   *us gayneth no raunsoun*: 'no ransom will be of any use to us'.

319ff.   cf. Aesop's fable of the lion and the bear (or tiger). A fox runs off with the bone of contention while they quarrel.

323–4   Proverbial. The use of proverb and fable, and the nearly colloquial vigour of his rhythms, distinguish Arcite's speech from the more formal tone used by Palamon.

328   The closing of the speech on *aventure* (mentioned in line 302 as well) emphasizes the importance of chance as a matter for consideration. It is no accident that the next paragraph introduces what looks like an inconsequential coincidence, Parotheus's visit to Athens. But it is only apparently chance; Chaucer hints that there is a chain of causality and custom behind the visit – it only looks fortuitous from the prisoners' point of view. The juxtaposition is also ironic, coming so soon after Arcite's certainty of perpetual imprisonment.

330   The *occupatio* avoids tedium and also reminds us that our story has a shape, that its 'effect' is what is ultimately of interest.

331   Chaucer introduces another pair of friends into the Tale: interestingly he follows the *Roman de la Rose* story (8148ff.) of Theseus's rescue of Peirithous from Hell rather than the version in Ovid (*Ex Ponto*, III.iii.43f.) which he must have known; in the latter, they both go off together to carry off Proserpina, the Queen of Hades. The values of friendship are thus emphasized, and also the irony that Parotheus's visit rescues Arcite from an analogue of Hell.

340   Chaucer inserts this small digression, or *diversio*: it is not in Boccaccio.

343   The *occupatio* is plainly inconsistent with a *Canterbury Tales* setting – evidence either of a lack of thorough revision, or of Chaucer being untroubled by any detailed link between the Tale and its teller.

347   It is stressed that Arcite is released without ransom, and that Theseus has been swayed to mercy by intercession.

Frely to goon wher that hym liste overal,
In swich a gyse, as I yow tellen shal.   350
   This was the forward, pleynly for tendite,
Bitwixen Theseus and hym Arcite:
That if so were, that Arcite were yfounde
Evere in his lyf, by day or nyght or stounde,
In any contree of this Theseus,   355
And he were caught, it was acorded thus,
That with a swerd he sholde lese his heed;
Ther nas noon other remedye ne reed,
But taketh his leve, and homward he hym spedde.
Lat hym be war, his nekke lith to wedde!   360
   How greet a sorwe suffreth now Arcite!
The deeth he feeleth thurgh his herte smyte.
He wepeth, wayleth, crieth pitously;
To sleen hym self he waiteth pryvely;

352 *hym Arcite*: the preposition governs the accusative of the pronoun, which is in apposition to 'Arcite'. Translate as 'this Arcite'.

354 *or stounde*: or for a single moment. Later this judgement, too, is waived by Theseus on intercession, even though its justice is accepted by Arcite.

360 *his nekke lith to wedde*: 'his neck is at stake'.

361ff. Chaucer gives us a short though careful build-up to Arcite's elaborate lament. The alliteration, *wepeth*, *wayleth*, followed by a verb, *crieth*, from the same conceptual group (or lexical set) might suggest hyperbolical overstatement to us, to be laughed at. I doubt whether this is so; Chaucer seems to want us to take this seriously – at the least, we have to accept that Arcite certainly does. (cf. the treatment of Aurelius in *The Franklin's Tale*, V. (F)1020ff.)

364 'He looks for a chance to kill himself quietly.'

He seyde, 'Allas the day that I was born!   365
Now is my prisoun worse than biforn!
Now is me shape eternally to dwelle
Noght in purgatorie, but in helle!
Allas, that evere knew I Parotheus!
For elles hadde I dwelled with Theseus   370
Yfetered in his prisoun everemo.
Thanne hadde I been in blisse, and nat in wo.
Oonly the sight of hire, whom that I serve,
Thogh that I nevere hir grace may deserve,
Wolde have suffised right ynogh for me.   375
   'O deere cosyn Palamon,' quod he,
'Thyn is the victorie of this aventure.
Ful blisfully in prisoun maistow dure.
In prisoun? certes nay, but in paradys!
Wel hath fortune yturned thee the dys,   380
That hast the sight of hire, and I thabsence.
For possible is, syn thow hast hir presence,
And art a knyght, a worthy and an able,
That by som caas, syn fortune is chaungeable,
Thow mayst to thy desir som tyme atteyne.   385
   But I, that am exiled, and bareyne
Of alle grace, and in so greet despeir
That ther nis erthe, water, fyr ne eyr,
Ne creature that of hem maked is,
That may me helpe or doon confort in this,   390

365ff. Chaucer, in inserting this lament, took the opportunity of widening the philosophical references of the Tale. The speaker, here and elsewhere, comments on the implications of his part in the story as he sees it. The speech is not intended to be realistic (cf. Introduction, p. 49f.); but it is as passionate, artificial and important as an aria in an opera. Just as the aria marks a moment of high significance and prepares us for further development, so does this. But no man in this position would or could produce so elaborately structured a speech.

The movement of thought is from the particular (himself, and his envy of Palamon) to the general (fortune and providence, and the irony of man's ignorant prayers), and then back to the particular, himself. The main argumentative device is to first make several general statements, exemplify them, and at the end of each paragraph draw a conclusion. The speech is meticulously worked, and therefore, like an aria, can be seen as a carefully crafted, distinct artefact within the whole. It has, of course, to be compared and contrasted with Palamon's (423ff.), and the result is not only a further deepening of the discussion of fortune and providence but also ironic comedy. Where Arcite sees a rudimentary wisdom in providence, by contrast Palamon sees *cruel goddes* manipulating an inexorable destiny and caring little about men (445ff.). (See Introduction, p. 56.)

The style is formal and elaborate, using anaphora (*repetitio*) and parison (*compar*) (e.g. 366–7, 402–3), apostrophe (376), rhetorical questions, climax (388–90), and *contentio* (strong and patterned contrast) strengthened by rhyme (412–13).

The sub-text of the speech repays attention. There is a strongly religious terminology just under the surface, which links up in the context with Theseus's prison and what it might symbolize: *prisoun* (366) ... *purgatorie* (368) ... *helle* (368) ... *prisoun* (371) ... *blisse* (372, always a loaded word in Chaucer, relating ironically or not to the true happiness that exists only in Heaven) ... *grace* (374; here it means Emelye's favour, but the word is interchangeable between amatory and religious contexts – cf. the ambiguous use of it in 387) ... *blisfully*, *prisoun* (378) ... *prisoun*, *paradys* (379) ... *grace* (387) ... *felicitee* (408); not just happiness. but blessedness ... *prisoun* (412) ... *joye and parfit heele* (413).

367 'I am now fated to live for ever ...'

384 Again, the emphasis is on changing fortune.

388 It was thought, following the Greeks, that different combinations of some or all of the four elements – earth, air, fire and water – compounded the created world and all that was in it.

Wel oghte I sterve in wanhope and distresse!
Farewel my lyf, my lust, and my gladnesse!
  'Allas, why pleynen folk so in comune
On purveiaunce of God, or of fortune,
That yeveth hem ful ofte, in many a gyse,   395
Wel bettre than they kan hem self devyse?
Som man desireth for to have richesse,
That cause is of his moerdre or greet siknesse;
And som man wolde out of his prisoun fayn,
That in his hous is of his meynee slayn.   400
Infinite harmes been in this matere;
We woot nat what thyng that we prayen heere.
We faren as he that dronke is as a mous;
A dronke man woot wel he hath an hous,
But he noot which the righte wey is thider,   405
And to a dronke man the wey is slider.
And certes, in this world so faren we;
We seken fast after felicitee,
But we goon wrong ful often, trewely.
  'Thus may we seyen alle, and nameliche I,   410
That wende and hadde a greet opinioun
That, if I myghte scapen from prisoun,
Than hadde I been in joye and parfit heele,
Ther now I am exiled fro my wele.
Syn that I may nat seen yow, Emelye,   415
I nam but deed; ther nis no remedye.'
  Upon that oother syde, Palamon,
Whan that he wiste Arcite was agon,
Swich sorwe he maketh that the grete tour
Resouneth of his yowlyng and clamour.   420
The pure fettres of his shynes grete
Were of his bittre salte teres wete.
  'Allas,' quod he, 'Arcite, cosyn myn,
Of al oure strif, God woot, the fruyt is thyn!
Thou walkest now in Thebes, at thy large,   425
And of my wo thou yevest litel charge.
Thou mayst, syn thou hast wisdom and manhede,
Assemblen alle the folk of oure kynrede,
And make a werre so sharp on this citee
That by som aventure, or som tretee,   430

394   *purveiaunce*: providence. Like the Lady's speech, this refers us to the central concerns of the Tale. However, this is the first time that providence has been mentioned as distinct from fortune. The ideas here are heavily dependent on Boethius (IV, p6; III, p2; II, p5).

396ff.   The idea of the wisdom of God in giving and the folly of men in asking is perfectly relevant to the present lament. Arcite's rehearsal of some fairly stereotyped philosophical ideas and proverbs – at 403, for instance – which he applies to his release from prison underlines an irony he perceives, but for us indicates another he does not perceive: he does not take his own advice. He is also far from the patience he recommended earlier.

    The view of providence here is much developed later in the Tale and particularly by Theseus's interpretation of the events at the end. Arcite's speech is a fair comment, too, on his own future career, including his and Palamon's prayers.

401   *Infinite ... matere*: 'There are great evils in this matter of trying to do better than providence.'

413   'Whereas I am now separated from all that makes for my well-being.' Emelye is seen in conventional lover's terms as the fount of all joy and health. We need to remind ourselves that the poor girl doesn't yet know what weight of devotion is being offered to her.

417   The ending of Arcite's formal speech is equally formally balanced by the speaker turning to Palamon to hear his reaction. Their speeches are meant to be seen as an ironic (yet serious) diptych; both start with the same word, both occupy in all fifty-two lines, and both deal with the same topics by similar procedures.

420   *yowlyng*: lamentation – not, as we might think from its modern descendant, a belittling word.

423ff.   The irony of each envying what makes the other miserable has already been mentioned (see Introduction, p. 52). Notice that the religious or devotional sub-text we saw in Arcite's speech is absent here. Yet – a nice irony – it was Palamon who at first saw Emelye as divine.

430   *aventure, or som tretee*: an odd zeugma – chance or treaty. It is not, given the concerns of the Tale, an insignificant one.

Thou mayst have hire to lady and to wyf
For whom that I moste nedes lese my lyf.
For, as by wey of possibilitee,
Sith thou art at thy large, of prisoun free,
And art a lord, greet is thyn avauntage,   435
Moore than is myn, that sterve here in a cage;
For I moot wepe and waille, whil I lyve,
With al the wo that prisoun may me yeve,
And eek with peyne that love me yeveth also,
That doubleth al my torment and my wo.'   440
 Ther with, the fyr of jalousie upsterte
With inne his brest, and hente hym by the herte
So woodly that he lyk was to biholde
The box tree or the asshen dede and colde.
 Thanne seyde he, 'O cruel goddes, that governe   445
This world with byndyng of youre word eterne,
And writen in the table atthamaunt
Youre parlement, and youre eterne graunt,
What is mankynde moore unto yow holde
Than is the sheep, that rowketh in the folde?   450
For slayn is man right as another beest,
And dwelleth eek in prisoun and areest,
And hath siknesse and greet adversitee,
And ofte tymes giltlees, pardee!
What governaunce is in this prescience   455
That giltlees tormenteth innocence?
And yet encreseth this al my penaunce,
That man is bounden to his observaunce
For Goddes sake, to letten of his wille,
Theras a beest may al his lust fulfille.   460
And whan a beest is deed, he hat no peyne;
But after his deeth, man moot wepe and pleyne,
Though in this world he have care and wo.
Withouten doute it may stonden so
 'The answere of this lete I to divynis,   465
But wel I woot that in this world greet pyne is.
Allas! I se a serpent, or a theef,
That many a trewe man hath doon mescheef,
Goon at his large, and wher hym list may turne.
But I moot been in prisoun thurgh Saturne,   470

441ff. A neat linking of the metaphorical fire of jealousy with the change of countenance in Palamon – ashen-faced, or greeny-yellow like boxwood. Jealousy is the green-eyed monster, of course.

445 The *exclamatio* balances Arcite's in 393ff. Palamon sees the gods as uncaring and cruel, and as binding man's future by their decree. There is a semantic emphasis on *cruel* (445), and the consequential innocent suffering of men – *giltlees* (454, 456). This cruelty anticipates the suffering in the *descriptiones* of the gods' temples in Book III.

456ff. '... which torments guiltless innocence' (the moving of *giltlees* forward is for emphasis). 'This makes my suffering even worse; that man is for God's sake bound to observe the moral law and give up his desires (and yet he gets no credit for it).' Chaucer returns again and again in his poetry to the problem of evil and suffering in a universe ruled by a just God, and it is of course a major issue in Boethius.

464 'Doubtless it may well turn out thus.'

465 *answere*: solution of the problem. Palamon implies here that he is not interested in an attempt to understand suffering – he has already made up his mind that the universe is cruel.

470ff. Palamon blames Saturn and Juno for his plight because of Juno's old enmity towards Thebes, originating in jealousy over Jove's relations with Semele and Alcmene. But Palamon is seeing Saturn as a god in the Classical sense, whereas Arcite saw Saturn as a planet (232). (Juno is not a planet.) See Appendix 2, pp. 219ff.

Both these important speeches deal with the issues of deserts, felicity, fortune and providence. The issues have been widened dramatically by them.

And eek thurgh Juno, jalous and eek wood,
That hath destroyed wel ny al the blood
Of Thebes, with his waste walles wyde.
And Venus sleeth me on that oother syde
For jalousie, and feere of hym Arcite.'   475

   Now wol I stynte of Palamon a lite,
And lete hym in his prisoun stille dwelle,
And of Arcita forth I wol yow telle.
The somer passeth and the nyghtes longe
Encresen double wise the peynes stronge   480
Bothe of the lovere and the prisoner.
I noot which hath the wofuller myster.
For shortly for to seyn, this Palamoun
Perpetuelly is dampned to prisoun,
In cheynes and in fettres to been deed;   485
And Arcite is exiled upon his heed
For evere mo as out of that contree,
Ne nevere mo he shal his lady see.

   Yow loveris axe I now this questioun,
Who hath the worse, Arcite or Palamoun?   490
That oon may seen his lady day by day,
But in prisoun moot he dwelle alway.
That oother wher hym list may ryde or go,
But seen his lady shal he nevere mo.
Now demeth as yow list, ye that kan   495
For I wol telle forth as I bigan.

           Explicit prima pars
         Sequitur pars secunda

476 A narratorial necessity, after so long a speech, to tell the audience that the focus of their attention is about to be changed.

480–81 A neat ambiguity; the conceit of the lover as the lady's prisoner was already current by this time.

482 *myster*: literally, 'job'; 'who had the hardest deal'.

484ff. The recapitulation is necessary to remind us, before this episode is closed, of the basic situation. Notice that it is repeated in the next paragraph.

489ff. *Demandes d'amour*, where a problem (ethical, usually) is set for the audience to consider, are common in medieval stories. Clearly this question, though it relates to the ideas of *blisse* and *felicitee* already raised, is not adequate as a summary of the concerns of the story so far. It is not meant to be; we have to guard against rushing to opinions in answering this question, only to see later that those opinions were irrelevant as they are overtaken by the events of the Tale. Thus this question is part of the ironic discussion of human knowledge and wisdom, including our own.

496 At this point, where clearly a break of some sort is indicated, some important manuscripts do not leave any gap. The Ellesmere manuscript, however, one of the most important, has what is probably a scribal insertion, two lines of Latin telling us the first part is over and the second will follow (the same thing happens at the end of Books II and III).

BOOK II

Whan that Arcite to Thebes comen was,
Ful ofte a day he swelte, and seyde, 'allas'.
For seen his lady shal he nevere mo.
And shortly to concluden al his wo   500
So muchel sorwe had nevere creature
That is, or shal, whil that the world may dure.
  His sleep, his mete, his drynke is hym biraft,
That lene he wex, and drye as is a shaft;
Hise eyen holwe, and grisly to biholde,   505
His hewe falow, and pale as asshen colde.
And solitarie he was, and evere allone,
And waillynge al the nyght, makynge his mone,
And if he herde song or instrument,
Thanne wolde he wepe – he myghte nat be stent;   510
So feble eek were his spiritz, and so lowe,
And chaunged so, that no man koude knowe
His speche nor his voys, though men it herde.
And in his gere, for al the world he ferde
Nat oonly lyk the loveris maladye   515
Of Hereos, but rather lyk manye
Engendred of humour malencolyk,
Biforn his celle fantastyk

502 The first six lines of the book serve as a brief and generalized overture
to the description, in very conventional terms, of Arcite's love-sickness.
The sufferings of the lover are a familiar topos from many romances,
and where it is used there is necessarily a generalizing effect. The sickness
itself should be recognized as serious; medieval physicians so regarded
it. Chaucer sometimes frames it ironically, as in the case of Aurelius
in *The Franklin's Tale*, or of Troilus in *Troilus and Criseyde* (see
Introduction, p. 36). The *repetitio* and *compar* enable the sketch to
be executed very swiftly through a series of rapid and distinct details.

507 *allone*: compare with Arcite *allone* in death (1921).

511 *spiritz*: according to medieval medical theory, derived ultimately
from the second-century Greek, Galen, three spirits, the natural, vital
and animal, were necessary to life. Natural spirit is the power of growth
and nutrition; this crude spirit is refined by air in the lungs and by heat
of the heart, and absorbs in the heart the principle of actual living, the
vital spirit. When some of this refined blood reaches the brain, it
generates the purest spirit of all, the animal – so called from the Latin
anima, 'soul'. This then circulates through the supposedly hollow
nerves, allowing motion and the higher bodily functions.

513 *though men it herde*: 'even though it was heard'.

514 *gere*: probably means here 'behaviour', but could refer to the
disordered clothing supposed in this and later centuries to be typical of
the unhappy lover (cf. Polonius's view of Hamlet in *Hamlet*, II.i.72ff.).

516 *Hereos*: the name for the lover's malady derives ultimately from the
Greek *eros*, 'love'. It was described as a medical condition by several
medieval physicians, and is so treated by Robert Burton in *The Anatomy
of Melancholy* (1621). Chaucer's details are all sound according to the
medical opinions of his day.

   manye: mania is one of the consequences of uncured *hereos*, and can
lead to death.

517 *humour malencolyk*: the ancient physicians recognized four com-
ponents or 'humours' in a man's make-up – blood, choler, phlegm
and melancholy. Their mixture or 'complexion' determined a man's
character and outlook. When one predominated, disorder was the
result – as here, where Arcite is suffering from an excess of melancholy
which causes his depression, lassitude, and the changes in his appearance
described below.

518 *celle fantastyk*: the brain was thought to be divided into three cells.
The forward one was that of fantasy, i.e. imagination, the middle of
reason, and the back of memory. Mania afflicts the front cell.

And shortly, turned was al up so doun
Bothe habit and eek disposicioun   520
Of hym, this woful lovere, daun Arcite.
What sholde I al day of his wo endite?
    Whan he endured hadde a yeer or two
This cruel torment, and this peyne and wo,
At Thebes in his contree as I seyde,   525
Upon a nyght, in sleep as he hym leyde,
Hym thoughte how that the wynged god Mercurie
Biforn hym stood, and bad hym to be murye.
His slepy yerde in honde he bar up righte;
An hat he wered upon his heres brighte.   530
Arrayed was this god (as he took keep)
As he was whan that Argus took his sleep;
And seyde hym thus: 'To Atthenes shaltow wende;
Ther is thee shapen of thy wo an ende.'
    And with that word, Arcite wook and sterte.   535
'Now trewely, how sore that me smerte,'
Quod he, 'to Atthenes right now wol I fare.
Ne for the drede of deeth shal I nat spare
To see my lady, that I love and serve;
In hir presence I recche nat to sterve.'   540
    And with that word he caughte a greet mirour,
And saugh that chaunged was al his colour,
And saugh his visage al in another kynde;
And right anoon it ran hym in his mynde
That, sith his face was so disfigured   545
Of maladie, the which he hadde endured,
He myghte wel, if that he bar hym lowe,
Lyve in Atthenes everemoore unknowe,
And seen his lady wel ny day by day.
    And right anoon he chaunged his array   550
And cladde hym as a poure laborer,
And al allone, save oonly a squyer
That knew his pryvetee and al his cas,
Which was disgised pourely, as he was,

520   *habit*: bodily condition. *Disposicioun*: not outlook or character, but frame of mind.

521   *this woful lovere*: a generalizing and distancing phrase closes the description. *Daun*: Latin *dominus*, 'lord'.

522   The *occupatio* once more reminds us that this is a story, and the description a mere element within it.

523   *a yeer or two*: Chaucer deliberately extends the time scale of the Tale to some seven years (cf. 568, 594); Boccaccio doesn't suggest a period anything like as long. It is medically somewhat remarkable that Arcite survived his love-sickness for so long.

527   *Hym ... Mercurie*: It is emphasized that it *seemed* Mercury was there. The ambiguity of dreams is a frequent topos in Chaucer's poetry. Some kinds were deceptive, some trustworthy, and the difficulty was to know which was which (cf. Proem to Book I of *The House of Fame*). This one is of the trustworthy kind, a *visio*, in which a god appears to a mortal. *Mercurie* was the messenger of the gods, and is instantly recognizable by his wings (on cap or feet) and his caduceus (*slepy yerde*). Chaucer links the gods into the Tale far more closely than Boccaccio did.

532   *Argus*: Argus of the hundred eyes was set by Juno to watch Io and to prevent Jove from approaching her. Mercury was sent by Jove to kill Argus, which he did after first sending him to sleep (Ovid, *Metamorphoses*, I.714ff.)

533–4   His words are deliberately ambiguous. Arcite's sufferings certainly come to an end.

536   *how sore that me smerte*: 'however it hurts me'.

540   As in 533–4, this is ironic; he gets his wish (cf. the irony of the prayers below, and their results in Books III and IV).

541–52   Notice how these twelve lines are constructed. The first four describe Arcite's perception of his state, closing on the germ of an idea that is developed in the middle four lines through the causal clause. The last four open with the climax of the plan – *seen his lady* – and then turn to his decisive action. The first and last four are linked not only by the obvious echoing *repetitio* on 'And', but also by having in common the key terms *saugh* and *seen* (542, 543, 549), and *chaunged* (542, 550). It is rhetorically so strongly marked because Chaucer needs to be sure the audience will grasp that Arcite is now, like many romance heroes, going to seek his lady in disguise, which by convention will be impenetrable. He even gives him a *squyer*, an echo of the faithful confidant and companion in many knightly tales of love. On a more serious level, the change of countenance and the disguise perhaps suggest the strange guises under which fortune is misunderstood.

113

To Atthenes is he goon the nexte way.   555
And to the court he wente upon a day,
And at the gate he profreth his servyse
To drugge and drawe, what so men wol devyse.
     And shortly of this matere for to seyn
He fil in office with a chamberleyn   560
The which that dwellyng was with Emelye.
For he was wys, and koude soone espye
Of every servant, which that serveth here.
Wel koude he hewen wode, and water bere,
For he was yong and myghty for the nones   565
And therto he was strong and byg of bones
To doon that any wight kan hym devyse.
     A yeer or two he was in this servyse,
Page of the chambre of Emelye the brighte,
And Philostrate he seyde that he highte.   570
But half so wel biloved a man as he
Ne was ther nevere in court, of his degree;
He was so gentil of condicioun
That thurgh out al the court was his renoun.
They seiden that it were a charitee   575
That Theseus wolde enhauncen his degree,
And putten hym in worshipful servyse
Theras he myghte his vertu excercise.
     And thus withinne a while his name is spronge,
Bothe of his dedes and his goode tonge,   580
That Theseus hath taken hym so ner
That of his chambre he made hym a squier,
And gaf hym gold to mayntene his degree.
And eek men broghte hym out of his contree
Fro yeer to yeer, ful pryvely, his rente;   585
But honestly and sleighly he it spente,
That no man wondred how that he it hadde.
And thre yeer in this wise his lyf he ladde,
And bar hym so, in pees and eek in werre,
Ther was no man that Theseus hath derre.   590
And in this blisse lete I now Arcite,
And speke I wol of Palamon a lite.

555 *nexte way*: the quickest or shortest way.

558ff.   Though several romance heroes perform such menial tasks, one is reminded of Jacob serving Laban for Rachel (Genesis, XXIX) – particularly with the other Biblical echo at line 564 (cf. Joshua, IX.21). Arcite is performing the sort of love-service some cruel ladies, playing hard to get, inflicted on their knights. But his lady still does not know of his existence, and so could not demand these services rom him. Chaucer doesn't underline the irony, but it is clearly there.

566 *strong*: Robinson's edition reads *long* ('tall'), following the majority of manuscripts.

570 *Philostrate*: Chaucer took this name not from the *Teseida* but from the title of another of Boccaccio's poems, *Il Filostrato*. Boccaccio coined the name to mean 'laid low by love' – appropriate enough for Arcite, both in his former state and now in his work.

570ff.   Notice how, by the use of the abbreviated style, Chaucer is able rapidly and efficiently to slip over a long period of time to reach the next significant action. He carefully leaves us on a note that emphasizes the double irony of Arcite's position – dear to the ruler who would, if he recognized him, condemn him to death, and still as far as ever from success with Emelye.

582 *made him a squier*: page of the chamber, then squire, was a normal course of promotion.

586 *honestly and sleighly*: honourably and discreetly.

591 *blisse*: always a dangerous word in later Chaucer, because it does a double job in referring both to the ineffable bliss of heaven and illusory bliss on earth. It is clearly ironic here.

592 The marking of the narrative block reminds us once more that this is a story, not reality, shaped and controlled by a narrator.

  In derknesse and horrible and strong prisoun
This seven yeer hath seten Palamoun
Forpyned, what for wo and for distresse.   595
Who feeleth double soor and hevynesse
But Palamon? that love destreyneth so
That wood out of his wit he gooth for wo;
And eek therto he is a prisoner
Perpetuelly, nat oonly for a yer.   600
Who koude ryme in englissh proprely
His martirdom? For sothe, it am noght I;
Therfore I passe as lightly as I may.
  It fil that in the seventhe yeer, of May
The thridde nyght (as olde bokes seyn,   605
That al this storie tellen moore pleyn)
Were it by aventure, or destynee
(As, whan a thyng is shapen, it shal be),
That soone after the mydnyght, Palamoun,
By helpyng of a freend, brak his prisoun   610
And fleeth the citee, faste as he may go.
For he had yeve his gailler drynke so
Of a clarree, maad of a certeyn wyn,
With nercotikes and opye of Thebes fyn,
That al that nyght, thogh that men wolde hym shake,   615
The gailler sleep; he myghte noght awake.
And thus he fleeth as faste as evere he may.
  The nyght was short, and faste by the day,
That nedes cost he moste hymselven hyde.
And til a grove faste ther bisyde   620
With dreedful foot thanne stalketh Palamoun.
For shortly, this was his opynyoun,
That in that grove he wolde hym hyde al day,
And in the nyght thanne wolde he take his way
To Thebesward, his freendes for to preye   625
On Theseus to helpe hym to werreye;
And shortly, outher he wolde lese his lyf
Or wynnen Emelye unto his wyf.
This is theffect and his entente pleyn.
  Now wol I turne to Arcite ageyn,   630
That litel wiste how neigh that was his care
Til that fortune had broght hym in the snare.

593–603   There is a remarkable concentration here on a group of related
words, or lexical set – *wo, distresse, soor, hevynesse, destreyneth, wood,
wo* – all suggesting pain, suffering, even madness. They are introduced
by a line very emphatically stressed on its key terms: the stresses fall on
*derk*nesse, *horr*ible, *strong, pris*oun, and the double caesura reinforces
them further. Moreover the line is built on a rhetorical figure rare in
Chaucer but common in Latin epic poetry, the *hendiadys* – the line
coordinates what is dependent, and means 'in the horrible darkness of
a strong prison'. (The emphasis on 'prison' may again have symbolic
force.) The passage is closed by three lines which are both *occupatio*
and *diminutio*, focussing on the very suggestive word *martirdom* (602).
The two rhetorical questions (596–7, 601–2) are recognized tools of
emphasis. Chaucer is writing in this way because we have spent a long
time with Arcite, and Palamon has dropped into the background. His
grief, too, has to be taken seriously.

604–5   *May*: the appropriate season for things to happen in a love story.
Commentators have spent a lot of time trying to fix the exact date, but
it hardly matters.

605–6   *olde bokes ... pleyn*: a general reminder of the authority of the
past again, and the indebtedness of the present to it. Also a self-
reference – Chaucer is inviting us to consider how well he is telling this
story as a story. (*pleyn*: fully; for *storie*, see note to line 1.)

607–8   An important parenthesis – chance (*aventure*), *destynee* (which
can't be chance), *shapen* ('decreed') all refer to the basic underlying
issues. Line 608 contains a proverb. (Cf. below, 632, 648.)

613   *clarree*: not claret, but a drink of wine, honey and spices; obviously,
here it is also a drug.

614   *Thebes*: opium came from Egyptian Thebes, but Chaucer is probably
echoing Boccaccio, who has a Greek Theban physician help Palamon
(*Teseida*, V.20).

619   *nedes cost*: of necessity.

621   'Palamon, full of fear, walks stealthily.' '*dreedful foot*' is an example
of hypallage, or transferred epithet. Note the cleverly imitative rhythms
of this and the previous line, mimicking Palamon's hesitant movement.

624ff.   Some irony; this is exactly what he thought Arcite would do.

630–32   Another transition, which explicitly makes Arcite's situation
ironical. It also underlines the narrator's overview of the Tale and the
'captivity' of his persons.

   The bisy larke, messager of day,
Salueth in hir song the morwe gray;
And firy Phebus riseth up so brighte,   635
That al the orient laugheth of the lighte
And with his stremes dryeth in the greves
The silver dropes hangynge on the leves.
And Arcita, that in the court roial
With Theseus, his squyer principal,   640
Is risen, and looketh on the murye day.
And, for to doon his observaunce to May,
Remembrynge on the poynt of his desir,
He, on a courser startlynge as the fir,
Is riden into the feeldes, hym to pleye,   645
Out of the court, were it a myle or tweye.
And to the grove, of which that I yow tolde,
By aventure his wey he gan to holde
To maken hym a gerland of the greves
Were it of wodebynde or hawethorn leves.   650

   And loude he song ayein the sonne shene,
'May, with alle thy floures and thy grene,
Welcome be thow, faire fresshe May,
In hope that I som grene gete may.'

   And from his courser with a lusty herte   655
Into the grove ful hastily he sterte,
And in a path he rometh up and doun
Theras by aventure this Palamoun
Was in a bussh that no man myghte hym se –
For soore afered of his deeth was he.   660
Nothyng ne knew he that it was Arcite –
God woot he wolde have trowed it ful lite!
But sooth is seyd, gon sithen many yeres,
That'feeld hath eyen and the wode hath eres'.
It is ful fair a man to bere hym evene,   665
For al day meeten men at unset stevene.
Ful litel woot Arcite of his felawe,
That was so neigh to herknen al his sawe,
For in the bussh he sitteth now ful stille.

   Whan that Arcite hadde romed al his fille,   670
And songen al the roundel lustily,
Into a studie he fil sodeynly,

633–8 A very brief use of the 'dawn' topos – the lark, the sun rising, the dew on the leaves. The formulae don't lose their charm for being so often used; and each item is linked responsively to another – the lark greets the day, and so on. The laughing of the orient echoes both Boccaccio (*Teseida*, III.5) and Dante (*Purgatorio*, I.21).

642 *observaunce*: cf. the *observaunce* of Emelye, walking in the garden (180ff.). That led to the quarrel; this leads to the first battle – again through someone being observed when they are unaware of the observer.

643 'Always keeping in mind the object of his desire.'

644 *startlynge as the fir*: prancing (leaping) like fire. The simile may pre-echo Arcite's Martial links later.

646 *were it*: it might be.

649 *maken hym a gerland*: as Emelye was doing. Hers was of flowers, Arcite's is of leaves. It is possible to see something symbolic in this, since Arcite's love is eventually sterile, but it is more likely to have some reference to a contemporary courtly love-controversy between the parties of the Flower and the Leaf – the subject of an anonymous fifteenth-century poem, *The Flower and the Leaf*. Chaucer seems to allude to the parties in the Prologue to *The Legend of Good Women* (F72).

654 Arcite may mean that he hopes Emelye will soon give him a garland; illustrations of the period often show a lady crowning her lover with a garland as a token of her acceptance of him.

663 'It was said many years ago, and it is true ...'

664 Proverbial. The use of *sententiae* was recommended by the *artes poeticae* as a means of anchoring the discussion.

665–6 Proverbial again: 'It is good if a man can keep on an even keel, for people always meet when they don't expect it.' Notice the emphasized irony here and the stress, both directly and through Arcite's ignorance of Palamon's proximity, on the limitedness of man's knowledge of the real parameters of his situation.

668 *al his sawe*: 'all he said'.

671 *roundel*: a song of between nine and fourteen lines, originally for dancing to, built on two rhymes and using repeated lines as a refrain. A roundel of sorts could be constructed from Arcite's three lines at 652–4.

672 *studie*: deep reverie.

As doon thise loveres in hir queynte geres –
Now in the croppe, now doun in the breres,
Now up, now doun, as boket in a welle. 675
Right as the Friday, soothly for to telle:
Now it shyneth, now it reyneth faste.
Right so kan gery Venus overcaste
The hertes of hir folk; right as hir day
Is gerful, right so chaungeth she array. 680
Selde is the Friday al the wike ylike.
    Whan that Arcite hadde songe, he gan to syke,
And sette hym doun withouten any moore.
'Allas,' quod he, 'that day that I was bore!
How longe, Juno, thurgh thy crueltee 685
Woltow werreyen Thebes the citee?
Allas! ybroght is to confusioun
The blood roial of Cadme and Amphioun;
Of Cadmus, which that was the firste man
That Thebes bulte, or first the toun bigan, 690
And of the citee first was crowned kyng;
Of his lynage am I, and his ofspryng
By verray ligne, as of the stok roial,
And now I am so caytif and so thral
That he, that is my mortal enemy, 695
I serve hym as his squyer pourely.
And yet doth Juno me wel moore shame,
For I dar noght biknowe myn owene name;
But ther as I was wont to highte Arcite,
Now highte I Philostrate, noght worth a myte. 700
Allas! thou felle Mars! allas ! Juno,
Thus hath youre ire oure lynage al fordo,
Save oonly me and wrecched Palamoun,
That Theseus martireth in prisoun.
    'And over al this, to sleen me outrely 705
Love hath his firy dart so brennyngly
Ystiked thurgh my trewe careful herte,
That shapen was my deeth erst than my sherte.
Ye sleen me with youre eyen, Emelye;
Ye been the cause wherfore that I dye. 710

673   *As doon thise loveres* ... : generalizing; once again Arcite is being related to the type. For the generalizing use of 'this', cf. *The Franklin's Tale*, V.(F)818, and see 265n., above.

674–5   The two similes exactly image vicissitude and reversal of fortune; each of them in its rhetorical formulation (the balanced opposites of *contentio*) echoes its sense. Neither is particularly ennobling, and their proverbial flavour once more generalizes the specific conflict we are to see. (Richard II uses the same image of the buckets to illustrate his fall and Bolingbroke's rise – *Richard II*, IV.i.185.)

676   *Friday*: Venus's day, *dies veneris* (cf. French *vendredi*), was proverbially unlike the rest of the week; it is changeable, as everything else about the goddess, and so are the hearts of lovers (678–9). There is little point in trying to fix the date on which Palamon and Arcite met, as some commentators have done, since Chaucer doesn't actually say that they met on a Friday.

684   Arcite's elaborately high-style soliloquy (*exclamatio*) contrasts with the hopefulness of his roundel. It is an important reminder of the wider context of the story, including the symbolically fallen city of Thebes. It also underlines once again the importance of change in human affairs.

685   *Juno*: see note to 470, above.

688   *Cadme and Amphioun*: the founders of Thebes. Cadmus sowed the dragon's teeth, which grew into fighting men, and Amphion's music built the walls of Thebes (Ovid, *Metamorphoses*, III; VI.176ff.).

704   *martireth*: the word keeps alive the idea of martyrdom for love.

706–7: cf. note to 238–9, above. The artificiality of the conceit (which is common enough) of the archer, love, allows Chaucer to make the speaker suggest his own powerlessness and passivity in the face of forces he does not understand.

708   'My death was destined before my first clothes (sc. body) were made.'

709   Note the semantic convergence between Emelye's glance and the god of Love's arrows (cf. 238–9, 706–7).

Of al the remenant of myn oother care
Ne sette I noght the mountaunce of a tare,
So that I koude doon aught to youre plesaunce!'
And with that word, he fil doun in a traunce
A longe tyme; and afterward he up sterte.   715
   This Palamoun, that thoughte that thurgh his herte
He felte a cold swerd sodeynliche glyde,
For ire he quook; no lenger wolde he byde.
And whan that he had herd Arcites tale,
As he were wood, with face deed and pale   720
He sterte hym up out of the buskes thikke,
And seyde, 'Arcite, false traytour wikke
Now artow hent that lovest my lady so,
For whom that I have al this peyne and wo,
And art my blood, and to my counseil sworn,   725
As I ful ofte have told thee her biforn,
And hast byjaped here duc Theseus,
And falsly chaunged hast thy name thus;
I wol be deed, or elles thow shalt dye.
Thow shalt nat love my lady Emelye,   730
But I wol love hire oonly, and namo.
For I am Palamon, thy mortal foo,
And thogh that I no wepne have in this place,
But out of prisoun am astert by grace,
I drede noght that outher thou shalt dye   735
Or thou ne shalt noght loven Emelye.
Chees which thow wolt, [f]or thow shalt noght asterte.'
   This Arcite, with ful despitous herte,
Whan he hym knew and hadde his tale herd,
As fiers as leoun pulled out his swerd,   740
And seyde thus: 'By God that sit above,
Nere it that thow art syk and wood for love,
And eek that thow no wepne hast in this place,
Thow sholdest nevere out of this grove pace,
That thow ne sholdest dyen of my hond.   745
For I diffye the seuretee and the bond
Which that thow seist that I have maad to thee.
What, verray fool, thynk wel that love is free
And I wol love hire, maugree al thy myght!
But, forasmuche thow art a worthy knyght,   750

714–15: As these lovers do; and with a rapid recovery.

717 Palamon's heart is also pierced, but with a cold sword – a deliberate contrast between the love Arcite has just been talking about and the anger Palamon feels.

724ff. Palamon's anger can be felt not only in the way he repeats the old claims of friendship and charges of treachery, but also in the cumulative structure of the sentence and the rhythmic build-up through the *repetitiones*. The climax is, typically, in a patterned contrast, rhythmically pointed (729).

730 cf. Arcite's reply to a similar attack at 306.

745 'Without being sure of death at my hand.'

746 *diffye*: *diffidatio* is the technical term for the formal rejection, by either party, of feudal obligation. Arcite is given the term here to emphasize that what is being revoked is the formal obligation of sworn brotherhood. It is reinforced by the legal terms *seuretee* and *bond*.

And wilnest to darreyne hire by bataille,
Have here my trouthe; tomorowe I wol nat faille,
With outen wityng of any oother wight,
That here I wol be founden as a knyght,
And bryngen harneys right ynogh for thee;   755
And chees the beste and leve the worste for me.
And mete and drynke this nyght wol I brynge
Ynogh for thee, and clothes for thy beddynge.
And if so be that thow my lady wynne,
And slee me in this wode ther I am inne,   760
Thow mayst wel have thy lady, as for me.'
   This Palamon answerde, 'I graunte it thee.'
And thus they been departed til amorwe,
Whan ech of hem had leyd his feith to borwe.

   O Cupide, out of alle charitee!   765
O regne, that wolt no felawe have with thee!
Ful sooth is seyd, that love ne lordshipe
Wol noght, his thankes, have no felaweshipe.
Wel fynden that Arcite and Palamoun.

   Arcite is riden anon unto the toun,   770
And on the morwe, er it were dayes light,
Ful pryvely two harneys hath he dight,
Bothe suffisaunt and mete to darreyne
The bataille in the feeld bitwix hem tweyne.
And on his hors, allone as he was born,   775
He carieth al this harneys hym biforn
And in the grove at tyme and place yset
This Arcite and this Palamon been met.

   T[h]o chaungen gan the colour in hir face;
Right as the hunters in the regne of Trace,   780
That stondeth at the gappe with a spere,
Whan hunted is the leoun or the bere,
And hereth hym come russhyng in the greves,
And breketh bothe bowes and the leves,
And thynketh, 'here cometh my mortal enemy;   785
Withoute faille, he moot be deed, or I;

751   *darreyne hire by bataille*: vindicate your claim to her by battle. On trial by battle, see note to 994ff., below.

759–61   The important middle lines of this book fall on the quarrel between Palamon and Arcite. These three lines ironically focus on Arcite's death and the possibility that Palamon may win Emelye.

765ff.   *O Cupide, out of alle charitee*: 'O Cupid, who art quite without generosity.' Charity is the highest, most selfless love (cf. I Corinthians, XIII).

    The apostrophe or *exclamatio*, closing with a *sententia* (767–8), inevitably generalizing yet again and inviting us to see the story as in some way typical and mythic, suspends the narrative to allow an increase in tension. Even with this narratorial interruption, notice the brevity of the narrative compared with the length and detailed articulation of the speeches.

768   *his thankes*: with his goodwill.

775   *allone as he was born*: again, the audience is reminded that Arcite is alone.

780ff.   An elaborate (epic) simile of unusual length for this Tale. Boccaccio uses this one, originally from Statius (*Thebaid*, IV.494–9), for the emotions of the rival armies a year later. Chaucer adapts it somewhat, and makes it extraordinarily vivid. The *repetitio* and *compar* of lines 783–5 capture the rapidity of the animal and of the hunter's feelings; note especially the momentary, almost cinematic, change of subject from the hunter to the quarry at line 784. The simile's tone and elaborate form signal that the fight between the lovers is to be taken very seriously indeed – a fit antecedent for the clash of armies later.

780   *hunters*: genitive; it was the colour of the hunter's face that changed. *Trace*: Thrace.

781   *stondeth at the gappe*: the hunters would be positioned to guard, with a long spear, the escape route of the hunted animal. The animal's force and speed would impale it on the spear if it was placed properly.

For outher I moot sleen hym at the gappe,
Or he moot sle me, if that me myshappe.'
So ferden they in chaungyng of hir hewe.

  As fer as everich of hem oother knewe 790
Ther nas no good day ne no saluynge;
But streight, withouten word or rehersynge,
Everich of hem heelp for to armen other
As frendly as he were his owene brother.
And after that with sharpe speres stronge 795
They foynen ech at other wonder longe.
Thou myghtest wene that this Palamoun
In his fightyng were a wood leoun,
And as a cruel tigre was Arcite.
As wilde bores gonnen they to smyte, 800
That frothen whit as foom, for ire wood.
Up to the ancle foghte they in hir blood.
And in this wise I lete hem fightyng dwelle,
And forth I wol of Theseus yow telle.

  The destinee, ministre general, 805
That executeth in the world overal
The purveiaunce that God hath seyn biforn,
So strong it is that, thogh the world had sworn
The contrarie of a thyng, by ye or nay,
Yet somtyme it shal fallen on a day 810
That falleth nat eft withinne a thousand yeer.
For certeynly, oure appetites heer,
Be it of werre or pees, or hate, or love,
Al is this ruled by the sighte above.
This mene I now by myghty Theseus, 815
That for to hunten is so desirus,
And namely at the grete hert in May,
That in his bed ther daweth hym no day
That he nis clad and redy for to ryde
With hunte and horn, and houndes hym bisyde. 820

790–94 Chaucer underlines the pathos behind the irony here: *as he were his owene brother* is exactly how each used to regard the other, but the subjunctive underlines the fact that that is long past.

796ff. It was usual, in medieval single combat between knights, to begin with the spear and then change to the sword. The combat is described quite differently in Boccaccio's account.

797ff. The distancing *thou myghtest wene* ('one might imagine') invites us to engage our imagination. There is actually little direct description of the fight. It is pretty generalized and conventional, and the epic simile does most of the work of visualization for us. Notice that in lines 798–800 the hunted animals of the simile are applied to Arcite and Palamon. Animals do, of course, have a moral or temperamental reference (cf. the description of the kings in Book III). Comparison of combatants with animals is a standard romance motif, however. The final effect is one of stabilized spectacle, with little sense of violent and uncontrolled action. We are watching this from a very long way away.

802 Comic to us, but probably quite serious, such an exaggeration is common in the heroic romances (cf. similar exaggeration in *The Ballad of Chevy Chase*). It thus signals that Chaucer is momentarily putting the combatants in that context of values.

803–4 The transition to Theseus, whom Chaucer must now bring on to the scene, is accomplished simply by halting in midstride and announcing the new subject. We have also to understand that there is a reason for his appearance at this point.

805 It is very significant indeed that Theseus's entry is preceded by an unambiguous narratorial comment on the irony of his narrative and on the importance of providence and destiny. His entry is specifically made an example of the general statement.

Cf. Boethius, *Consolation*, IV, prose 6: 'God disponith in his purveaunce singulerly and stablely the thinges that ben to doone; but he amynistreth in many maneris and in diverse tymes by destyne thilke same things that he hath disponyd.' See also Appendix 3, p. 223.

809 *by ye or nay*: definitely.

817 *grete hert*: a noble quarry and an aristocratic pursuit; but the standard pun on 'heart' is also present.

820 *hunte*: huntsman. A finely rhythmical alliterative line, suggesting the energy Theseus properly brings to all he does.

For in his huntyng hath he swich delit
That it is al his joye and appetit
To been hymself the grete hertes bane;
For after Mars he serveth now Diane.

   Cleer was the day, as I have told er this;   825
And Theseus, with alle joye and blis,
With his Ypolita, the faire quene,
And Emelye, clothed al in grene,
On huntyng been they riden roially.
And to the grove that stood ful faste by,   830
In which ther was an hert (as men hym tolde),
Duc Theseus the streighte wey hath holde;
And to the launde he rideth hym ful right,
For thider was the hert wont have his flight,
And over a brook and so forth on his weye.   835
This duc wol han a cours at hym or tweye
With houndes swiche as that hym list comaunde.

   And whan this duc was come unto the launde
Under the sonne he loketh, and anon
He was war of Arcite and Palamon   840
That foghten breme, as it were bo[r]es two.
The brighte swerdes wenten to and fro
So hidously, that with the leeste strook,
It semed as it wolde felle an ook.
But what they were nothyng he ne woot.   845

   This duc his courser with his spores smoot,
And at a stert he was bitwix hem two,
And pulled out a swerd, and cried,'Ho!
Na moore, up peyne of lesyng of youre heed!
By myghty Mars, he shal anon be deed   850
That smyteth any strook that I may seen!
But telleth me, what myster men ye been
That been so hardy for to fighten here
Withouten juge or oother officere,
As it were in a lystes roially.'   855

   This Palamon answerde hastily,
And seyde, 'Sire, what nedeth wordes mo?
We have the deeth disserved, bothe two.
Two woful wrecches been we, two caytyves,
That been encombred of oure owene lyves.   860

824 *Mars ... Diane*: Diana here is obviously the goddess of Hunting, Diana Venetrix, in which role she appears to Emelye in her temple below. But Diana is also the moon goddess, the symbol of fortune. A nice irony that the servant of Mars is now serving as the goddess whose moon represents fortune (cf. 805n.).

828 Emelye is wearing green because she is properly dressed for hunting, a highly formal and ceremonial pursuit.

831 *In which ther was an hert*: A 'harbourer' had the job of spying out where the animals habitually lay up, in order to direct the hunters to a likely spot. Theseus has been told that a hart can usually be found in this thicket. There is, again, the obvious pun on 'heart'.

833 *launde*: a glade or clearing in the wood.

839 *Under the sonne*: he is looking to the east and shading his eyes with his hand against the sun, which is still low.

840 In Boccaccio it is Emelye, not Theseus, who discovers the quarrelling knights. Chaucer speeds the action up considerably at this point.

841 The simile, which echoes those in lines 798ff., neatly links what is happening with what could be the proper quarry of the hunter.

846ff. cf. the intervention of Adrastus in the fight between Tydeus and Polyneices in Statius, *Thebaid*, I.438ff.

848ff. Note Theseus's quickness of response and decisiveness of action. What shocks him is that the combat *à l'outrance* is being fought without any of the proper legal forms being observed, and as ruler he is justly angry since such combat is a breach of the King's (or Duke's) Peace. Palamon (861) recognizes Theseus's right in this – an important touch.

852 *what myster men*: 'what kind of men'.

And as thow art a rightful lord and juge,
Ne yeve us neither mercy ne refuge.
But slee me first, for seinte charitee!
But slee my felawe eek as wel as me,
Or slee hym first; for thogh thow knowest it lite,   865
This is thy mortal foo, this is Arcite
That fro thy lond is banysshed on his heed,
For which he hath deserved to be deed;
For this is he that cam unto thy gate
And seyde that he highte Philostrate.   870
Thus hath he japed thee ful many a yeer,
And thow hast maked hym thy chief squyer,
And this is he that loveth Emelye.
For sith the day is come that I shal dye,
I make pleynly my confessioun,   875
That I am thilke woful Palamoun,
That hath thy prisoun broken wikkedly.
I am thy mortal foo, and it am I
That loveth so hoote Emelye the brighte
That I wol dye present, in hir sighte.   880
Wherfore I axe deeth and my juwise –
But slee my felawe in the same wise
For bothe have we deserved to be slayn.'

   This worthy duc answerde anoon agayn,
And seyde, 'This is a short conclusioun!   885
Youre owene mouth, by youre confessioun,
Hath dampned yow, and I wol it recorde;
It nedeth noght to pyne yow with the corde.
Ye shul be deed, by myghty Mars the rede!'
The queene anoon, for verray wommanhede,   890
Gan for to wepe, and so dide Emelye,
And alle the ladyes in the compaignye.

   Greet pitee was it, as it thoughte hem alle,
That evere swich a chaunce sholde falle,
For gentil men they were, of greet estaat,   895
And nothyng but for love was this debaat;
And sawe hir blody woundes, wide and soore,
And alle cryden, bothe lasse and moore,
'Have mercy, lord, upon us wommen alle!'
And on hir bare knees adoun they falle,   900

863–4 cf. 881–2. Palamon's jealousy, emphasized by the rhetorical pattern, is hardly attractive. This is one of the nastier aspects of affective love – cf. the narrator's apostrophe to 'Cupide, out of alle charitee' (765).

881 *juwise*: sentence.

884 Theseus's response is in accordance with his own laws, which Palamon accepts. It is entirely just in a legal sense.

888 *corde*: possibly a reference to the torture in which the victim's arms were tied behind his back in a full Nelson by a rope passing over a pulley, which was then jerked up and down.

889 Again Theseus swears by Mars.

890ff. This scene has no precedent in Boccaccio. It is an important and exact balance to the intercession of the ladies at the opening of the Tale, and is a powerful symbol. Through intercession, the just ruler may be persuaded to show mercy. Note especially line 903. Chaucer uses this line four times in his work, and it emphasizes again the key qualities of *gentillesse* (cf. Prologue to *The Legend of Good Woman*, F503; *The Canterbury Tales*, E1986 and F479, and cf. B660).

There seems to me to be a symbolic parallel between the justice of Theseus moderated by the intercession of the queen and her ladies and the justice of God moderated by the intercession of the Blessed Virgin and the saints. A man of Chaucer's day, when this intercession was a theological commonplace, can hardly have failed to notice the similarity. Such a symbol, of course, does relate to the central discussion of what the parameters of human life on earth really are.

895–6 *gentil . . . love: Gentillesse* is not only rank, but nobility of character; and love is, in romance, the cause most worth fighting for.

896ff. Note the summarizing *repetitio*. Lines 893–7 are virtually in reported speech.

900 A standard suppliant's gesture.

And wolde have kist his feet, theras he stood,
Til at the last aslaked was his mood,
For pitee renneth soone in gentil herte.
  And thogh he first for ire quook and sterte,
He hath considered shortly, in a clause,   905
The trespas of hem bothe, and eek the cause,
And althogh that his ire hir gilt accused,
Yet in his resoun he hem bothe excused,
As thus: he thoghte wel, that every man
Wol helpe hymself in love, if that he kan,   910
And eek delivere hymself out of prisoun.
And eek his herte had compassioun
Of wommen, for they wepten evere in oon;
And in his gentil herte he thoghte anoon,
And softe unto hymself he seyde, 'Fy   915
Upon a lord that wol have no mercy,
But be a leoun, bothe in word and dede,
To hem that been in repentaunce and drede
As wel as to a proud despitous man
That wol mayntene that he first bigan!   920
That lord hath litel of discrecioun
That in swich caas kan no divisioun,
But weyeth pryde and humblesse after oon.'
  And shortly, whan his ire is thus agoon,
He gan to loken up with eyen lighte,   925
And spak thise same wordes al on highte:
'The god of love, a, benedicitee!
How myghty and how greet a lord is he!
Agayns his myght ther gayneth none obstacles.
He may be cleped a god for his miracles;   930
For he kan maken, at his owene gyse,
Of everich herte as that hym list devyse.
  'Lo, here, this Arcite and this Palamoun,
That quitly weren out of my prisoun,
And myghte have lyved in Thebes roially,   935
And witen I am hir mortal enemy,
And that hir deeth lyth in my myght also;
And yet hath love, maugree hir eyen two,
Broght hem hyder bothe for to dye.
Now looketh, is nat that an heigh folye?   940

904ff. His just wrath (which punished Creon) is turned aside by the intercession, and by recognition of himself as being subject to the same passions as Arcite and Palamon.

911ff. The *repetitio* summarizing the reported processes of Theseus's mind climaxes in the direct speech (915ff.) that emphasizes the basic qualities of mercy and judgement in the good ruler – a speech that obviously reflects on himself. A very important passage, both in itself and in the way it provides a prelude for Theseus's long speech of judgement, in which he decisively intervenes in the quarrel and sets up a way of setting it (927–1011). See Introduction, p. 58.

927ff. The speech parallels Theseus's speech at the end of Book IV. Both are serious philosophical reflections on the situation as Theseus can understand it at that point. Here, love is seen as a lawless human affection, which all men in their own way are subject to; at the end of Book IV, love is seen as an ordered cosmic principle.

Seeing the comic side to the love felt by the type figures, Arcite and Palamon, does not mean that love is being sent up or satirized. Love is seen as potentially comic, at least for the observer, in such respected love-poems as the *Roman de la Rose* (cf. 4229ff. for parallels with this speech).

927 *benedicitee*: a common exclamation – 'Bless us!' or 'Ye Gods!'.

933 After the general statement, Theseus now uses Arcite and Palamon as specific examples of love's power.

935ff. The clauses pile up, *repetitio* and *compar* rushing to a climax on the idea of love bringing them to the point of death. The example shows the self-defeating folly that can attend love; Theseus carefully points the serious comedy of the situation.

Who may been a fool but if he love?
Bihoold, for goddes sake, that sit above,
Se how they blede! Be they noght wel arrayed?
Thus hath hir lord, the god of love, ypayed
Hir wages and hir fees for hir servyse   945
And yet they wenen for to be ful wyse
That serven love, for aught that may bifalle.
  'But this is yet the beste game of alle,
That she, for whom they have this jolitee,
Kan hem therfore as muche thank as me.   950
She woot namoore of al this hoote fare,
By god, than woot a cokkow o[r] an hare!
  'But al moot been assayed, hoot and coold;
A man moot been a fool, or yong or oold –
I woot it by myself ful yore agoon,   955
For in my tyme a servant was I oon.
And therfore, syn I knowe of loves peyne
And woot how sore it kan a man distreyne,
As he that hath been caught ofte in his laas,
I yow foryeve al hoolly this trespaas,   960
At requeste of the queene, that kneleth here,
And eek of Emelye, my suster dere.
And ye shal bothe anoon unto me swere
That nevere mo ye shal my contree dere,
Ne make werre upon me nyght nor day,   965
But been my freendes in al that ye may.
I yow foryeve this trespas everydel.'
  And they hym sworen his axyng faire and wel,
And hym of lordshipe and of mercy preyde,
And he hem graunteth grace, and thus he seyde: 970
'To speke of roial lynage and richesse,
Thogh that she were a queene or a princesse,
Ech of yow bothe is worthy, doutelees,
To wedden whan tyme is, but nathelees
I speke as for my suster Emelye,   975
For whom ye have this stryf and jalousye.
Ye woot yourself she may nat wedden two
Atones, thogh ye fighten everemo.
That oon of yow, al be hym looth or lief,
He moot go pipen in an yvy leef.   980

941 'Who can be a fool unless he is a lover?' (i.e. 'it takes love to make a real fool of you'. cf. the irony at line 943 – Be they noght wel arrayed? ('Don't they look marvellous?')

949 *jolitee*: a beautifully understated word – 'a bit of fun' (cf. *hoote fare*, line 951).

950 *kan ... thank*: 'owes them as much obligation as I do'.

952 A belittling simile; the cuckoo and the hare are traditionally stupid.

956 *servant*: lover, in the abjectly subordinate relationship to the beloved that we see in so many romances. A nice touch; Theseus is made to recognize his common ground with them, and now that he is wedded to Ypolita it alludes to the concord in marriage that follows the struggles of the lover.

960 *foryeve*: an important word; see also line 967. The forgiveness completely upstages Arcite and Palamon, who are now surrounded by irony.

964 *dere*: injure.

969 Probably they asked to be accepted as vassals, with the reciprocal obligations of dependence and protection that would imply. Hence mercy (970); for one is an escaped prisoner, and both are breakers of the Peace.

971ff. The next section of the speech underlines the fact that one of them must remain unsatisfied, and attempts to set up a fair way of deciding which it is to be. 'One of you, whether he likes it or not, may as well go and whistle with an ivy leaf' (980) – as one might with a blade of grass.

This is to seyn, she may nat now have bothe,
Al be ye nevere so jalous ne so wrothe,
And forthy I yow putte in this degree,
That ech of yow shal have his destynee
As hym is shape; and herkneth in what wyse.   985
Lo, here youre ende of that I shal devyse.
   'My wyl is this for plat conclusioun,
Withouten any replicacioun –
If that yow liketh, take it for the beste:
That everich of yow shal goon wher hym leste   990
Frely, withouten raunsoun or daunger,
And this day fifty wykes, fer ne ner,
Everich of yow shal brynge an hundred knyghtes,
Armed for listes up at alle rightes,
Al redy to darreyne hire by bataille.   995
   'And this bihote I yow withouten faille,
Upon my trouthe, and as I am a knyght,
That wheither of yow bothe that hath myght –
This is to seyn, that wheither he or thou
May with his hundred, as I spak of now,   1000
Sleen his contrarie or out of listes dryve,
Thanne shal I yeve Emelye to wyve
To whom that fortune yeveth so faire a grace.
The lystes shal I maken in this place,
And God so wisly on my soule rewe,   1005
As I shal evene juge been and trewe.
Ye shul noon oother ende with me maken
That oon of yow ne shal be deed or taken.
And if yow thynketh this is wel ysayd
Sey youre avys and holdeth yow apayd.   1010

983   *degree*: situation.

984   It is important that Theseus sees his solution as a way of discovering what is the destined end of each of them (cf. the reference to fortune at 1003, below).

986   'Hear the result of what I shall say.'

994ff.   Trial by battle was an accepted legal means of settling disputes where merit or truth was difficult to ascertain. It was of course limited to those of high enough rank to deserve such honourable treatment. The theory behind it was that God would intervene to ensure the triumph of the right and a just result. The battle, single combat or with supporters, might continue until the death, surrender or capture of one of the principals.

1002ff.   Emelye, of course, has no feelings that we need to take into consideration. The syntactical parallel in the two lines makes us see her as a gift of fortune, and Theseus as fortune's agent: Theseus gives Emelye *to wyve* (as a wife) as fortune gives *so faire a grace*.

1006   Another emphasis on Theseus's justice.

1007–8   'You shall make no agreement with me save that one of you must be killed or taken prisoner.'

1009   *yow thynketh*: it seems to you.

This is youre ende and youre conclusioun.'
   Who looketh lightly now but Palamoun?
Who spryngeth up for joye but Arcite?
Who koude telle, or who koude it endite,
The joye that is maked in the place   1015
Whan Theseus hath doon so fair a grace?
But doun on knees wente every maner wight
And thonken hym, with al hir herte and myght,
And namely the Thebans ofte sythe.
And thus with good hope and with herte blythe   1020
They take hir leve, and homward gonne they ryde
To Thebes, with olde walles wyde.

        Explicit secunda pars
        Sequitur pars tercia

1012ff.   A neatly patterned last paragraph closes Book II. The paradox
of the end of Book II has brought closer the possibility of a physical
resolution by a higher power. The rhetorical questions and the *occupatio*
are a clever way of making the audience do the work of visualization.

1016: 'When Theseus performed so noble and gracious an action.'

BOOK III

I trowe men wolde deme it necligence,
If I foryete to tellen the dispence
Of Theseus, that gooth so bisily   1025
To maken up the listes roially,
That swich a noble theatre as it was,
I dar wel seyn in this world ther nas.
The circuit a myle was aboute,
Walled of stoon and dyched al withoute.   1030
Round was the shap, in maner of compas,
Ful of degrees, the heighte of sixty paas,
That whan a man was set on o degree
He letted noght his felawe for to see.
Estward, ther stood a gate of marbul whit;   1035
Westward, right swich another in the oposit.
And shortly to concluden, swich a place
Was noon in erthe, as in so litel space.
For in the lond ther was no crafty man
That geometrie or ars metrik kan,   1040
Ne purtreyour, ne kerver of ymages,
That Theseus ne yaf mete and wages
The theatre for to maken and devyse.
And for to doon his ryte and sacrifise,
He estward hath upon the gate above,   1045
In worship of Venus goddesse of love,
Doon make an auter and an oratorie,
And on the westward, in memorie
Of Mars, he maked hath right swich another
That coste largely of gold a fother.   1050
And northward, in a touret on the wal,
Of alabastre whit and reed coral,
An oratorie, riche for to see,
In worship of Dyane of chastitee

1023ff. The narrator's intervention, in a sort of cancelled *occupatio*, once more emphasizes that this is a story whose manner of telling is interesting in itself. It also is a necessary build-up to the elaborate *descriptio* of the temples in the theatre. The description proceeds from the practicalities of the first paragraph, which link it firmly to fourteenth-century experience, to the general layout, and then to detailed descriptions of the temples. The theatre needs such a full treatment because its layout and buildings are important symbols of the world we inhabit. (See Introduction, p. 56.) Description of a work of art – or, as here, a temple – is itself a topos. All subsequent descriptions of temples and buildings owe something to Virgil's description of Juno's temple (*Aeneid*, I.446ff.). The three here have a close similarity in style, procedure and matter: a great deal of *repetitio* and *compar* in the lists of personifications, a list (medieval rhetoricians liked lists) of examples of the particular god's power (mainly malign reversals of fortune – cf. 67n.), and at the end a description of the god's statue. Each god's power is represented in lists of end-stopped lines, each one containing a single vivid vignette (for example, 1073ff., 1139ff., 1207ff.).

1027ff. Chaucer, when Clerk of the King's Works, had to have scaffolds constructed for two tournaments at Smithfield in 1390; he knew what was required. He adds a north gate, and the oratories, to the description of the theatre in Boccaccio. It is obviously a large building – a mile in circumference, and sixty yards high (1032).

1033–4 Here speaks a man with knowledge of the problems! *degree*: level or tier of seats.

1040–41 The elaborateness of some medieval sets for pageants and tournaments was extreme – and extremely expensive.

1048 The line is in some way corrupt. The reconstructed reading adopted by F. N. Robinson in his edition is better: 'And on the gate westward, in memorie'. The placing of the temples is important. Mars and Venus, in planetary and astrological terms the Lesser Infortune and the Lesser Fortune, are diametrically opposed, like the knights who serve them. To the north, equidistant between them, is the Temple of Diana, goddess of Maidens as well as of the Moon (Fortune), representing her servant Emelye.

Hath Theseus doon wroght in noble wyse.   1055
But yet hadde I forgeten to devyse
The noble kervyng and the purtreitures,
The shap, the contenance and the figures
That weren in thise oratories thre.

First, in the temple of Venus maystow se   1060
Wroght on the wal, ful pitous to biholde,
The broken slepes and the sykes colde,
The sacred teerys, and the waymentynge,
The firy strokes of the desirynge
That loves servantz in this lyf enduren;   1065
The othes that hir covenantz assuren;
Plesance and hope, desir, foolhardynesse,
Beautee and youthe, baudrye, richesse,
Charmes and force, lesynges, flaterye,
Despence, bisynesse, and jalousye,   1070
That wered of yelowe gooldes a gerland
And a cokkow sittyng on hir hand;
Festes, instrumentz, caroles, daunces,
Lust and array, and alle the circumstaunces
Of love, whiche that I rekned and rekne shal,   1075
By ordre weren peynted on the wal,
And mo than I kan make of mencioun.
For soothly, al the mount of Citheroun
Ther Venus hath hir principal dwellynge,
Was shewed on the wal in purtreyynge,   1080
With al the gardyn and the lustynesse.
Nat was foryeten the porter Ydelnesse,
Ne Narcisus the faire of yore agon,
Ne yet the folie of kyng Salomon,

1055 *doon wroght*: had had made.

1060 Note the exactly similar stylistic procedure and terms of these three *descriptiones*, and their very careful thematic and structural balance (see Introduction, p. 56). Each reflects back on the relevant devotee and his or her values.

1060 *Venus*: abbreviated from Boccaccio's account in the *Teseida*, which Chaucer uses in full (though with extremely important modifications of order) in *The Parliament of Fowls*, 183ff. (cf. also *The House of Fame*, 119–39). But Boccaccio in turn was drawing on a common iconographic tradition, which still had a long life ahead of it in the Renaissance.

Note that what is described is itself art – in all cases, it is what is painted on the walls. It thus represents how human beings have experienced and conceptualized that god's power, which may be only a relative truth.

1062ff. The externalization of mental states owes a lot to allegory (cf. the personifications of the *Roman de la Rose*). Here, as with Mars, the atmosphere is not pleasant. Cruelty is near the surface – the effects of Venus's influence include jealousy and unfaithfulness (1070), and the influence of Mars can lead to felony and murder (1137ff.). There is an obvious application here to the sufferings of Arcite and Palamon.

1066 'The oaths they swear to confirm their vows.'

1071 *gooldes*: marigolds. Colours were often symbolic – yellow for jealousy, green for inconstancy, blue for faithfulness, and so on.

1075 Probably 'which I'm giving an account of, and which I shall be telling you about'. Again there is corruption in the text, and no manuscript gives a completely satisfactory reading.

1078 *Citheroun*: Chaucer (he is not alone) confuses Mount Cithaeron, near Athens, with Venus's island of Cythera, whence she derives her name Cytherea.

1081 *gardyn*: the love garden, of course, and possibly a direct allusion to the garden in the *Roman de la Rose*, where the porter is also Ydelnesse (Chaucer's translation, 531ff.).

1082 *foryeten*: the word governs all the following *repetitiones*, each line of which exemplifies Venus's power and the danger associated with it.

1083 *Narcisus*: when Echo's unrequited love for him caused her death, Nemesis punished him by causing him to fall in love with his own reflection, and to pine away to death in his turn (Ovid, *Metamorphoses*, III.407ff.).

1084 *Salomon*: Solomon, King of Israel, was renowned for his wisdom; his *folie* was to give in to the blandishments of his foreign wives and to allow their gods to be worshipped in the Temple at Jerusalem (I Kings, XI).

Ne yet the grete strength of Ercules – 1085
Thenchauntementz of Medea and Circes –
Ne of Turnus with the hardy fiers corage,
The riche Cresus, caytif in servage.
Thus may ye seen that wisdom ne richesse,
Beautee ne sleighte, strengthe, hardynesse 1090
Ne may with Venus holde champartie;
For as hir lust the world than may she gye.
Lo, al thise folk so caught were in hir laas
Til they for wo ful ofte seyde, 'Allas!'
Suffiseth here ensamples oon or two 1095
And though I koude rekne a thousand mo.

The statue of Venus, glorious for to see,
Was naked, fletyng in the large see,
And fro the navele doun al covered was
With wawes grene, and brighte as any glas. 1100
A citole in hir right hand hadde she,
And on hir heed, ful semely for to se,
A rose gerland, fressh and wel smellynge;
Above hir heed hir dowves flikerynge.

1085 *Ercules*: Hercules' love for Iole made his wife Deianira jealous; thinking to win back his love, she sent him a shirt which was soaked in the blood of the centaur Nessus, who had told her that his blood was a love-charm. But he wanted revenge on Hercules, and it was in fact a deadly poison.

1086 *Medea*: Medea used her magic to help her love Jason win the Golden Fleece; later, when he rejected her, she used her enchantments to kill his new wife Creusa and her children. *Circes*: Circe, the enchantress of Aeaea, who turned men into animals (*Odyssey*, X) – a symbol of the way in which sexual love can turn a man into a beast, lacking discourse of reason.

1087 *Turnus*: Turnus, king of the Rutuli, fought Aeneas for Lavinia, to whom he was betrothed, and was killed (*Aeneid*, VIII and XII).

1088 *Cresus*: the proverbially rich King of Lydia, deposed and later killed by Cyrus. It is not clear why he should be in this list, except that the examples given match the abstract nouns in lines 1089–90. Croesus exemplifies the powerlessness of riches.

1091 *holde champartie*: share power with. The general conclusion summarizes the paragraph, leaving an impression of distinct danger; all the specific examples are tragic, the pleasant concepts are outweighed by the unpleasant, and one is left with a dominant impression of pain and cruelty.

1095–6 The descriptions of the Temples of Venus and Mars both begin with the same word and have closely parallel *occupationes* before the final icon of the deity. This stylistic pattern alerts us to the structural balance between the two, who are ultimately interdependent (see Introduction, p. 56).

1097 Chaucer is here drawing on a very standard picture going back to Classical times, which Botticelli, in 'The Birth of Venus', was to use later. The iconography of the gods was fairly fixed, and was of course symbolic of that god's nature and operation. (cf. the exactly similar picture of Venus in *The House of Fame*, 120ff.)

1098 Venus is in the sea because legend had it that she was born of the sea foam (Aphrodite: 'daughter of the foam'). The sea is also an image of her inconstancy.

1103 *rose gerland*: the flowers of love.

Biforn hire stood hir sone Cupido; 1105
Upon his shuldres wynges hadde he two.
And blynd he was, as it is ofte sene;
A bowe he bar, and arwes brighte and kene.

Why sholde I nat as wel eek telle yow al
The purtreyture that was upon the wal 1110
Withinne the temple of myghty Mars the rede?
Al peynted was the wal in lengthe and brede
Lyk to the estres of the grisly place
That highte the grete temple of Mars in Trace,
In thilke colde, frosty regioun 1115
Theras Mars hath his sovereyn mansioun.

First, on the wal was peynted a forest,
In which ther dwelleth neither man ne best,
With knotty, knarry, bareyne trees olde,
Of stubbes sharpe and hidouse to biholde, 1120
In which ther ran a rumbel in a swough,
As thogh a storm sholde bresten every bough.

And dounward from an hil, under a bente,
Ther stood the temple of Mars armypotente,
Wroght al of burned steel, of which the entree 1125
Was long and streyt, and gastly for to see.
And ther out cam a rage, and swich a veze,
That it made al the gate for to rese.
The northren light in at the dores shoon,
For wyndow on the wal ne was ther noon 1130
Thurgh which men myghten any light discerne.
The dore was al of athamant eterne,
Yclenched overthwart and endelong
With iren togh; and for to make it strong,
Every piler, the temple to sustene, 1135
Was tonne greet of iren, bright and shene.

Ther say I first the derke ymagynynge
Of felonye, and al the compassynge;
The cruel ire, reed as any gleede;
The pikepurs, and eek the pale drede; 1140
The smylere, with the knyf under the cloke;
The shepne brennyng with the blake smoke;
The tresoun of the mordryng in the bed;
The open werre with woundes al bibled;

1107   Cupid's blindness signifies the inexplicability of falling in love.

1109ff.   The narratorial intervention is necessary to signal a change of direction from one very complex long passage to another equally important one (cf. 1193ff.). Chaucer mainly follows Boccaccio in this description, though there are details that he seems to have added or to have borrowed from Statius (VII.34–73).

1113   *estres*: interior.

1114   *Trace*: Thrace, the cold north of Greece. Note the emphasis on coldness, barrenness, hideousness and violence in the description of Mars' temple.

1121–2   'Through which came a rushing, rumbling sound of wind, as if a storm was about to break every bough.'

1124   *armypotente*: powerful in battle. The central lines of the entire Tale fall in this block describing Mars, whose temple is described as being between those of Venus and Diana.

1127–8   'Out of it came such a fierce blast, such a rush of wind, that it made the whole gate shake.'

1129   *northren light*: possibly the cold daylight of the northern regions (like Thrace?), where the temple is supposed to be.

1132   *athamant*: a very hard substance (adamant), usually the diamond, but sometimes applied to the magnet or loadstone.

1134   Iron is Mars' metal, as copper is Venus's and silver Diana's.

1137   *say I*: this formula, which Chaucer uses elsewhere to structure a description (cf. *The House of Fame*, 150–255), occurs some seven times in the descriptions of the temples. It is obviously inappropriate; the narrator has never claimed to have time-travelled to ancient Athens.

1138ff.   Another summarizing list – personifications and symbols of Mars' cruel effects. As in Venus's case, the total impression is of pain, suffering and horror; the immediacy of some of the visual impressions is most telling, for example in lines 1141, 1150 and 1155. The passage focusses all the war and battle images of the poem.

1143   There may be a reminiscence here of the fifty daughters of Danaus, who all, except for Hypermnestra, agreed to his order to murder their new husbands in bed (cf. *The Legend of Good Women*, 2561ff.).

Contek, with blody knyf and sharp manace.   1145
Al ful of chirkyng was that sory place.
   The sleere of hymself yet saugh I ther;
His herte blood hath bathed al his heer;
The nayl ydryven in the shode anyght;
The colde deeth, with mouth gapyng upright.   1150
   Amyddes of the temple sat meschaunce,
With disconfort and sory contenaunce.
Yet saugh I woodnesse, laughyng in his rage,
Armed compleynt, outhees, and fiers outrage;
The caroyne in the bussh, with throte ycorve;   1155
A thousand slayn, and noght of qualm ystorve;
The tiraunt with the praye by force yraft;
The toun destroyed, ther was nothyng laft.
Yet saugh I brent the shippes hoppesteres;
The hunte, strangled with the wilde beres;   1160
The sowe freten the child, right in the cradel;
The cook yscalded, for al his longe ladel.
Naught was forgeten by the infortune of Marte;
The cartere overryden with his carte
Under the wheel ful lowe he lay adoun.   1165
Ther were also, of Martes devysioun,
The barbour and the bochier and the smyth,
That forgeth sharpe swerdes on his styth.
   And al above, depeynted in a tour,
Saugh I conquest, sittyng in greet honour,   1170
With the sharpe swerd over his heed
Hangynge by a subtil twynes threed.
Depeynted was the slaughtre of Julius,
Of grete Nero, and of Anthonius.
(Al be that thilke tyme they were unborn,   1175
Yet was hir deeth depeynted ther biforn,
By manasynge of Mars, right by figure.)
So was it shewed in that purtreyture
As is depeynted in the [sterres] above,
Who shal be slayn or ellis deed for love.   1180

1146   *chirkyng*: strident noise.

1149   A reference to the story of Jael, who killed Sisera by driving a tent-peg into his temple as he slept (Judges, IV.17).

1153   *rage*: passion (cf. Latin *rabies*, 'fury').

1156   *qualm*: pestilence.

1156   Possibly an echo of the destruction of Thebes.

1159   *shippes hoppesteres*: this is a real tangle. Statius (VII.57) has *bellatricesque carinae* ('warships'), and is followed correctly by Boccaccio, *navi bellatrici*. Chaucer either had a text which read 'ballatrices', or misunderstood and connected the word with *ballare*, 'to dance'. Hence *hoppesteres*, 'dancing'. Ships do, one supposes, dance on the water.

1160   *hunte*: hunter.

1163   *by the infortune of Marte*: 'that referred to (or was accounted for by) the ill-fortune Mars ruled'.

1164   'The charioteer run over by his own chariot.' The next line momentarily glances at the Wheel of Fortune. The Classical idea of the chariot seems not to have been distinguished from an ordinary cart in the Middle Ages.

1166   *of Martes devysioun*: subject to Mars' astrological influence.

1167   The barber was also, as his pole still reminds us, a bloodletter and surgeon, and thus under Mars.

1170ff.   The reference is to the sword of Damocles, suspended over the king's head by a single hair, and underlines the precariousness of rule and conquest.

1173   Julius Caesar was murdered when apparently in supreme control of Rome in 44 B.C.

1174   Nero stabbed himself in A.D. 68. Mark Antony, defeated by Octavian at Actium in 31 B.C., committed suicide in Alexandria.

1175   The neat reminder of the distant context of the Tale turns aside the charge of indecorous anachronism.

1177   *by figure*: probably a reference to the horoscope.

1179–80   See Appendix 2, p. 219.

Suffiseth oon ensample in stories olde,
I may nat rekne hem alle, thogh I wolde.
   The statue of Mars upon a carte stood,
Armed, and loked grym as he were wood.
And over his heed ther shynen two figures   1185
Of sterres, that been cleped in scriptures,
That oon Puella, that oother Rubeus.
This god of armes was arrayed thus.
A wolf ther stood bifore hym at his feet
With eyen reed, and of a man he eet.   1190
With subtil pencel was depeynted this storie
In redoutynge of Mars and of his glorie.
   Now to the temple of Diane the chaste,
As shortly as I kan, I wol me haste,
To telle yow al the descripcioun.   1195
Depeynted been the walles up and doun
Of huntyng and of shamfast chastitee.
   Ther saw I how woful Calistopee,
Whan that Diane agreved was with here,
Was turned from a womman til a bere   1200
And after was she maad the lodesterre.
Thus was it peynted; I kan seye yow no ferre.
Hir sone is eek a sterre as men may see.
   Ther saw I Dane yturned to a tree –
I mene nat the goddesse Diane,   1205
But Penneus doghter which that highte Dane.
   Ther saw I Attheon an hert ymaked,
For vengeaunce that he saw Diane al naked;
I saugh how that his houndes have hym caught
And freten hym, for that they knewe hym naught.   1210
   Yet peynted was a litel forther moor
How Atthalante hunted the wilde boor,
And Meleagree, and many another mo,
For which Diane wroghte hym care and wo.
Ther saugh I many another wonder storie   1215
The which me list nat drawen to memorie.

1183   Again Chaucer draws, like his predecessors, on an established
iconographic and mythological tradition. *carte*: chariot.

1185–7   In a form of divination, geomancy, four rows of stars were
randomly jotted down, each row having one or two dots. *Puella* and
Rubeus are two of the sixteen possible combinations that result, and
were usually assigned to Mars.

Puella	*Rubeus*
*	**
**	*
*	**
*	**

1189   Venus has at her feet the emblem of Cupid; Diana, the emblem of
a woman in childbirth; Mars, a red-eyed wolf eating a man, fit emblem
of his violence, and possibly connected with the supposed etymology
of Mavors, his old name, from *mares vorans*, 'devouring men'.

1193   There is no model in Boccaccio for the temple of the moon goddess,
Diana, patroness of chastity and hunting, and of childbirth.

1198   *Calistopee*: Diana's nymph Callisto was one of Jove's many loves.
Angered by her unchastity, Diana turned her into a bear, and later,
mistaking her for the real thing, shot her. Jove then made her into the
constellation Ursa Major, the Great Bear (Ovid, *Fasti*, II.153ff.). There
is some confusion, for the Pole Star (*lodesterre*, 1201) is in Ursa Minor,
and Callisto's son Arcas was turned into the constellation Bootes, not
a *sterre* (1203). But it is Diana's vengeance that is really the issue.

1204   *Dane*: Daphne, daughter of the river god Peneus, who, rejecting
Apollo's amorous pursuit, prayed successfully for help and was
promptly and disconcertingly turned into a laurel tree (Ovid, *Metamorphoses*, I.548ff.).

1207   *Attheon*: Actaeon, turned into a stag by Diana after he had seen
her bathing, was killed by his own hounds (Ovid, *Metamorphoses*,
III.138ff.).

1212–13   *Atthalante*: Atalanta was a virgin huntress, who, with Meleager
(*Meleagree*) and other heroes, killed a wild boar that Diana had sent
to ravage Calydon because sacrifices to her had been forgotten.
Meleager, jealous for his beloved Atalanta's honour in this quest, killed
his two uncles who wished to take the spoils from her; whereupon his
mother brought about his death by casting into the fire a log of wood
which, it had been prophesied, would last as long as Meleager's life. As
the wood burned, Meleager died in torment (cf. Ovid, *Metamorphoses*,
VIII.298ff.).

This goddesse on an hert ful hye seet,
With smale houndes al aboute hir feet.
And undernethe hir feet she hadde a moone –
Wexynge it was, and sholde wanye soone.   1220
In gaude grene hir statue clothed was,
With bowe in honde, and arwes in a cas.
Hir eyen caste she ful lowe adoun
Ther Pluto hath his derke regioun.
A womman travaillyng was hir biforn –   1225
But for hir child so longe was unborn,
Ful pitously Lucyna gan she calle,
And seyde, 'Help for thow mayst best of alle!'
Wel koude he peynte lyfly that it wroghte;
With many a floryn he the hewes boghte.   1230

Now been thise listes maad, and Theseus,
That at his grete cost arrayed thus
The temples and the theatre every del,
Whan it was doon, hym liked wonder wel.

But stynte I wol of Theseus a lite,   1235
And speke of Palamon and of Arcite.

The day approcheth of hir retournynge,
That everich sholde an hundred knyghtes brynge
The bataille to darreyne, as I yow tolde.
And til Atthenes hir covenant for to holde   1240
Hath everich of hem broght an hundred knyghtes,
Wel armed for the werre at alle rightes.

And sikerly ther trowed many a man
That nevere, sithen that the world bigan,
As for to speke of knyghthod of hir hond,   1245
As fer as god hath maked see and lond,
Nas of so fewe so noble a compaignye.
For every wight that loved chivalrye,
And wolde, his thankes, han a passant name,
Hath preyed that he myghte been of that game;   1250
And wel was hym that ther to chosen was.

For if ther fille tomorwe swich a cas,
Ye knowen wel that every lusty knyght
That loveth paramours and hath his myght,
Were it in Engelond or elles where,   1255
They wolde, hir thankes, wilnen to be there

1217 Diana's statue echoes her three forms (cf. 1455), of Luna (the moon, planet of fortune and change), Diana the chaste huntress on earth, and Hecate in the Underworld.

1219–20 The moon is a prime symbol of fortune and change; note that it is coming to its full, as the Tale is reaching its crisis.

1221 The huntress dressed in green has more than a hint of menace. Like Apollo's arrows, hers too caused disease and suffering on earth.

1227 *Lucyna*: Diana's aspect as helper of women in childbirth – those who bring children into the light of day (Latin, *lux, lucis*, 'light').

1230ff. The astonishing and daring bathos, after the most elaborate section of the Tale so far, jerks us right back to our practical world and reminds us that what we have heard described in the illusion of story was itself illusion, a summary of mortals' understanding and experience, not a final truth. Colours were, however, very expensive – particularly the blue, made of powdered lapis lazuli. The patron of the de Limbourg brothers, the Duc de Berri, in an inventory of his extreme wealth, mentioned as really valuable a stock of colours.

1231–69 Structurally this is a bridge passage, in a rapid, direct, and concise style, between the set-pieces of the temples and the kings. The entire Book VI of the *Teseida* consists of descriptions of the individual knights in the opposing companies; Chaucer has concentrated on the two symbolic figures of the kings, symmetrically disposed in passages of roughly equal length.

1242 *at alle rightes*: in every respect.

1245 *knyghthod of hir hond*: knightly prowess in practice.

1249 'And would willingly have a reputation above all others.' The attraction of such a gathering in Chaucer's own day was real enough, and of course in romances knights are constantly going off to prestigious away fixtures.

1255–6 The parenthesis links this imagined ancient world to the values of Chaucer's own day.

To fighten for a lady. Benedicitee,
It were a lusty sighte for to see!
   And right so ferden they with Palamon.
With hym ther wenten knyghtes many oon;   1260
Som wol ben armed in an haubergeoun,
And in a brestplate and in a light gypoun;
And som wol have a peire plates large;
And som wol have a Pruce sheeld, or a targe;
Som wol be armed on his legges weel,   1265
And have an ax, and som a mace of steel –
Ther nis no newe gyse that it nas old.
Armed were they, as I have yow told,
Everich after his opinyoun.
   Ther maystow seen, comynge with Palamoun,   1270
Lygurge hymself, the grete kyng of Trace.
Blak was his berd, and manly was his face;
The cercles of his eyen in his heed,
They gloweden bitwixen yelow and reed,
And lyk a griffoun loked he aboute,   1275
With kempe heres on his browes stoute;
His lymes grete, his brawnes harde and stronge,
His shuldres brode, his armes rounde and longe.
   And as the gyse was in his contree,
Ful hye upon a chaar of gold stood he,   1280
With foure white boles in the trays.
In stede of cotearmure, over his harnays,
With nayles yelwe, and brighte as any gold,
He hadde a beres skyn colblak, for old.

1261 *haubergeoun*: coat-of-mail.

1262 *gypoun*: surcoat.

1263 *peire plates large*: a leather jerkin with metal plates riveted to it, worn over the coat-of-mail; sometimes two large plates buckled together.

1264 *Pruce*: Prussia. *targe*: a small round shield.

1267 'There is no new fashion that hasn't been old before' – proverbial, but again it closes the distance between Athens and London.

1270ff. cf. Introduction, p. on 57, on the *descriptiones* of the two kings. Emetreus is Chaucer's invention; his inclusion once more stresses Chaucer's interest in this Tale in balancing more or less equal opposites. Note the similarity of rhetorical procedure in the two descriptions – the use of animal similes, the selection of similar details, the use of similar sentence structures (mainly statement in a list pattern), ending on the animals that accompanied them. It has been suggested, with plausibility but not absolute conclusiveness, that Lygurge and Emetreus represent respectively the Saturnine and the Martial man. Emetreus is certainly specifically compared with Mars (1301), and supports Arcite who soon will pray to Mars. But on the other hand, Lygurge comes from Mars' region, looks like that mythical northern beast the gryphon (1275), and has a metal crown, while Emetreus, from the warm east, has a leafy garland like the one gathered by Arcite. It seems more likely that these elaborate descriptions are meant to lift the level of this part of the Tale to something like the epic tone (cf. the description of the battle itself at 1741ff., and notes); it seems to suggest in its resourceful detail that the four corners of the earth are in arms as a result of the quarrel between Arcite and Palamon. The remarkable amount of physical detail helps the audience to form a very rich visual impression. Cecil B. De Mille would have had a field-day here.

1275 *griffoun*: this fabulous animal had the head and wings of an eagle and the body of a lion, and was reputed to live in the cold northern regions. It combines the qualities of two symbolically royal animals, and thus is an appropriate similitude for a king. Note also the other animal similes below.

1280 *chaar*: chariot.

1283 The ancient practice was to gild the claws and teeth of an animal skin when it was worn as a cloak.

1284 *for old*: very old. The prefix 'for' is usually intensive (cf. 1286).

His longe heer was kembed bihynde his bak.   1285
As any ravenes fethere it shoon for blak.
A wrethe of gold, arm greet, of huge wighte
Upon his heed, set ful of stones brighte,
Of fyne rubyes and of dyamauntz.
    Aboute his chaar ther wente white alauntz   1290
Twenty and mo, as grete as any steer,
To hunten at the leoun or the deer,
And folwed hym with mosel faste ybounde,
Colered of gold, and turrettes filed rounde.
    An hundred lordes hadde he in his route,   1295
Armed ful wel, with hertes sterne and stoute.
    With Arcita, in stories as men fynde,
The grete Emetrius, the kyng of Inde,
Upon a steede bay trapped in steel,
Covered in clooth of gold, dyapred weel,   1300
Cam ridynge, lyk the god of armes, Mars.
His cote armure was of clooth of Tars,
Couched with perles, white and rounde and grete;
His sadel was of brend gold newe ybete;
A mantelet upon his shulder hangynge,   1305
Bret ful of rubies rede as fyr sparklynge.
    His crispe heer lyk rynges was yronne,
And that was yelow, and glitred as the sonne.
His nose was heigh, his eyen bright citryn,
His lippes rounde; his colour was sangwyn.   1310
A fewe fraknes in his face yspreynd,
Bitwixen yelow and somdel blak ymeynd;
And as a leoun he his lookyng caste.
Of fyve and twenty yeer his age I caste.
His berd was wel bigonne for to sprynge;   1315
His voys was as a trompe thonderynge.
Upon his heed he wered, of laurer grene,
A gerland, fressh and lusty for to sene.
Upon his hand he bar, for his deduyt,
An egle tame, as any lilie whyt.   1320
    An hundred lordes hadde he with hym there,
Al armed, save hir heddes, in al hir gere,
Ful richely in alle manere thynges.
For trusteth wel that dukes, erles, kynges,

1287   *arm greet*: thick as his arm.

1290   *alauntz*: massively-built, tall hunting-dogs.

1294   *turrettes*: the rings on the dogs' collars.

1299ff.   Armour for horses in tournaments was not unknown, and all horses would wear richly decorated caparisons.

1300   *dyapred*: worked with small regular patterns.

1302   *clooth of Tars*: a silken cloth, also referred to in the contemporary *Sir Gawain and the Green Knight* (77). Though the word could derive from Tarsus, it is perhaps significant that at this time, when it is first recorded in English, appeared Mandeville's description of the lands of the Far East, including Tharsia (*Travels*, Ch. 26).

1303   *couched*: studded.

1304   *brend gold newe ybete*: refined gold newly stamped, i.e. the saddle was covered with gold leaf.

1306   The astonishing effect of this line is achieved by the use of four words which have in common an idea of redness and brightness.

1320   White eagles are unknown except in heraldry, and so a falcon may be meant. The word 'eagle' was used more loosely than it is now.

    The centre of Book III lies here, at the close of the descriptions of the two kings and of the preparations for the tournament.

1322   *save hir heddes*: until battle was joined, the knights would not have their helmets on.

Were gadred in this noble compaignye, 1325
For love and for encrees of chivalrye.
Aboute this kyng ther ran on every part
Ful many a tame leoun and leopart.
    And in this wise thise lordes, alle and some,
Been on the Sonday to the citee come 1330
Aboute pryme, and in the toun alight.
    This Theseus, this duc, this worthy knyght,
Whan he had broght hem into his citee,
And inned hem everich at his degree,
He festeth hem, and dooth so gret labour 1335
To esen hem, and doon hem al honour,
That yet men wenen that no mannes wit
Of noon estaat ne koude amenden it.
    The mynstralcye, the servyce at the feeste,
The grete yiftes to the meeste and leeste, 1340
The riche array of Theseus paleys,
Ne who sat first ne last upon the deys,
What ladyes fairest been or best daunsynge,
Or which of hem kan daunsen best and synge,
Ne who moost felyngly speketh of love, 1345
What haukes sitten on the perche above,
What houndes liggen on the floor adoun –
Of al this make I now no mencioun,
But al theffect, that thynketh me the beste.
Now comth the point; and herkneth if yow leste. 1350
    The Sonday nyght, er day bigan to sprynge,
Whan Palamon the larke herde synge,
(Althogh it nere nat day by houres two
Yet song the larks) and Palamon right tho
With holy herte, and with an heigh corage, 1355
He roos to wenden on his pilgrymage
Unto the blisful Citherea benygne –
I mene Venus, honurable and digne.
    And in hir hour he walketh forth a paas
Unto the lystes ther hir temple was, 1360

1328   There were a number of menageries in Europe at this time, in which exotic animals were kept. Mandeville mentions leopards being used for hunting in Cyprus (*Travels*, Ch. 5), though this needs taking with a pinch of the salt he says was produced there.

1331   *Aboute pryme*: about 9 a.m., or early morning.

1332   Note the repetition of the essential categories defining Theseus.

1334   'And gave them lodging according to their rank.'

1339ff.   A neat abbreviated sketch of the feast provides the bridge passage to the next important block, the prayers.

1342   Seating was strictly according to precedence, the most important folk of all being at the High Table (as in an Oxford or Cambridge college), and again set according to their rank.

1345   Talking of love seems to have been a favoured courtly diversion, especially in romances, when problems like that at the end of Book I of the Tale may have been set (cf. *Sir Gawain and the Green Knight*, 927, where a similar accomplishment is expected of the visitor to a Court).

1346   The hygienic risks of this practice were disregarded; the hawks, hooded, were an important symbol of status.

1348–50   The *occupatio* reminds us again of the shaping intelligence of the poet, and underlines the importance of *theffect*, which is what we are now going to be told about.

1351ff.   In his *Treatise on the Astrolabe* (II, para. 12), Chaucer explains the system whereby the planets govern certain hours of the day. Each day is divided into twelve hours from sunrise to sunset, and twelve from sunset to sunrise. The first hour from sunrise is ruled by the planet whose day it is, and the following hours, through the twenty-four, are assigned in the series Saturn, Jupiter, Mars, sun, Venus, Mercury, moon. On Sunday the hour after sunrise is the sun's, the second Venus's, and so on, repeating the series through the twenty-four hours. So on a Sunday, when Palamon got up two hours before the first hour of Monday, the hour is dedicated to Venus. The first hour of Monday is the moon's, when Emelye rose and prayed to Diana. Arcite, getting up at the *nexte houre of Mars folwynge this* (1509), made his sacrifice at the fourth hour after sunrise.

     Chaucer has not only altered Boccaccio's order of the prayers; he has given an entirely appropriate astrological time to them, and underlined the conscious following by Arcite, Palamon and Emelye of their appropriate planets.

1357   *blisful Citherea*: so he believes her to be, but in her temple we saw a different and much more dangerous Venus.

And doun he kneleth, and with humble cheere
And herte soor, he seyde, as ye shal heere:
'Faireste of faire, o lady myn, Venus,
Doghter to Jove, and spouse to Vulcanus,
Thow gladere of the mount of Citheron,   1365
For thilke love thow haddest to Adoon,
Have pitee of my bittre teeres smerte,
And taak myn humble prayere at thyn herte.
Allas, I ne have no langage to telle
Theffect ne the tormentz of myn helle;   1370
Myn herte may myne harmes nat biwreye;
I am so confus that I kan noght seye
But "Mercy, lady bright, that knowest wele
My thoght, and seest what harmes that I feele!"
Considre al this, and rewe upon my soore   1375
As wisly as I shal for everemoore,
Emforth my myght, thy trewe servaunt be,
And holden werre alwey with chastitee.
That make I myn avow, so ye me helpe!
   'I kepe noght of armes for to yelpe,   1380
Ne I ne axe noght tomorwe to have victorie
Ne renoun in this cas, ne veyne glorie
Of prys of armes blowen up and doun;
But I wolde have fully possessioun
Of Emelye, and dye in thy servyse.   1385
Fynd thow the maner how, and in what wyse;
I recche nat but it may bettre be
To have victorie of hem, or they of me,
So that I have my lady in myn armes.
For thogh so be that Mars is god of armes,   1390
Youre vertu is so greet in hevene above
That, if yow list, I shal wel have my love.
Thy temple wol I worshipe everemo,
And on thyn auter, wher I ryde or go,
I wol doon sacrifice, and fyres beete;   1395
And if ye wol noght so, my lady sweete,
Than praye I thee tomorwe with a spere
That Arcita me thurgh the herte bere.
Thanne rekke I noght, whan I have lost my lyf,
Thogh that Arcita wynne hire to his wyf.   1400

1363ff. The prayers are very similar in structure and in their high style. All begin with an *invocatio*, an apostrophizing of the god, supported by a relative clause outlining his or her nature, the sentence concluding with an imperative main clause: a formal structure like a Collect (see note to 57ff.). The middle of the prayer extends the ideas here, before the speech closes with a repetition of the key request. Palamon and Arcite both promise undying service in gratitude if they are helped. Then follows the moment of actual sacrifice and the response of the god, just as the prayers were preceded by an underlining of the correct time at which they were being made.

The three prayers are deliberately put into a significant order: Palamon – Venus, Lesser Fortune; Emelye – Diana, moon, Fortune; Arcite – Mars, Lesser Infortune. Each forms a discrete unit, like a panel in a triptych, where the full significance only emerges when they are seen in relation to each other.

1365 See note to 1078.

1366 *Adoon*: Adonis, beloved by Venus. When he died in a hunting accident, her grief persuaded Pluto and Proserpine to allow him to return to earth for six months of each year (cf. Ovid, *Metamorphoses*, X.519ff.).

1369 A neat use of the 'inexpressibility' topos! The repetition of the same idea in different guises is *expolitio* – a most useful amplificatory figure.

1380 'I'm not concerned with boasting about prowess in arms.'

1384–5 Notice the singlemindedness of Palamon, and his rejection, in the preceding lines, of what Arcite will equally singlemindedly pray for. There may be a pun on *dye* in 1385.

1390ff. We are reminded once more of the cosmic dimension of the struggle, and we are being prepared for the discussion among the gods at the end of Book III.

This is theffect and ende of my prayere:
Yif me my love, thow blisful lady deere.'
  Whan the orisoun was doon of Palamon,
His sacrifice he dide, and that anon,
Ful pitously, with alle circumstaunces,   1405
Al telle I nat as now his observaunces;
But at the laste, the statue of Venus shook,
And made a signe wherby that he took
That his prayere accepted was that day.
For thogh the signe shewed a delay,   1410
Yet wiste he wel that graunted was his boone,
And with glad herte he wente hym hoom ful soone.

  The thridde hour inequal that Palamon
Bigan to Venus temple for to gon
Up roos the sonne and up roos Emelye,   1415
And to the temple of Diane gan hye.
Hir maydens, that she thider with hire ladde,
Ful redily with hem the fyr they hadde,
Thencens, the clothes, and the remenant al
That to the sacrifice longen shal;   1420
The hornes ful of meeth, as was the gyse:
Ther lakked noght to doon her sacrifise.
Smokynge the temple, ful of clothes faire,
This Emelye, with herte debonaire
Hir body wessh with water of a welle   1425
But how she dide hir ryte I dar nat telle,
But it be anythyng in general;
And yet it were a game to heren al;
To hym that meneth wel it were no charge
But it is good a man be at his large.   1430
Hir brighte heer was kembed, untressed al;
A corone of a grene ook cerial
Upon hir heed was set ful fair and meete.

  Two fyres on the auter gan she beete,
And dide hir thynges, as men may biholde   1435
In Stace of Thebes, and thise bokes olde.
Whan kyndled was the fyr, with pitous cheere
Unto Diane she spak, as ye may heere:
'O chaste goddesse of the wodes grene,
To whom bothe hevene and erthe and see is sene,   1440

1402 The prayer closes with a very effective simple request.

1415 It is difficult, after *The Rape of the Lock*, not to feel comedy in this line, with its *compar* of such different elements suggesting equivalence. I am not sure we should, however.

1423 *Smokynge*: almost certainly, Chaucer had in mind the use of incense – or, at least, thought Boccaccio did. Boccaccio's text reads 'fu mondo il tempio' – 'the temple was clean'; Chaucer seems to have read 'fumando il tempio' – 'the temple smoking'.

1426ff. 'I dare not say exactly what she did, except in very general terms; yet it would be fun to have all the details. To a man of pure mind it would cause no offence; it is good for a man to have freedom (to imagine for himself).' The comic *occupatio*, with is suggestion of a coy prurience, prevents us from taking things too seriously. The narrator's intrusion, with its drop in tone (and taste!), again deliberately reminds us of his controlling presence, and draws attention to the way in which we are imperceptibly drawn into illusion and lose our objectivity (cf. the shock administered at 1230). What Chaucer actually omits from Boccaccio is in fact nothing to do with Emelye's ablutions; it is the detailed description of her rites after taking her bath.

1432 *ook cerial*: evergreen oak.

1435 *dide her thynges*: performed her rites – a standard sense.

1436 Although he is following Boccaccio, it does no harm to have a distancing reference to a book of ancient and grave authority.

1437 *pitous cheere*: downcast countenance.

Queene of the regne of Pluto, derk and lowe,
Goddesse of maydens, that myn herte hast knowe
Ful many a yeer, and woost what I desire,
As keep me fro thy vengeaunce and thyn ire,
That Attheon aboughte cruelly.   1445
Chaste goddesse, wel wostow that I
Desire to been a mayden al my lyf,
Ne nevere wol I be no love ne wyf.
I am, thow woost, yet of thy compaignye,
A mayde, and love huntyng and venerye,   1450
And for to walken in the wodes wilde
And noght to been a wyf, and be with childe,
Noght wol I knowe compaignye of man.
    'Now help me, lady, sith ye may and kan,
For tho thre formes that thow hast in thee.   1455
And Palamon that hath swich love to me,
And eek Arcite that loveth me so soore,
This grace I preye thee withoute moore,
As sende love and pees bitwix hem two;
And fro me turne awey hir hertes so   1460
That al hir hote love and hir desir,
And al hir bisy torment and hir fyr,
Be queynt, or turned in another place.
And if so be thow wolt noght do me grace,
Or if my destynee be shapen so   1465
That I shal nedes have oon of hem two,
As send me hym that moost desireth me.
Bihoold, goddesse of clene chastitee,
The bittre teeres that on my chekes falle.
Syn thow art mayde and kepere of us alle,   1470
My maydenhode thow kepe and wel conserve,
And whil I lyve a mayde, I wol thee serve.'
    The fyres brenne upon the auter clere
Whil Emelye was thus in hir prayere;
But sodeynly, she saugh a sighte queynte,   1475
For right anon oon of the fyres queynte,
And quyked agayn, and after that, anon,
That oother fyr was queynt, and al agon.
And as it queynte, it made a whistlynge
As doon thise wete brondes in hir brennynge,   1480

1441 This is Diana in her third aspect: Hecate (cf. 1455, and note to 1217, above).

1444 *As keep*: a standard form of the imperative or command – 'Keep me ...'

1445 *Attheon*: Actaeon. See note to 1207, above.

1446ff. The great irony – she desires neither knight.

1459 Note that she prays for reconciliation and harmony, and then, if that is impossible, the triumph of the highest love. She also accepts her destiny (1465, emphasized at 1505ff.).

1476ff. The *significacio* of the odd (*queynte*) happening is that one knight will be defeated but survive, and the other will be killed.

1479–80 A brilliant touch. The exact detail of a fire of wet wood hissing, and boiling sap bubbling out of the ends of the logs, is linked with the old concept of twigs that bleed human blood as a portent, as in the Polydorus episode in the *Aeneid* (III.19ff.).

And at the brondes ende, out ran anoon
As it were blody dropes many oon.
   For which so soore agast was Emelye
That she was wel neigh mad, and gan to crye,
For she ne wiste what it signyfied.   1485
But oonly for the fere thus hath she cried,
And weep, that it was pitee for to heere.
And therwithal Diane gan appeere,
With bowe in honde, right as an hunteresse,
And seyde, 'Doghter, stynt thyn hevynesse!   1490
Among the goddes hye it is affermed,
And by eterne word writen and confermed,
Thou shalt be wedded unto oon of tho
That han for thee so muche care and wo.
But unto which of hem, I may nat telle.   1495
Farewel! For I ne may no lenger dwelle.
The fires whiche that on myn auter brenne
Shul thee declaren er that thow go henne
Thyn aventure of love as in this cas.'
   And with that word, the arwes in the caas   1500
Of the goddesse clateren faste and rynge,
And forth she wente and made a vanysshynge.
   For which this Emelye astoned was,
And seyde, 'What amounteth this, allas!
I putte me in thy proteccioun,   1505
Diane, and in thy disposicioun.'
And hoom she gooth anoon, the nexte weye.
This is theffect, ther is namoore to seye.
   The nexte houre of Mars folwynge this,
Arcite unto the temple walked is   1510
Of fierse Mars, to doon his sacrifise,
With alle the rytes of his payen wise.
With pitous herte, and heigh devocioun,
Right thus to Mars he seyde his orisoun.
'O stronge god, that in the regnes colde   1515
Of Trace honoured art, and lord yholde,
And hast in every regne and every lond
Of armes al the brydel in thyn hond,
And hem fortunest as thee list devyse,
Accepte of me my pitous sacrifise.   1520

1488   Diana (Fortune) is the only immortal actually to have a theophany in this poem.

1492, 1499   Note the connection in her speech between destiny and what appears as fortune.

1515   Arcite's prayer is much less generous than Emelye's or Palamon's. Palamon concentrated on love, and any other consideration was completely irrelevant. Arcite wants victory, and victory only, thinking it will give him Emelye – even though it may mean the defeat and death of Palamon.

If so be that my youthe may deserve,
And that my myght be worthy for to serve
Thy godhede, that I may be oon of thyne,
Thanne praye I thee to rewe upon my pyne.
For thilke peyne, and thilke hote fyr,   1525
In which thow whilom brendest for desir
Whan that thow usedest the beautee
Of faire yonge fresshe Venus free,
And haddest hire in armes at thy wille –
Although thee ones on a tyme mysfille,   1530
Whan Vulcanus had caught thee in his laas
And foond thee lyggyng by his wyf, allas! –
For thilke sorwe that was in thyn herte,
Have routhe as wel upon my peynes smerte.
I am yong and unkonnyng, as thow woost,   1535
And, as I trowe, with love offended moost
That evere was any lyves creature;
For she, that dooth me al this wo endure
Ne reccheth nevere wher I synke or fleete
And wel I woot, er she me mercy heete,   1540
I moot with strengthe wynne hire in the place;
And wel I woot, withouten help or grace
Of thee, ne may my strengthe noght availle.
Thanne help me, lord, tomorwe in my bataille,
For thilke fyr that whilom brente thee,   1545
As wel as thilke fyr now brenneth me;
And do that I tomorwe have victorie.
Myn be the travaille, and thyn be the glorie!
Thy sovereyn temple wol I moost honouren
Of any place, and alwey moost labouren   1550
In thy plesaunce, and in thy craftes stronge,
And in thy temple I wol my baner honge
And alle the armes of my compaignye
And everemo, unto that day I dye,
Eterne fyr I wol bifore thee fynde.   1555
And eek, to this avow I wol me bynde:
My berd, myn heer that hangeth long adoun,
That nevere yet ne felte offensioun
Of rasour ne of shere, I wol thee yive,
And been thy trewe servaunt whil I lyve.   1560

1525ff. The old story of the adultery of Mars with Venus, whose husband, Vulcan, trapped them in a golden net.

1536–7 'I have been more injured by love, so I believe, than has any creature that ever lived.'

1541 *in the place*: in the lists.

1549 Like Palamon, Arcite promises undying devotion to the god.

Now, lord, have routhe upon my sorwes soore;
Yif me the victorie; I axe thee namoore.'
   The prayere stynt of Arcita the stronge.
The rynges on the temple dore that honge,
And eek the dores clatereden ful faste,   1565
Of which Arcita somwhat hym agaste.
The fires brenden upon the auter brighte
That it gan al the temple for to lighte;
A swete smel anoon the ground up yaf,
And Arcita anoon his hand up haf,   1570
And moore encens into the fyr he caste,
With othere rytes mo; and at the laste,
The statue of Mars bigan his hauberk rynge,
And, with that soun, he herde a murmurynge,
Ful lowe and dym, and seyde thus: 'Victorie!'   1575
For which he yaf to Mars honour and glorie
And thus with joye, and hope wel to fare,
Arcite anoon unto his in is fare,
As fayn as fowel is of the brighte sonne.
   And right anoon, swich stryf ther is bigonne   1580
For thilke grauntyng, in the hevene above
Bitwixe Venus, the goddesse of love,
And Mars, the sterne god armipotente,
That Juppiter was bisy it to stente;
Til that the pale Saturnus the colde,   1585
That knew so many of aventures olde,

1562   The irony is that he will be given no more than victory. Palamon and Arcite get exactly what they ask for (which is what they think they want), no more and no less. Sentimentalists need to remember this point. It is not just a question on a mortal level; the fabric of the universe is involved.

1578   *in*: 'lodging' – not necessarily an inn.

1580ff.   A sudden and unexpected shift of perspective. (On the gods, see Appendix 2, p. 219.) The gods' signals to the mortals had involved, of course, a mutual contradiction, it seemed, yet Diana's had clearly referred to an unchangeable destiny over which she – and therefore the other gods – had no control. So before Venus and Mars quarrel the issue is already settled, and Fortune knows about it.

The force the planet gods have in the poem is twofold. First, they provide a powerful and, in fourteenth-century terms, scientific mechanism of causality within a Christian conception of the universe. Though powerful, no one is all-powerful or all-knowing. (It is in just this way that Robert Henryson, who seems to some degree to be drawing on this passage, uses them in his *Testament of Cresseid* about a hundred years later.) Second, Chaucer is using a topos in Classical epic, imitated later, of debates among the gods about human fate – familiar, if from nowhere else, from Virgil's *Aeneid*. The widening of the vision reinforces the importance of the human struggle. Moreover, *The Knight's Tale* is set in a pagan world, long before the revelation of Christianity, where the Classical pattern is decorous. Without that revelation, only limited perceptions of truth, inferences from experience, are possible. One such perception is that of Egeus – all is change and decay; another is that of Theseus, who sees behind change and decay and the causality operated by the gods to the One who is all-knowing and all-powerful. (See Introduction, p. 59, and below, 2129ff.)

The introduction of the supernatural mechanism of causality and destiny, which is inscrutable but logical, at the end of this book again reminds us of the paradigmatic nature of the story: it signifies a great deal more than appears on the surface, and acts as a test-bed for some important philosophical ideas. Even the particular gods do not possess total knowledge; Jupiter tries to reconcile them, but only Time (Saturn) knows the outcome, and Time alters the rules of the game. At the end of the poem we see the force of the One that rules even the powerful Time.

Foond in his olde experience an art
That he ful soone hath plesed every part.
As sooth is seyd, elde hath greet avantage;
In elde is bothe wisdom and usage;   1590
Men may the olde atrenne, and nat atrede.
Saturne anoon, to stynten stryf and drede,
Al be it that it is agayn his kynde,
Of al this stryf he gan remedie fynde.
'My deere doghter Venus, 'quod Saturne,   1595
'My cours, that hath so wyde for to turne,
Hath moore power than woot any man.
Myn is the drenchyng in the see so wan;
Myn is the prisoun in the derke cote;
Myn is the stranglyng and hangyng by the throte,   1600
The murmur and the cherles rebellyng,
The groynyng, and the pryvee empoysonyng;
I do vengeance and pleyn correccioun,
Whil I dwelle in the signe of the leoun;
Myn is the ruyne of the hye halles,   1605
The fallyng of the toures and of the walles,
Upon the mynour or the carpenter.
I slow Sampson, shakyng the piler;
And myne be the maladies colde,
The derke tresons, and the castes olde;   1610
My lokyng is the fader of pestilence.
Now weep namoore; I shal doon diligence
That Palamon, that is thyn owene knyght,
Shal have his lady, as thow hast hym hight.
Thogh Mars shal helpe his knyght, yet, nathelees,   1615
Bitwixe yow ther moot be som tyme pees,
Al be ye noght of o complexioun,
That causeth al day swich divisioun.
I am thyn aiel, redy at thy wille.
Weep now namoore, I wol thy lust fulfille.'   1620
    Now wol I stynten of the goddes above,
Of Mars, and of Venus, goddesse of love,
And telle yow as pleynly as I kan
The grete effect, for which that I bigan.
                    Explicit tercia pars
                    Sequitur pars quarta

172

1587ff. Note the extreme insistence on words connected with age and time. This note is picked up at the end of Book IV by the aged Egeus. The preparation for Saturn's utterance pre-echoes Egeus's human understanding of vicissitude and age (1985ff.); yet, conversely, Theseus's deeper understanding that supersedes his father's also reflects back on Saturn. The answer to the puzzle of life is not just the Greater Infortune.

1591 'One can run faster than an old man, but you can't beat his advice.'

1595ff. Saturn describes himself in exactly the same conceptual and rhetorical terms as Mars, Venus and Diana were described in the pictures in the temples. (Boccaccio does not mention Saturn.) We have here a list of the attributes of the Greater Infortune. Venus was, strictly, his granddaughter.

1596 Saturn's was then thought to be the largest orbit, taking thirty years to complete.

1599 *derke cote*: madmen were confined in the dark – a possible explanation. But in line 230 Arcite recognized that his imprisonment was brought about by the power of Saturn.

1601 *cherles rebellyng*: possibly a reference to various disturbances like the Jacquerie or the Peasants' Revolt (1381).

1604 *the signe of the leoun*: the constellation Leo, where Saturn is at his most malignant.

1605 A reference to Thebes?

1608 *Sampson*: for the story of Samson, who was killed when he pulled down the pillars of the Temple of Dagon, causing the death of a number of Philistines at the same time, see Judges, XIII–XVII.

1617 *complexioun*: temperament. Complexion is the mixture of the four humours (cf. above 517n.).

1624 Again, the narratorial emphasis is on the outcome. Book III leaves us with a sudden widening of the issues. Causality and justice have become central considerations, and their working out occupies Book IV. Note the parallel between Books II and IV – similar mutual exclusions in both, the quarrel, and the imposition of order and control by an older and more authoritative figure.

BOOK IV

Greet was the feeste in Atthenes that day,   1625
And eek the lusty sesoun of that May
Made every wight to been in swich plesaunce
That al that Monday justen they and daunce,
And spenden it in Venus heigh servyse.
And by the cause that they sholde ryse   1630
Erly, for to seen the grete fight,
Unto hir reste went they at nyght.
  And on the morwe, whan the day gan sprynge,
Of hors and harneys noyse and claterynge
Ther was in hostelryes al aboute.   1635
And to the paleys rood ther many a route
Of lordes, upon steedes and palfreys.
Ther maistow seen devysynge of harneys
So unkouth and so riche, and wroght so weel
Of goldsmythrye, of browdyng, and of steel;   1640
The sheldes brighte, testeres, and trappures,
Gold hewen helmes, hauberkes, cote armures;
Lordes in parementz on hir coursers,
Knyghtes of retenue, and eek squyers
Naylynge the speres, and helmes bokelynge;   1645
Gyggynge of sheeldes, with layners lasynge.
Ther as nede is they were nothyng ydel.
The fomy steedes on the golden brydel
Gnawynge, and faste the armurers also
With fyle and hamer prykyng to and fro;   1650
Yemen on foote, and communes many oon
With shorte staves, thikke as they may goon;
Pipes, trompes, nakers, clariounes,
That in the bataille blowen blody sounes;
The paleys ful of peple up and doun,   1655
Heer thre, ther ten, holdynge hir questioun,
Dyvynynge of thise Thebane knyghtes two.
Somme seyden thus, somme seyde, 'It shal be so';
Somme helden with hym with the blake berd;
Somme with the balled, somme with the thikke herd;   1660

1626   All the crucial events of the Tale take place in May, the season of love – the first sight of Emelye, the first duel between Arcite and Palamon, and now the battle. Notice how the service of Venus is here linked with strife (1629–31, and cf. Introduction, p. 56).

   This passage, to line 1664, is a beautifully vivid evocation of the bustle before a tournament. Notice how it is executed. The list of sights and noises gradually becomes more specific and in sharper focus, and so much activity gives a sense of importance and tension. The *repetitiones*, often governed by present participles, sounds urgent; and through the clear visual impressions our focus gradually closes in to the point where we overhear the gossip of an excited crowd.

1633   *on the morwe*: i.e Tuesday, the day dedicated to Mars. His is the first hour, *whan the day gan sprynge*.

1637   a steed is a warhorse, a palfrey merely a riding-horse.

1638–9   'There could be seen such strange and such rich fashions of armour, made extremely well in goldsmith's work, in embroidery, in steel.'

1643   *parementz*: robes. *coursers*: horses used either in battle or, for their speed, in hunting.

1644   *Knyghtes of retenue*: knights in the service of greater lords.

1645–6   Spearheads were being fitted on to shafts, new straps and buckles on to helmets and shields, and lanyards were being laced into the right places.

1648   *fomy steedes*: hypallage; it was only the bits that were foamy so far. The horses are getting excited.

1652   *thikke as they may goon*: i.e. 'so crowded that they could hardly move'.

1654   *blody sounes*: sounds (that summon to) bloodshed.

1656   *holdynge hir questioun*: discussing or debating, and speculating about the two Theban knights. The sense of tension and excitement is increased by the jerky rhythm and double caesura of this line. The *repetitio* and *compar* of the next lines give us a very vivid impression of excited talk and argument.

1660   *thikke herd*: 'with a good head of hair'.

Somme seyde he looked grym, and he wolde fighte;
He hath a sparth of twenty pound of wighte.
Thus was the halle ful of devynynge,
Longe after that the sonne gan to sprynge.
   The grete Theseus, that of his sleep awaked   1665
With mynstralcye and noyse that was maked
Held yet the chambre of his paleys riche
Til that the Thebane knyghtes, bothe yliche
Honoured, weren into the paleys fet.
Duc Theseus is at a wyndow set,   1670
Arrayed right as he were a god in trone.
The peple preeseth thiderward ful soone
Hym for to seen, and doon heigh reverence,
And eek to herkne his heste and his sentence.
   An heraud on a scaffold made an 'Oo!'   1675
Til al the noyse of the peple was ydo;
And whan he say the peple of noyse al stille,
Thus shewed he the myghty dukes wille:
'The lord hath, of his heigh discrecioun,
Considered that it were destruccioun   1680
To gentil blood to fighten in the gyse
Of mortal bataille now in this emprise.
Wherfore, to shapen that they shal noght dye,
He wol his firste purpos modifye:
No man therfore, up peyne of los of lyf,   1685
No maner shot, ne polax, ne short knyf
Into the lystes sende, or thider brynge;
Ne short swerd for to stoke, with poynt bitynge,
No man ne drawe, ne bere it by his syde.
Ne no man shal unto his felawe ryde   1690
But o cours with a sharp ygrounde spere;
Foyne, if hym list, on foote, hymself to were.
And he that is at meschief shal be take,
And noght slayn, but be broght unto the stake
That shal been ordeyned on either syde.   1695
But thider he shal by force and ther abyde.
And if so falle the chiefteyn be take
On either syde, or ellis sleen his make,
No lenger shal the turneyinge laste.
God spede yow; go forth and ley on faste.   1700

1661   *he ... he*: like the Latin *is ... ille*, 'this one, that one' (cf. 1754ff.).

1663–4   The two summarizing lines mark off the end of this vivid picture, and push it into the background to make ready for Theseus's proclamation.

1665   In Boccaccio, Theseus makes the proclamation himself. Chaucer's use of the Herald increases our impression of Theseus's power and august dignity. (And note the important simile at 1671, which underlines the symbolic links he has with the gods.)

1675   *made an 'Oo!'*: The Herald said 'Oyez' – in Old French, 'Listen!'.

1679   The first point of the proclamation is that Theseus does not want life to be wasted – his mercy and good sense are again stressed.

1682   *mortal*: this will not be a fight *à l'outrance*, or to the death, hence the prohibition of really lethal weapons, though even the ones used could cause a lot of damage. These conditions are not in Boccaccio.

1690–91   'No man is to tilt at his opponent more than once with a sharpened spear.' (Blunt ones were sometimes used in tournaments.)

1693   *at meschief*: in trouble, distress.

1694   *unto the stake*: the defeated knights will be, by agreement, *hors de combat*, and will be conducted to a symbolic prison marked in some such way as by a small palisade of stakes.

With long swerd and with maces fighteth your fille.
Go now youre wey; this is the lordes wille.'
   The voys of peple touched the hevene,
So loude cride they with mury stevene,
'God save swich a lord, that is so good   1705
He wilneth no destrucioun of blood!'
   Up goon the trompes and the melodye,
And to the lystes rit the compaignye,
By ordinaunce, thurgh out the citee large,
Hanged with clooth of gold and noght with sarge.   1710
Ful lyk a lord this noble duc gan ryde,
Thise two Thebans upon either syde;
And after rood the queene, and Emelye,
And after that another compaignye
Of oon and oother after hir degree.   1715
And thus they passen thurgh out the citee,
And to the lystes come they bityme.
It nas nat of the day yet fully pryme
Whan set was Theseus ful riche and hye,
Ypolita the queene and Emelye,   1720
And othere ladyes in degrees aboute.
Unto the setes preeseth al the route.
   And westward, thurgh the gates under Marte,
Arcite and eek the hundred of his parte,
With baner reed is entred right anon;   1725
And in that selve moment Palamon
Is under Venus estward in the place,
With baner whit and hardy cheere and face.
In al the world, to seken up and doun,
So evene, with outen variacioun,   1730
Ther nere swiche compaignyes tweye.
For ther was noon so wys that koude seye
That any hadde of oother avauntage
Of worthynesse, ne of estaat, ne age,
So evene were they chosen, for to gesse.   1735
And in two renges faire they hem dresse.
Whan that hir names rad were everichon,
That in hir nombre gyle were ther noon,
Tho were the gates shet, and cried was loude,
'Do now your devoir, yonge knyghtes proude!'   1740

1701 *long swerd*: unsharpened at the end, this sword was used for the slashing stroke. The short, sharp, stabbing sword (1688) was more lethal at close quarters.

1705–6 The point is stressed that Theseus wishes to avoid any deaths. *destrucioun of blood* might well mean 'death of anyone of noble family'.

1709 *By ordinaunce*: in due order – i.e. the procession was organized with careful attention to rank and hierarchy. Chaucer adopts an appropriately high and serious tone to describe this ceremonial progress and the seating of the spectators.

1710 The city was hung with cloth of gold, not the cheaper serge cloth.

1715 *after hir degree*: according to their rank.

1717 *bityme*: early, betimes.

1721 *in degrees*: either 'according to their rank', or 'on the tiers'.

1723, 1727 The two knights enter under the temples of their gods, but Chaucer deliberately allows an ambiguity. The lines suggest the gods themselves are present – as, in a way, they are. The knights are very evenly matched (1729–31).

1737–8 There is a roll-call to make sure no one has cheated by having more than the agreed hundred combatants. (*gyle*: deception.)

    The heraudes lefte hir prikyng up and doun.
Now ryngen trompes loude, and clarioun.
Ther is namoore to seyn, but west and est,
In goon the speres ful sadly in tharest;
In gooth the sharpe spore into the syde;   1745
Ther seen men who kan juste and who kan ryde.
Ther shyveren shaftes upon sheeldes thikke;
He feeleth thurgh the herte spoon the prikke.
Up spryngen speres twenty foot on highte;
Out goon the swerdes, as the silver brighte.   1750
The helmes they to hewen and to shrede;
Out brest the blood with sterne stremes rede.
With myghty maces the bones they to breste.
He thurgh the thikkest of the throng gan throste.
Ther stomblen steedes stronge, and doun gooth al,   1755
He rolleth under foot as dooth a bal.
He foyneth on his feet with his tronchoun,
And he hym hurtleth with his hors adoun.
He thurgh the body is hurt, and sithen ytake,
Maugree his heed, and broght unto the stake,   1760
As forward was; right ther he moste abyde.
Another lad is on that oother syde.
And somtyme dooth hem Theseus to reste,
Hem to refresshe and drynken if hem leste.

1742ff. Here and in the description of the Battle of Actium (*The Legend of Good Women*, 635ff.) – the only two battle set-pieces in his work – Chaucer uses verse which is deliberately made to sound like the alliterative verse of his day.

Alliterative poetry, drawing on the resources of a highly developed poetic diction and a metrical tradition reaching a long way back into English history, seems to have been written mainly in the Western and Northern Midland varieties of English. That, of course, is no guarantee that it was unknown in the South, because a dialect, or a manuscript, are pretty portable pieces of baggage. Langland, who wrote his great spiritual poem in alliterative verse, was clearly writing against a London background for as wide an audience as possible. Alliterative verse had particularly good resources for the description of physical events or happenings, and is very effective indeed for descriptions of nature, or of battles. The nearest thing to an epic poem that has survived in English of the period, the Alliterative *Morte Arthure*, is a fine example. I would suggest that Chaucer deliberately adopted the mode at this point because he felt it to be the appropriate one for the graphic and physical handling of a serious battle; he is signalling that the battle was of great importance, and that it was on a large scale. (The poet of the nearly contemporary *Ywain and Gawain* seems to have thought in a similar way.) There is no suggestion of parody.

Chaucer does not, in fact, exactly imitate the metre, nor does he conform exactly to its rules of alliteration; nevertheless, the pastiche is a good one. Allowing for his usually decasyllabic line, Chaucer has managed to suggest the four heavy stresses on alliterating words, two on each side of the caesura. The lines are balanced against each other, as are the opposing sides in the battle. The headlong movement is sustained by the use of each line as a separate sense unit, and the use of *compar* and *repetitio*.

1744   *in tharest*: i.e. the lances were couched in the rests for the charge.

1748   *herte spoon*: hollow in the breast bone (cf. 1852).

1749   Probably 'bits of the broken lances sprang twenty feet into the air' – though lances were about that long.

1751   *to hewen and to shrede*: *to* is intensive, as in line 1753.

1754, 1756, etc. *he*: 'this man ... that man'.

1757   'On his feet, this (unhorsed) knight thrusts with the broken shaft of his lance.'

1762   *lad*: is led away captive.

   Ful ofte a day have thise Thebanes two 1765
Togydre ymet, and wroght his felawe wo;
Unhorsed hath ech oother of hem tweye,
Ther nas no tygre in the vale of Galgopheye,
Whan that hir whelp is stole, whan it is lite,
So cruel on the hunte as is Arcite 1770
For jalous herte upon this Palamoun:
Ne in Belmarye ther nis so fel leoun
That hunted is, or for his hunger wood,
Ne of his praye desireth so the blood,
As Palamon to sleen his foo Arcite. 1775
The jalous strokes on hir helmes byte;
Out renneth blood on bothe hir sydes rede.
Somtyme an ende ther is of every dede.
For, er the sonne unto the reste wente,
The stronge kyng Emetrius gan hente 1780
This Palamon as he faught with Arcite,
And made his swerd depe in his flessh to byte,
And by the force of twenty is he take
Unyolden, and ydrawen to the stake.
And in the rescus of this Palamoun 1785
The stronge kyng Lygurge is born adoun;
And kyng Emetrius, for al his strengthe,
Is born out of his sadel a swerdes lengthe,
So hitte hym Palamon er he were take.
But al for noght; he was broght to the stake. 1790
His hardy herte myghte hym helpe naught;
He moste abyde, whan that he was caught,
By force, and eek by composicioun.
Who sorweth now but woful Palamoun
That moot namoore goon agayn to fighte? 1795
   And whan that Theseus had seen this sighte,
Unto the folk that foghten thus echon
He cryde, 'Hoo! namoore, for it is doon!
I wol be trewe juge, and nat partie.
Arcite of Thebes shal have Emelye, 1800
That by his fortune hath hir faire ywonne.'
   Anon ther is a noyse of peple bigonne
For joye of this, so loude and heigh withalle,
It semed that the lystes sholde falle.

1765   The general mêlée established, Chaucer now focusses on the two principal combatants – again, evenly matched.

1768–75   The first of the two epic comparisons (animals again!) is from Boccaccio; the other Chaucer adds. The tone (and bloodiness) echoes the first fight at the end of Book II. They balance exactly, four lines against four. The structures are nearly identical: animal + region – hunting, cause of ferocity – Arcite against Palamon/Palamon against Arcite.

1768   *Galgopheye*: probably Gargaphia in Boeotia, where Actaeon was turned into a stag.

1770   *hunte*: hunter.

1772   *Belmarye*: Benmarin, in Morocco. North Africa was noted for its lions.

1783–4   The enjambement carries the full weight of line 1783 over to the emphatic *unyolden* ('not admitting defeat'), further emphasized by the following caesura.

1793   He was overpowered by force, and also had to keep by the agreement (*composicioun*).

1799   Theseus again stresses his impartiality as a judge in awarding Emelye to Arcite. His judgement on the human level is parallelled by that of Saturn on the part of the gods; Saturn speaks in a style as firm and impartial as Theseus (1810–12).

1794–1801, 1805–12   These two passages, of equal length, are deliberately balanced on each side of the reaction of the crowd. Both start with the same sort of subject – impotent sorrow – in the same sort of rhetorical structure. One deals with human judgement, the other with divine, and both give us a longer perspective on the immediate action.

What kan now faire Venus doon above? 1805
What seith she now? What dooth this queene of love,
But wepeth so, for wantyng of hir wille,
Til that hir teeres in the lystes fille.
She seyde, 'I am ashamed, doutelees.'
   Saturnus seyde, 'Doghter, hoold thy pees. 1810
Mars hath his wille; his knyght hath al his boone;
And, by myn heed, thow shalt been esed soone.'
   The trompours, with the loude mynstralcye,
The heraudes, that ful loude yelle and crye,
Been in hir wele for joye of daun Arcite. 1815
But herkneth me, and stynteth noyse a lite,
Which a myracle ther bifel anon.
This fierse Arcite hath of his helm ydon,
And on a courser, for to shewe his face,
He priketh endelong the large place, 1820
Lokyng upward upon this Emelye;
And she agayn hym caste a freendlich eye
(For wommen, as to speken in comune,
They folwen al the favour of fortune)
And [she] was al his cheere, as in his herte. 1825
   Out of the ground a furye infernal sterte,
From Pluto sent at requeste of Saturne,
For which his hors for feere gan to turne,
And leep asyde, and foundred as he leep;
And, er that Arcite may taken keep, 1830
He pighte hym on the pomel of his heed,
That in the place he lay as he were deed,
His brest to brosten with his sadel bowe.
As blak he lay as any cole or crowe,
So was the blood yronnen in his face. 1835
   Anon he was yborn out of the place,
With herte soor, to Theseus paleys.
Tho was he corven out of his harneys,

1805 A significant alteration from the source, where Venus knows what the outcome will be and has already arranged for the appearance of a fury. Chaucer's change underlines the incompleteness of Venus's knowledge and therefore power; the triple *repetitio* of questions powerfully draws attention to it. Chaucer may be remembering Venus's appeal to Jupiter in *Aeneid*, I.223ff.

1809 *ashamed*: humiliated.

1811 Saturn states the exact truth; Mars promised no more and no less than victory.

1817 *Which a*: what a.

1820 *endelong*: down the length of.

1823–4 These lines are not in the important Ellesmere, Hengwrt or Cambridge Gg.4.27 manuscripts, though it seems certain they are Chaucer's. He may have cancelled them, of course. But if we allow them to stand, there need be no problem; Emelye is the gift of a momentarily favourable fortune, she is smiling at him, and women are frequently linked with the moon and fortune. The remark would emphasize the penetration of fortune into all reaches of human experience. Further, if Chaucer's mind was running on the *Aeneid*, as I suggest above (1805ff.), he might well have remembered Virgil's remark, *varium et mutabile semper femina* ('woman is a changeable thing, always different') (*Aeneid*, IV.569).

1825 Probably 'she was all his heart's delight'.

1826–8 cf. 1805n.; Chaucer makes Saturn arrange this. In Boccaccio, much more is made of the fury – Chaucer is interested purely in what it caused to happen.

1833 cf. 1895.

1838 *corven out*: i.e. the laces and thongs holding the armour together were cut for easier removal.

And in a bed ybroght ful faire and blyve,
For he was yet in memorie and alyve, 1840
And alwey cryinge after Emelye.
   Duc Theseus, with al his compaignye
Is comen hoom to Atthenes his citee,
With alle blisse and greet solempnytee,
Al be it that this aventure was falle. 1845
He nolde noght disconforten hem alle.
Men seyde eek that Arcite shal nat dye,
He shal been heled of his maladye.
And of another thyng they were as fayn:
That of hem alle was ther noon yslayn, 1850
Al were they sore yhurt, and namely oon
That with a spere was thirled his brest boon.
To oothere woundes, and to broken armes,
Somme hadden salves, and somme hadden charmes,
Fermacies of herbes, and eek save 1855
They dronken, for they wolde hir lymes have.
   For which this noble duc, as he wel kan,
Conforteth and honoureth every man,
And made revel al the longe nyght
Unto the straunge lordes, as was right. 1860
   Ne ther was holden no disconfitynge,
But as a justes or a tourneyinge;
For soothly ther was no disconfiture,
For fallyng nis nat but an aventure;
Ne to be lad by force unto the stake 1865
Unyolden, and with twenty knyghtes take,
O persone allone, with outen mo,
And haryed forth by arm, foot, and too,
And eek his steede dryven forth with staves,
With footmen, bothe yemen and eek knaves – 1870
It nas arretted hym no vileynye;
Ther may no man clepe it cowardye.
   For which anoon duc Theseus leet crye
To stynten alle rancour and envye,
The gree as wel of oo syde as of oother, 1875
And either syde ylyk, as otheres brother.

1840 *in memorie*: conscious.

1842–84 This deliberately amplified digression of over forty lines is inserted here to increase the tension of the narrative. We are at this point far less interested in what happened to the other combatants than in what Arcite is suffering; but the widening of vision, as in lines 1794–1801 and 1805–12, reminds us of a perspective and a context in which we are to see it.

1843 *comen hoom*: as he did after a previous battle, at the beginning of the poem – a suggestive parallel.

1845 *aventure*: cf. line 1864 – the word is stressed.

1852 *was thirled his brest boon*: 'whose breastbone was pierced'. This is obviously the casualty of line 1748 – a good example of Chaucer's attention to detail. No one is actually killed; Boccaccio despatches several.

1854 *charmes*: incantations were used by physicians in conjunction with herbal remedies.

1855 *save*: sage was highly regarded as a medicinal plant, but here surely a draught (called 'save') made from many different herbs is meant. Recipes have survived.

1856 *lymes*: limbs – but this word could apply to any part of the body.

1861ff. The heat of the tournament could lead to real quarrelling, and grudges taken home afterwards could spawn feuds. So Theseus, supporting public opinion, declares that everyone has done equally well and that it was a good clean fight.

1873 *leet crye*: 'had it proclaimed'.

1876 *brother*: an interesting echo, after the battle, of the brotherhood that once linked Arcite and Palamon. The summary *repetitio* in these lines gets rid of the visitors very quickly.

And yaf hem yiftes, after hir degree,
And fully heeld a feeste dayes three;
And conveyed the kynges worthily
Out of his toun a journee largely.   1880
And hoom wente every man the righte way.
Ther was namoore but 'Farewel, have good day!'
Of this bataille I wol namoore endite,
But speke of Palamon and of Arcite.
   Swelleth the brest of Arcite, and the soore   1885
Encreeseth at his herte moore and moore.
The clothered blood, for any lechecraft,
Corrupteth, and is in his bouk ylaft,
That neither veyne blood, ne ventusynge,
Ne drynke of herbes, may been his helpynge.   1890
The vertu expulsif or animal,
Fro thilke vertu cleped natural,
Ne may the venym voyden ne expelle;
The pipes of his longes gan to swelle,
And every lacerte in his brest adoun   1895
Is shent with venym and corrupcioun.
Hym gayneth neither, for to gete his lyf,
Vomyt upward ne dounward laxatyf.
Al is to brosten, thilke regioun;
Nature hath no dominacioun,   1900
And certeinly ther nature wol nat werche,
Farewel, phisik! go ber the man to cherche!
   This al and som, that Arcita moot dye;
For which, he sendeth after Emelye,
And Palamon, that was his cosyn deere;   1905
Thanne seyde he thus, as ye shal after heere.
   'Nat may the woful spirit in myn herte
Declare o point of alle my sorwes smerte
To yow, my lady, that I love moost.
But I byquethe the servyce of my goost   1910
To yow aboven every creature,
Syn that my lyf may no lenger dure,
Allas, the wo! Allas, the peynes stronge
That I for yow have suffred, and so longe!

1883–4 The narrator's rounding-off the block is a clever way of drawing attention to its rambling digressions, thus highlighting the importance of what we must wait for him to give us.

1885ff. Chaucer adds most of these details; this suggests he had some fairly detailed knowledge of medical treatises.

1887 *for any lechecraft*: despite any medical skill.

1889 *veyne blood ... ventusynge*: bloodletting by opening a vein, and cupping (applying a vacuum to the skin, thus blistering it).

1891 The old physiology recognized three 'virtues' or 'spirits': the natural, seated in the liver; the vital, in the heart; and the animal (Latin, *anima*, 'soul'), in the brain. The last controlled the muscles, and is thus the *expulsif*. Arcite's could not expel the poison from his natural virtue. (cf. 511n.)

1894 *pipes*: possibly 'veins'.

1898 *Vomyt*: emetic. Purging in either direction was a major resource of the physician. It is remarkable how many people survived.

1901–2 *Nature* probably means the 'natural spirit', essential to life. But it almost certainly implies a distinction between natural healing and physic.

1902 The proverb's summarizing and dismissive tone signals the closing of the block, whose function has been to prepare for Arcite's great set-piece deathbed speech. Comparison of Chaucer's composition with Dryden's fine re-handling of it reveals a lot about the essential qualities of both poets.

1907ff. The elaborately patterned first paragraph of the speech consists mainly of a series of *exclamationes*, arranged cumulatively in *repetitio*.

1908 *o point*: a single jot.

Allas, the deeth! Allas, myn Emelye!   1915
Allas, departyng of oure compaignye!
Allas, myn hertes queene! Allas, my wyf!
Myn hertes lady, endere of my lyf!
What is this world? What axeth men to have?
Now with his love, now in his colde grave,   1920
Allone, withouten any compaignye.
Farewel, my swete foo, myn Emelye!
And softe take me in your armes tweye,
For love of God, and herkneth what I seye.
    'I have heer with my cosyn Palamon   1925
Had strif and rancour, many a day agon,
For love of yow, and for my jalousye;
And Juppiter so wys my soule gye,
To speken of a servaunt proprely,
With circumstaunces alle trewely –   1930
That is to seyn, trouthe, honour, knyghthede,
Wisdom, humblesse, estaat, and heigh kynrede,
Fredom, and al that longeth to that art –
So Juppiter have of my soule part,
As in this world right now ne knowe I non   1935
So worthy to ben loved as Palamon,
That serveth yow, and wol doon al his lyf.
And if that evere ye shal been a wyf,
Foryet nat Palamon, the gentil man.'
    And with that word, his speche faille gan,   1940
For from his feet up to his brest was come
The coold of deeth, that hadde hym overcome.
And yet mooreover, for in his armes two
The vital strengthe is lost, and al ago.
Oonly the intellect, withoute moore,   1945
That dwelled in his herte syk and soore,
Gan faillen, whan the herte felte deeth;
Dusked his eyen two, and failled breeth,
But on his lady yet caste he his eye;
His laste word was, 'Mercy, Emelye!'   1950

1917   *wyf*: though in Boccaccio a marriage has taken place, none has in Chaucer. *Wyf* is probably no more than a term of devotion.

1918   *endere of my lyf*; 1922: *swete foo*. A moving recurrence of the paradoxes and oxymora of love poetry, here in a real sense true. Also, perhaps, an ironic echo of 710.

1919–22   The generalization widens the perspective, emphasizes again that *allone*-ness in Arcite already noted, and throws much weight on line 1920, whose balanced *contentio* and *compar* highlight the speed and unpredictability of change in human life – a major issue, first raised by the ladies in Book I.

1925ff.   Arcite is here making a sort of verbal will. In it he recovers the old generosity that sworn brotherhood would imply; and – delicate irony! – he pleads his rival's cause as a friend in romances might be expected to.

1926–7   *strif ... rancour ... love ... jalousye*: the combination demonstrated in the temples.

1928ff.   The disordered syntax, the repeated wish that Jupiter should look after his soul and that Emelye 'Foryet nat Palamon', cleverly convey Arcite's failing powers.

1929   *servaunt*: lover.

1930–33   The list of qualities of the noble lover is very similar to the qualities attributed to Troilus. Several are applied to the Knight of the *General Prologue*, who figures, of course, an accepted norm of true knighthood.

1936ff.   The central lines of this book lie here, where Arcite recommends Palamon to Emelye. The central lines of Book I fall on Palamon's prayer for mercy to the Venus he sees through Emelye (246ff.).

1939   *gentil*: a very strong term of recommendation. See Introduction, pp. 28, 71, and the ballade *Gentilesse*.

1943   *yet mooreover*: still further.

1945   *intellect*: the seat of the intellect was held to be the heart. Translate as: 'Nothing was left but the intellect ...; it failed when ...'

His spirit chaunged hous, and wente ther
As I cam nevere, I kan nat tellen wher.
Therfore I stynte; I nam no dyvynystre.
Of soules fynde I nat in this registre,
Ne me ne lyst thilke opynyons to telle   1955
Of hem, thogh that they writen wher they dwelle.
Arcite is coold, ther Mars his soule gye.
  Now wol I speken forth of Emelye.
Shrighte Emelye, and howleth Palamon,
And Theseus his suster took anon   1960
Swownynge, and baar hire fro the corps away.
What helpeth it to tarien forth the day,
To tellen how she weep, bothe eve and morwe?
For in swich caas wommen have swich sorwe,
Whan that hir housbondes been from hem ago,   1965
That for the moore part they sorwen so,
Or ellis fallen in swich a maladye,
That at the laste certeinly they dye.
  Infinite been the sorwes and the teeres
Of olde folk, and folk of tendre yeeres,   1970
In al the toun for deeth of this Theban.
For hym ther wepeth bothe child and man.
So greet wepyng was ther noon, certayn,
Whan Ector was ybroght, al fressh yslayn,
To Troye. Allas, the pitee that was ther,   1975
Cracchynge of chekes, rentyng eek of heer.

1951ff. *chaunged hous*: changed its dwelling-place. The next few lines have no counterpart in Boccaccio. With this deliberately tedious passage Chaucer punctures the sublimity by an intrusion of narratorial clumsiness; this both heightens the sublimity and distances it. The passage emphasizes human ignorance and the provisional nature of what knowledge we have.

He glances at the discussions of the philosophers and theologians about the soul's place after death, and about what happened to virtuous pagans (cf. the ironic handling of Dante's *Divina Commedia* in *The House of Fame*, and here, perhaps, in line 1956). Boccaccio (*Teseida*, XI.1ff.) has Arcite's soul ascending to the eighth heaven (see Appendix 2, p. 219) and looking down on the little earth. (He draws on a long tradition of heavenly ascents going back to Cicero's *Somnium Scipionis*.) Chaucer uses this important passage in *Troilus and Criseyde* (V.1827ff.). Here it is excluded because one of the interests of the Tale is in how mortals still on earth can understand the heavens; drawing away the veils by imposing a celestial overview would ruin this purpose.

1954 *in this registre*: in my table of contents, i.e. what I set out to speak about.

1957 *ther Mars his soule gye*: 'May Mars look after his soul.'

1959–61 We might find the verbs undignified. Medieval men would have expected such an extreme display of grief. The enjambement of lines 1960–61 stresses *Swownynge*. The pattern of the lines throws our attention on to Emelye's reaction and Theseus's intervention.

1962–3 Another crashing narratorial remark: *tarien forth the day* ('waste time') is hardly the appropriate register for high grief. The narrator goes on to generalize on women's readiness to be sorrowful. There is irony, of course, in that Emelye doesn't die of sorrow, but lives to marry Palamon (1968); but the generalization about women's grief at bereavement is a common one, whose ultimate source is St Augustine's sensitive commentary on *Genesis*.

1969ff. The generalizing 'long-focus' continues. The events have to be not merely experienced but understood – this is why Chaucer is deliberately preventing us from becoming too involved emotionally.

1974 *Ector*: the comparison with Hector suggests the scale of the grief. Possibly the mention of Troy, symbol of earthly cities that must fall, is a reminder of the precariousness of human life, and thus prepares for Egeus's speech.

   'Why woldestow be deed?' thise wommen crye,
'And haddest gold ynow, and Emelye?'
   No man myghte gladen Theseus
Savyng his olde fader Egeus,   1980
That knew this worldes transmutacioun,
As he hadde seyn it up and doun –
Joye after wo, and wo after gladnesse;
And shewed hem ensample and lyknesse.
   'Right as ther deyed nevere man,' quod he,   1985
'That he ne lyved in erthe in som degree,
Right so ther lyved nevere man,' he seyde,
'In al this world that somtyme he ne deyde.
This world nis but a thurghfare ful of wo,
And we been pilgrymes passynge to and fro.   1990
Deeth is an ende of every worldly soore.'
And over al this yet seyde he muchel moore
To this effect, ful wysly to enhorte
The peple, that they sholde hem reconforte.
   Duc Theseus, with al his bisy cure,   1995
Caste now wher that the sepulture

1977   *Why woldestow be deed?*: 'Why did you have to die?' – an entirely
normal – even unavoidable – human reaction; yet the poem goes on to
suggest that it is not the logical one.

1978   The women's laments close on the emphasis that Arcite died when
he was at the top of Fortune's wheel, having got all he wanted. They
feel this to be terrible; but see lines 2200ff.

1979ff.   Theseus, deeply affected (for it is part of his nobility that *pitee
renneth soone in gentil herte* – 903), turns for immediate consolation to
Egeus, his aged father. The similarity between this and Venus's turning
for consolation to her aged father is obvious. Egeus, like Saturn (cf.
1591n.), offers the wisdom of age, which mainly consists in seeing
nothing as stable. Egeus's view is generalization from observation of
human life; Saturn is merely a god/planet among gods/planets. Neither
has a comprehensive answer. Fuller understanding must come from
putting new factors into the equation – which Theseus does in his
speech.

     Chaucer's brilliant change to his source here is to take the sentiments
Boccaccio gives to Teseo (XI.2843–9), and with them to create a vivid
glimpse of a nice but platitudinous old man. Then, later, he gives
Theseus a much more profound speech, fully in keeping with his
seriousness in the tale. Egeus's trivial commonplaces thus highlight the
profundity of Theseus's view: yet they are not incompatible, merely
based on a different level of vision and knowledge.

1983   The emphasis on change is here crystallized. The structure of the
line is chiasmic, a *commutatio* where the second half reverses the
structure of the first. This admirably figures the cyclic change Egeus is
talking of. (cf. the similar chiasmic structure *deyed ... lyved ... lyved
... deyde* in lines 1985–8.)

1989–91   The familiar figure of the pilgrimage (scriptural in origin? cf.
Hebrews, XI.13f.) is not as simple as it seems. Where is the pilgrimage
leading? The best answer Egeus can give is that death ends woe – not
adequate to the seriousness of the issues raised in the Tale.

1995ff.   Leaving the issue suspended, as is done elsewhere, the Tale now
turns to the funeral rites for Arcite. The description is modelled on
Boccaccio, who was closely following Statius, *Thebaid*, VI, where the
funeral of Archemorus is described. Choosing to follow the source in
this way indicates that Chaucer was aiming to capture something of the
grandeur and dignity of the funerals described in Classical epic. There
are a number of features in this account which are specifically not
Christian and not contemporary.

Of good Arcite may best ymaked be,
And eek moost honurable in his degree.
And, at the laste, he took conclusioun
That theras first Arcite and Palamoun   2000
Hadden for love the bataille hem bitwene,
That in the selve grove, swoote and grene,
Theras he hadde his amorouse desires,
His compleinte, and for love his hote fyres,
He wolde make a fyr in which the office   2005
Funeral he myghte al acomplice.
And leet anoon comaunde to hakke and hewe
The okes olde, and leyen hem on a rewe
In colpons wel arrayed for to brenne.
His officers with swifte feet they renne,   2010
And ryde anoon at his comandement.
    And after this, Theseus hath ysent
After a beere, and it al overspradde
With clooth of gold, the richeste that he hadde.
And of the same suyte he cladde Arcite.   2015
Upon his handes [hadde he] gloves white,
Eek on his heed a coroune of laurer greene,
And in his hand a swerd, ful bright and keene.
He leyde hym, bare the visage, on the beere.
Ther with he weep that pitee was to heere.   2020
And for the peple sholde seen hym alle,
Whan it was day, he broghte hym to the halle,
That roreth of the cryyng and the soun.
    Tho cam this woful Theban Palamoun,
With flotry berd, and ruggy asshy heerys,   2025
In clothes blake, ydropped al with teerys;
And passyng othere of wepyng, Emelye,
The rufulleste of al the compaignye.
    Inasmuche as the servyce sholde be
The moore noble, and riche in his degree,   2030
Duc Theseus leet forth thre steedes brynge
That trapped were in steel, al gliterynge,
And covered with the armes of daun Arcite.
Upon thise steedes grete and white

2002 Some discrepancy here with line 1004; there, the theatre is said to be on the site of the battle in the woods. But poetically it feels right for the funeral to be there too, and the discrepancy is hardly noticed in reading or hearing. The brief amplification of the narrative (1999–2004) underlines the irony. The metaphorical fire (2004) becomes literal (2005).

2016 Gloves were given as presents to mourners at funerals until well into the eighteenth century. Arcite's white gloves are appropriate to an unmarried person.

2017 *a coroune of laurer greene*: the wreath of green laurel reminds us of the garland Arcite sought in the grove (649–53). Chaucer underlines this touch by the addition of the word *grene* to Boccaccio's crown; and he also gives Arcite a drawn sword to remind us of his battle with Palamon on that first occasion.

2019 *bare the visage*: with his face uncovered.

2024ff. Palamon's mourning is formal and ceremonial, as was decorous. This emphasizes its genuineness.

2028 *rufulleste*: most sorrowful.

2029 *servyce*: funeral service.

2030 *in his degree*: for (Arcite's) rank.

2032ff. It was usual at important funerals to have the dead man's warhorses in the procession, carrying his arms. The funeral hatchment (cf. 2033) is a relic of this. The custom lasted in state funerals until the nineteenth century.

Ther seten folk, of which oon baar his sheeld,   2035
Another his spere up on his hondes heeld;
The thridde bar with hym his bowe Turkeys.
Of brend gold was the caas, and eek the harneys;
And ryden forth a paas with sorweful cheere
Toward the grove, as ye shul after heere.   2040
   The nobleste of the Grekes that ther were
Upon hir shuldres carieden the beere,
With slakke paas, and eyen rede and wete,
Thurgh out the citee, by the maister strete,
That sprad was al with blak; and wonder hye   2045
Right of the same is the strete ywrye.
   Upon the right hand wente olde Egeus,
And on that oother syde, duc Theseus,
With vessels in hir hand of gold ful fyn,
Al ful of hony, melk, and blood, and wyn.   2050
Eek Palamon, with ful greet compaignye;
And after that cam woful Emelye,
With fyr in hande, as was that tyme the gyse,
To do the office of funeral servyse.
   Heigh labour, and ful greet apparaillynge,   2055
Was at the servyce and the fyr makynge,
That with his grene top the hevene raughte,
And twenty fadme of brede the armes straughte –
This is to seyn, the bowes were so brode.
   Of stree first ther was leyd many a lode.   2060

2037 *bowe Turkeys*: the Turkish bow was heavily curved (rather like the one Cupid is represented as holding), and was frequently made of horn with elaborate mountings in precious metal (cf. *brend gold*, 2038). Chaucer, writing in an age when the straight English yew bow had proved its superiority to all others, is clearly seeking a consciously antiquarian and exotic effect; such a bow could plausibly have been carried by a warrior of this remote period.

2038 *harneys*: chasing or decoration.

2039 *ryden forth a paas*: rode forth at walking pace.

2043 *With slakke paas*: at a slow speed.

2044ff. *maister strete*: i.e. the principal street of the town. The buildings along the route are hung with black cloth, and the same black cloth covers the road itself.

2049ff. The libations to be poured on the pyre and Emelye's carrying of the fire with which to light it echo funeral practices in Virgil and Homer. Chaucer, imagining this distant past, intends us in this passage to feel the grandeur, seriousness and strangeness of the proceeding and at the same time underlines the differences between past and current practice. This distance between the world of *The Knight's Tale* and the world for which it was written is important: see Introduction, p. 41.

2055 *labour*: hard work. *apparaillynge*: preparation.

2056ff. *fyr makinge ... straughte*: '... the making of the fire, whose green top reached up to the heavens, and the sides stretched some twenty fathoms (120 feet)'. Chaucer is referring to the size of the trees and of the unlit pyre.

But how the fyr was maked upon highte,
Ne eek the names how the trees highte,
As ook, fir, birch, asp, alder, holm, popler,
Wylow, elm, plane, assh, box, chestayn, lynde, laurer,
Mapul, thorn, beech, hasyl, ew, whippultree, 2065
How they were feld, shal nat been told for me.
Ne how the goddes ronnen up and doun,
Disherited of hir habitacioun,
In which they woneden in reste and pees –
Nymphes, fawnes and Amadrides – 2070
Ne how the beestes, and the briddes alle,
Fledden for fere whan the wode was falle,
Ne how the ground agast was of the light,
That was nat wont to seen the sonne bright;
Ne how the fyr was couched, first with stree, 2075
And than with drye st[o]kkes cloven a three,
And thanne with grene wode and spicerye,
And thanne with clooth of gold and with perrye,
And gerlandes hangynge with ful many a flour,
The mirre, thencens, with al so greet odour; 2080
Ne how Arcite lay among al this,
Ne what richesse aboute his body is;
Ne how that Emelye, as was the gyse,
Putte in the fyr of funeral servyse;
Ne how she swowned, whan men made the fyr, 2085
Ne what she spak, ne what was hir desir;
Ne what juels men in the fyr caste,
Whan that the fyr was greet and brente faste;
Ne how somme caste hir sheeld, and somme hir spere,
And of hir vestimentz, whiche that they were, 2090
And coppes ful of milk, and wyn, and blood,
Into the fyr, that brente as it were wood;
Ne how the Grekes, with an huge route,
Thries ryden al the fyr aboute
Upon the left hand, with a loud shoutynge, 2095
And thries with hir speres claterynge;
And thries how the ladyes gonne crye;
And how that lad was homward Emelye;
Ne how Arcite is brent to asshen colde;
Ne how that lychewake was yholde 2100

2061–2108   A huge *occupatio*. It certainly does abbreviate as it pretends, but is itself a *tour de force* of rhetorical virtuosity which courts admiration. It is structurally a balance to the *occupatio* with which the Tale begins (17ff.); both *occupationes* close with a return to Athens after labours.

The surprising thing is that the *occupatio* is probably the most efficient way of describing the subject forcefully. It is a masterpiece of syntactical and rhetorical control, using *repetitio*, *compar*, anacoluthon, asyndeton, all focussed round visual impressions. In this sentence of over forty lines, the audience is constantly required to draw on its own literary and practical experience, and though it is governed by negatives there is in fact a lot of *amplificatio* to indicate to us what to draw on. There is a serious attempt to catch something of the atmosphere of an epic pagan ceremony, and the audience is forced to contribute its own visions of the past by the reticence of the description.

2062ff.   Catalogues of trees are a common convention in medieval and Renaissance poetry (cf. *The Parliament of Fowls*, 176ff.). This is a pretty cursory one, shorn of the usual adjectives that link the trees to the activities and concerns of men.

2065   *whippultree*: probably dogwood, a smallish bush with red bark. It might also be the cornel tree.

2067   *the goddes*: the (Classical) beings supposed to live in the woods as spirits of the trees, etc.

2070   *fawnes*: creatures with the hind legs of a goat, the torso of a man and small horns, whose chief occupation is playing with nymphs. *Amadrides*: hamadryads, wood nymphs.

2075   *couched*: laid.

2078   *perrye*: jewellery.

2083–4   Emelye lights it because she is chief mourner.

2094ff.   The triple shout, clashing of arms, and riding round the pyre all derive from epic rituals and deliberately evoke a distant and heroic pagan past.

2100   *lychewake*: in some parts of the country it is still customary to sit up all night with the dead body.

Al thilke nyght, ne how the Grekes pleye
The wake pleyes, ne kepe I noght to seye;
Who wrastleth best, naked, with oille enoynt,
Ne who that baar hym best, in no disjoynt.
I wol nat tellen al how they goon   2105
Hoom til Atthenes, whan the pleye is doon.
But shortly to the poynt than wol I wende,
And maken of my longe tale an ende.

    By proces and by lengthe of certeyn yerys
Al stynted is the moornynge and the terys   2110
Of Grekes, by oon general assent.
Thanne semed me ther was a parlement
At Atthenes, upon a certeyn point and caas:
Among the whiche pointes yspoken was
To have with certyn contrees alliaunce,   2115
And have fully of Thebans obeisaunce.

    For which this noble Theseus anon
Leet senden after gentil Palamon,
Unwist of hym what was the cause, and why;
But in his blake clothes, sorwefully,   2120
He cam at his comandement in hye.
Tho sente Theseus for Emelye.

    Whan they were set, and hust was al the place,
And Theseus abiden hath a space
Er any word cam from his wise brest,   2125
His eyen sette he theras was his lest,
And with a sad visage he siked stille,
And after that, right thus he seyde his wille.

2102 *wake pleyes*: possibly a deliberate fusing of the funeral games of Classical times with the games and diversions that in Chaucer's day sometimes punctuated the *lychewake*.

2103 Another Classical echo (possibly from *Aeneid*, V).

2104 *bar hym best, in no disjoynt*: conducted himself best, without getting into difficulty.

2106 *pleye*: games.

2109 The fixed period of Court mourning, appropriate for one of Arcite's standing, was over.

2112 *Thanne semed me*: then it would appear ...

2114ff. It is very important to notice here that Palamon's marriage to Emelye is firmly linked to the achievement of political harmony and peace. The connection between human affective love and cosmic love is one Chaucer, like Gower, never allows to be forgotten (cf. *Troilus and Criseyde*, III.1–49).

2118 'Had noble Palamon sent for.'

2121 *in hye*: in haste.

2124ff. Note Theseus's dignity, and the clever way in which Chaucer signals to us that this speech is going to be important. It will be helpful to outline its structure:

2129–44 Proposition 1: the God who created and sustains all is loving, and in his loving providence has ordered different things with different tendencies justly and fairly, using time as one of his tools. Time is a part of his pattern.

2145–58 Proposition 2: the part is necessarily less perfect than the whole. Recognition of imperfection presupposes a perfection from which it must derive. The imperfect is subject to time, the perfect is not.

2159–76 Exemplification: four examples of mortality and mutability.

2177–82 Re-statement of first principle – God's absolute power and wisdom, using change to achieve an ultimate good.

2183–98 First (general) application: accept what cannot be changed anyway as part of the basic parameters of living. Death is not the only evil; a man dying at the height of fortune is lucky, for if he lives on he can only decline from that point – he has avoided pain and ignominy.

2199–208 Second (specific) application: one must no longer mourn Arcite, delivered from *foule prisoun*.

2209–16 Conclusion (general): accept, and act.

2217ff. Action: the political and emotional marriage that makes *parfit joye* out of *sorwes two*.

'The firste moevere of the cause above,
Whan he first made the faire cheyne of love, 2130
Greet was theffect, and heigh was his entente.
Wel wiste he why, and what therof he mente;
For with that faire cheyne of love he bond
The fyr, the eyr, the water, and the lond
In certeyn boundes, that they may nat flee. 2135
That same prince and that same moevere,' quod he,
'Hath stabliced in this wrecched world adoun
Certeine dayes and duracioun
To al that is engendred in this place,
Over the whiche day they may nat pace, 2140
Al mowe they yet tho dayes abregge.
Ther nedeth noon auctoritee to allegge,
For it is proved by experience;
But that me list declaren my sentence.
   'Thanne may men wel by this ordre discerne 2145
That thilke moevere stable is, and eterne.
Wel may men knowe, but it be a fool,
That every part diryveth from his hool.
For nature hath nat taken his bigynnyng
Of no partie or of cantel of a thyng, 2150
But of a thyng that parfit is, and stable,
Descendynge so, til it be corrumpable;
And therfore, for his wise purveiaunce,
He hath so wel biset his ordinaunce,
That speces of thynges and progressiouns 2155
Shullen enduren by successiouns,
And noght eterne [be,] with outen lye.
   'This maistow understonde and seen at eye.
Lo the ook, that hath so long a norisshynge
Fro the tyme that it first bigynneth sprynge, 2160
And hath so long a lyf, as ye may see,
Yet at the laste wasted is the tree,
Considereth eek, how that the harde stoon
Under oure feet, on which we trede and goon,
Yit wasteth it as it lyth by the weye. 2165
The brode ryver somtyme wexeth dreye;
The grete townes se we wane and wende.
Than ye se that al this thyng hath ende.

2129 *The firste moevere*: in medieval Scholastic philosophy, God is conceived of as both First Cause, on which all depends for its being, and as First Mover, who sets the circling spheres in motion.

2130 *cheyne of love*: the chain of love is a not infrequent metaphor for God's control of the four elements (2134), the basic units of matter (cf. *Roman de la Rose*, 16785–8, and the important discussion in A. Lovejoy, *The Great Chain of Being*. Cambridge, Mass., 1950).

2131–2 Note the memorable balance and alliteration in these two lines, with their emphasis on God's knowledge and purpose.

2139ff. Time is part of a loved creation, for it is an integral part of space; matter exists in space–time. Nothing may last longer than its nature allows. This begins to look behind Egeus's view.

2141 'Even though they can cut them short.'

2142–4 'No authority is needed to support this, for it is proved by experience; but it pleases me to declare my own view.'

2146 *stable*: impassive, not subject to change.

2151–2 The principle was accepted that the entire creation was ordered hierarchically; the lower down the hierarchy, the less perfect, and one reaches a point where corruptibility becomes part of the conditions of existence – e.g., only below the low sphere of the moon are things subject to change.

2153 *purveiaunce*: providence. See Appendix 3, p. 225.

2155 *speces*: a technical philosophical term – 'kinds'. *progressiouns*: the meaning is uncertain: possibly 'things that are not originals but proceed from an original'.

2156–7 'Following each other, and not each living eternally.'

2158 *at eye*: at a glance.

2159ff. The *exempla* lead up to the final crucial one – human life.

    'Of man and womman se we wel also,
That nedes, in oon of thise termes two,   2170
(That is to seyn, in youthe or elles age)
He moot be deed, the kyng as shal a page;
Som in his bed, som in the depe see,
Som in the large feeld, as ye may se.
Ther helpeth noght; al gooth that ilke weye.   2175
Thanne may I seyn that al this thyng moot deye.
    'What maketh this, but Juppiter the kyng?
That is prince and cause of alle thyng,
Convertyng al unto his propre welle
From which it is deryved, sooth to telle,   2180
And heer agayns no creature on lyve,
Of no degree, availleth for to stryve.
    'Thanne is it wisdom, as it thynketh me,
To maken vertu of necessitee,
And take it wel, that we may nat eschue;   2185
And nameliche that to us alle is due.
And who so gruccheth oght, he dooth folye,
And rebel is to hym that al may gye.
    'And certeinly a man hath moost honour
To dyen in his excellence and flour,   2190
Whan he is siker of his goode name;
Thanne hath he doon his freend ne hym no shame,
And gladder oghte his freend been of his deeth,
Whan with honour yolden is his breeth,
Than whan his name appalled is for age,   2195
For al forgeten is his vasselage.
Thanne is it best, as for a worthy fame,
To dyen whan he is best of name.
The contrarie of this is wilfulnesse.
    Why grucchen we? Why have we hevynesse   2200
That goode Arcite, of chivalrie flour,
Departed is with duetee and honour
Out of this foule prisoun of this lyf?
Why grucchen heere his cosyn and his wyf

2173–4 The preceding lines had reiterated, but in a vastly different context, Egeus's idea (cf. notes to 1580ff. and 1979ff.). The balanced *repetitio* of these two lines reminds us of the similar ideas in similar rhetorical pattern in the temples of the gods. *in the large feeld* could mean 'in the battlefield'.

2177 When Jupiter made a brief appearance above (1584) he is attempting (as is his astrological nature) a reconciliation. Theseus as a figure in Classical Antiquity can't with decorum ignore the ruler of Olympus in Classical times, but the sudden appearance of Jupiter is awkward to us. Chaucer knew well, of course, that Saturn had been deposed by Jupiter. Even the similarity between old Egeus (time) and Theseus (wisdom), and Saturn (time) and Jupiter (eternal wisdom), doesn't completely dispel the unease. It is, I think, clear that Chaucer is using two conceptions of Jupiter in the poem: first, as a planet, and second, as the only name he can allow Theseus to use for the First Mover.

2179 *his propre welle*: 'turning it back to its own source of being'.

2184ff. the *repetitiones* and *comparationes* have a strong cumulative force, emphasizing the necessary sequence of related conclusions.

2186 'And above all what is due to us all' – (death).

2189–98 A difficult view to hold, either by the victim or his friend, but sound sense, given that fortune is indeed fickle and unstable.

2195 *name*: reputation. *appalled*: faded.

2196 *his vasselage*: i.e. his loyal service as a servant of his lord.

2200 The repetition of *grucchen* links the special instance of Arcite back to general principles (2187). Notice the *comparatio* at 2204ff., below, echoing this sentence, and the word *grucchen*, for emphasis.

2203 The idea of life as a prison is not unfamiliar in ancient philosophy, but here the *foule prisoun* must remind us of that specific symbolic prison where Palamon and Arcite became enslaved by an affection for another created being, at the opening of the poem.

Of his welfare that loveth hem so weel?   2205
Kan he hem thank? Nay, god wot, never a deel,
That bothe his soule and eek hemself offende;
And yet they mowe hir lustes nat amende.
   'What may I conclude of this longe serye,
But, after wo, I rede us to be merye,   2210
And thanken Juppiter of al his grace?
And, er we departen from this place,
I rede we make, of sorwes two,
O parfit joye, lastynge evere mo.
And loketh now, wher moost sorwe is herinne,   2215
Ther wol I first amenden and bigynne.
Suster,'quod he, 'this is my ful assent,
With al thavys heer of my parlement,
That gentil Palamon, youre owene knyght,
That serveth yow with wille, herte and myght,   2220
And evere hath doon, syn ye first hym knewe,
That ye shul of youre grace upon hym rewe,
And taken hym for housbonde and for lord.
Lene me youre hond, for this is oure accord.
Lat se now of youre wommanly pitee.   2225
He is a kynges brother sone, pardee,
And, thogh he were a poure bachiler,
Syn he hath served yow so many a yeer,
And had for yow so greet adversitee,
It moste been considered, leveth me;   2230

2210–11   cf. Psalm 30.10.

2213–14   A powerful couple of lines. *Parfit* and *evere mo* must be qualified by the discussion of perfection and eternity earlier in the speech, and though we know that Palamon and Emelye are mortal, their symbolic marriage is an echo of a divine harmony. Also, the reference to *sorwes two*, literally the loss of a fiancé and the loss of a friend, must remind us of their astrological helpers and the sorrows they typify. I think the idea, which the Renaissance was later to explore, of the harmony to be found when strife (Mars) married concord (Venus), or the balance in the soul when chastity was reconciled to love, may be usefully brought to bear on this line. Moreover, the marriage echoes the marriage of the martial Theseus and the warlike Ypolyta at the beginning of the poem.

2225   'Let us see proof of your womanly compassion.'

2227   'Even if he were a mere bachelor', i.e. merely a probationary knight.

For gentil mercy oghte passen right.'
　　Thanne seyde he thus to Palamon the knyght:
'I trowe ther nedeth litel sermonyng
To make yow assente to this thyng.
Com neer, and taketh youre lady by the hond.' 2235
　　Bitwixen hem was maad anon the bond
That highte matrymoigne or mariage
By al the conseil and the baronage.
And thus with alle blisse and melodye
Hath Palamon ywedded Emelye, 2240
And God, that al this world hath wroght,
Sende hym his love, that hath it deere aboght.
　　For now is Palamon in alle wele,
Lyvynge in blisse, in richesse, and in hele;
And Emelye hym loveth so tendrely 2245
And he hir serveth so gentilly,
That was ther no word hem bitwene
Of jalousie, or any oother tene.
　　Thus endeth Palamon and Emelye;
And God save al this faire compaignye. Amen 2250

Here is ended the knyghtes tale

2231 The last line of the speech has great force. The link of love with
Christian thought has been mentioned above (p. 37), and no lover can
deserve his lady; she yields to him through her grace or mercy. But the
context of the remark extends its significance to something far wider
than just sexual love: a principle in the universe, which Theseus has
himself demonstrated in action – against the strict principle of his own
justice – on several occasions in the Tale. An important idea in Chaucer:
cf. *The Legend of Good Women*, F160ff.

2237 The pleonasm, *matrymoigne or mariage*, is for emphasis.

2239–40 An important symbol: cf. line 14.

2241–2 'May God, who created all this wide world, grant Palamon his
love (Emelye), which he has bought so dearly.' The smooth transition
begins the return to the contemporary world of the pilgrimage.

2248 The balanced line is a fit summary of their happiness. The bad
aspects of the gods are not present.

Appendix 1
Language, Pronunciation and Metre

In the England of Chaucer's day there were several varieties of spoken and written English. It is somewhat misleading to call these dialects, since the word 'dialect' now implies a provincial deviation from or variation on what can be recognized as a standard English. This was not the case in the fourteenth century: the English of the North-west Midland district, the East Midland, Kent, the North and other regions all grew from a different though often closely related mix of roots, depending on the history of settlement in those regions. Thus in the North, for example, there was (and still is) a much higher proportion of words deriving from Old Norse or Danish than in the South, where invasions by those peoples did not lead to extensive settlement. But, of course, Danish, Anglian, Saxon, Jutish and Norse are all related members of the Germanic group of languages, and the real differences should not blind us to the fact that there is a lot of etymological and grammatical common ground. At the beginning of the fourteenth century, moreover, no one of those separate kinds of speech could have been called a standard English, though East Midland was to become the basis of modern standard English and was already beginning to show signs of developing in that direction. That it was the language spoken in the economically (and politically) crucial area was one factor pushing it in this direction; another contributory element was the fact that the greatest poet of the period wrote in it and vastly extended its range. But even in the fifteenth century, the other forms of English were practised and were still vigorous.

Because his language eventually became modern English, readers will find far fewer words that are strange to them in Chaucer's writing than in the works of contemporary poets who wrote in other 'dialects', and they will also find fewer syntactical difficulties. Compared with its parent Anglo-Saxon (and even with some of the other contemporary 'dialects') its inflections are simple and easily mastered by intelligent reading. Problems will occur, however, in recognizing that an apparently familiar word in fact carries a different force from that of its modern descendant; in appreciating the beauty of Chaucer's verse, because of different sounds conveyed by familiar letters; and in recognizing when the sounding or not of a final 'e' affects the rhythmical balances of his lines. The solution to the first is quite simply the diligent use of the Glossary and Commentary, where I have attempted to anticipate the difficulties that may be encountered. This note mainly addresses itself, therefore, to the second and third problems.

Vocabulary

The basic vocabulary and syntactical structures Chaucer uses are those of the everyday speech of his own day and place. But a good number of his words, idioms and constructions are adopted or adapted from the Norman-French used in England until his own lifetime, or from the fashionable literary French. Sometimes, clearly, the adoption is conscious – where, for example, the French expression has no direct counterpart in English and is needed to convey an exact shade of meaning. Sometimes the French word exists alongside an English near-equivalent, and the difference is one of register rather than meaning. Not only did the French element add considerably to the flexibility and fluency of the language, it also gave English a range of near-synonyms and doublets that down to our own day allows it to be a uniquely expressive instrument.

Pronunciation

The conventions used in Middle English spelling are in general based on the sound the word actually made. Consonants, for example, are often to be given a sound value even where they are silent in a modern descendant of the word. Thus the initial 'k' or 'w' should be sounded in 'knight' and 'write': consonants in the middle of words (like 'l' in 'half') should be sounded, and 'gh' and 'ch', even where silent in modern English, should be given a sound like 'ch' in the modern German 'ich'. 'R' is rolled. The letters 'gg' can sound either like the double 'gg' in modern 'beggar', or as 'dg' in 'judge'. Generally the modern pronunciation, which does after all derive from the medieval, is a good guide. The syllables '-tion', '-cion' and '-cioun' are each treated as a double syllable, unlike '-tion' in modern 'situation', and a stress can fall on the '-o(u)n' part of the word. (This is metrically important, and this pronunciation continued until well into the seventeenth century.) The only silent consonants are the initial 'h' in words of French origin ('honour', 'harneys') and 'g' preceding 'n', again in words of French derivation – thus 'resigne' can rhyme with 'diffyne'.

Vowels can be short or long. Long vowels can be indicated in their spelling, either by doubling them, or, in the case of 'o', by adding 'w' or 'u'; or, as in modern English, by putting an 'e' after a single consonant ('cap', 'cape'). The values of vowels and diphthongs are best summarized in a table:

Spelling	Example	Sound
a, aa	name, caas	f<u>a</u>ther
a	man, that	m<u>a</u>n
e, ee	bete, sweete	l<u>a</u>te
e	tendre	p<u>e</u>t
e (final)	tendre, yonge	uh
i, y (long)	shires	rav<u>i</u>ne
i, y (short)	thyng	s<u>i</u>t
o, oo	(1) bote, goode	r<u>o</u>te
	(2) rood, holy	<u>oa</u>r
o	oft	c<u>o</u>t
ou, ow	(1) founde, fowles	r<u>oo</u>t
	(2) soule, growen	gr<u>ow</u>
u, o	but, yong	f<u>u</u>ll
u, ew	vertu, salewe	as French 'tu'
ai, ay, ei, ey	day, seith, wey	h<u>igh</u>
au, aw	cause	h<u>ouse</u>
eu, ew	Theseus, knew	f<u>ew</u>
oi, oy	joye	boy

There is also the problem of the final 'e'. In modern English, the final 'e' in words like 'take', 'cascade' and 'there' is silent; Middle English retained a good number of syllabic 'e's, either final (a relic of a syllable in the word's ancestor) or in the inflections '-es' or '-en'. Even in Chaucer's day some were beginning to be dropped. (This tendency to iron them out was to produce metrical chaos at the beginning of the sixteenth century.) It is clearly essential to the correct reading of the poetry that we get this right. In general, the final 'e' is pronounced except when it occurs before a vowel or silent 'h' not separated from it by a pause or caesura; in the latter case it elides (e.g. 'theffect' instead of 'the effect'). (The 'o' in 'to' can elide in the same way, so that 'to ask' will sound like 't'ask'.) Where final 'e' is pronounced, it is sounded as a neutral vowel (like 'u' in 'ugh!').

Inflections

The job of inflections, which indicate the relationship of words to each other, has largely been taken over by prepositions in modern English, and this process was already advanced by Chaucer's day. We still retain, however, a rudimentary inflexion in the genitive singular and in the plurals of most nouns – the addition of 's'. Middle English retains some less

215

familiar inflections, though none of them will cause serious difficulty in comprehension.

Nouns

In Anglo-Saxon, nouns are classed as strong or weak. Weak nouns had their genitive in '-an', while strong ones had it in '-(e)s'. Gradually all nouns came to take the strong form, but in Chaucer's English some weak nouns had dropped the weak genitive form and not yet taken up the strong: thus 'the sonne upriste' (the Anglo-Saxon form was 'sunnan', 'the rising of the sun'). Again, some Anglo-Saxon nouns had no inflection in the genitive singular, or nominative, or accusative plural – for example, 'faeder', 'brother', 'hors', 'thing' – and these can occur in this form in Chaucer. So 'fader soul' or 'lady grace' ('father's soul', lady's favour'), and 'thyng' is plural in line 2178.

Adjectives

In Anglo-Saxon, a weak form of the adjective followed the definite article, demonstrative adjective, and sometimes possessives. Occasionally indication of this weak form survives as a final 'e' – for instance in line 951. 'hoote'.

Pronouns

The nominative 'ye' is still distinct from accusative and dative 'yow'. The genitive of '(h)it' is 'his', just as it is of 'he'. In the plural, the nominative 'they' is followed by accusative 'hem' and genitive 'hire'.

Verbs

The infinitive ending '-an' of Anglo-Saxon verbs sometimes survives as '-en'. This ending can also indicate a plural in the present indicative.

Plural verbs in the past tense often close with '-en'. The plural imperative, now obsolete, still survives in '-eth' – for instance, 'herkneth' in line 985.

Past participles of strong verbs in Anglo-Saxon had the prefix 'ge-' as well as the ending '-en'. 'Ge-' survives in many cases as 'y-' but sometimes has been dropped, while '-en' survives as '-e' or '-en'. Verbs from French usually took the form of the past participle of weak verbs, adding '-ed'.

Adverbs

The most usual endings of adverbs are '-e', '-ly' and '-liche' (the last two come from adjectives with the adverbial ending). A few – 'ones', 'twyes', 'hennes', 'aboven' – have an ending that derives from the Anglo-Saxon '-es' and '-an'.

Metre

In *The Knight's Tale*, Chaucer uses a metrical form from which was to descend the popular decasyllabic rhyming couplet. He is the first to use in English anything approximating to the decasyllabic line of some of the fashionable French poetry that influenced him so strongly, and he clearly admired its weight and dignity. There are, however, important differences. Chaucer has developed a line which is extremely flexible, the basic scaffolding of which is a group of (usually five) stresses; he varies the position of the caesura for emphasis, regularly enjambes the lines, and often alters the expected stress pattern. Not all the lines have ten syllables: the first syllable, if unstressed, is sometimes omitted, and the resulting nine-syllable line then opens with a strong stress; or the line may include an extra light syllable, often at the end, or more commonly before the caesura.

The commonest pattern is a ten-syllable line, in what might later be described as iambics:

> Bŭt Mércy,|lădȳ bright,|thăt knówĕst wēle (line 1373).

Omission of the initial unstressed syllable gives us lines such as:

> Ō pĕrsóne ăllóne,|wĭth oŭtĕn mo (line 1867).

The order of stresses can be reversed:

> Fáire ĭn ă feeld,|ther ăs hĕ thóghte tŏ fíghte (line 126).

Stresses can be put together for emphasis:

> Ŏf brénd gōld wăs the cáas (line 2038).

Lines can have extra syllables:

> Víctóriĕ,|ănd ăs ă cónquĕrour tŏ lȳvĕn (line 58).

Here the extra weight of the line and the enjambement to its predecessor emphasizes the central idea of Theseus's power as the gift of Fortune.

There is little doubt that Chaucer had a very good ear, and a feeling for the way in which rhythms of the spoken language could counterpoint and highlight the rhythmical form of the line. His verse is very rarely unmusical or clumsy, and is itself the surest guide a modern reader can have – provided he takes the trouble to master the pronunciation and to read the poem aloud. Very rapidly the beat of the lines will set up a rhythmical norm in the ear, the rhyme words will mark off musical and metrical units, and the reader will then become aware of the varieties of pattern Chaucer uses; will realize, too, that they are part of his method of controlling how we accept and understand the poem. It will also become clear how a line, or a pair of lines, is frequently treated as a sense unit.

Appendix 2   The Gods

To us, it may well seem extraordinary for a Christian artist in a Christian society to talk of and use the gods of the Greeks and the Romans as if they had real vitality and power. The excuse that a poem or a painting is set in a Classical past and uses a Classical story might seem to have some force; but this could never explain the almost universal use, even in Christian contexts, of the Classical pantheon in medieval and Renaissance art.

It is an argument already deployed by Classical writers – for instance, Plato and Cicero – that the stories of the gods do not contain a literal but a mythic truth, a truth about the nature and operation of the world, hidden in a fable. The early Christians, of course, set their faces very firmly against any worship of the ancient gods, regarding it as blasphemous idolatry. But the belief that the wisdom of the one God lay behind everything in the universe necessarily meant that the errors of the pagans were based on some sort of truth, however misunderstood, and several of the early Church writers recognize that behind the persons of the Classical gods and the fables of their doings lay some useful intuitions about the universe whose maker was the God of Abraham, Isaac and Jacob. At the end of the fifth century, for example, Fulgentius of Ruspe in his *Mythologiae* systematically demonstrated that the myths of the pagans could be seen to contain allegorical glimpses of the truth revealed in Holy Scripture, and that the various gods of the Greeks and Romans were, in fact, the servants of the One and had been mistakenly worshipped as gods themselves. Fulgentius's work is an early representative of a type of discussion that recurs right down to the seventeenth century; two encyclopedias and interpretations of mythology that Chaucer could have used were Boccaccio's *De Genealogia Deorum* and Albericus's *De Deorum Imaginibus*. Even the unedifying stories of the gods' amours can be interpreted symbolically.

The basis for the reconciliation of pagan and Christian was provided by a conception of the physical universe which lasted substantially unchanged from Aristotle's adoption of the system of Eudoxus (c. 370 B.C.) to Copernicus's researches in the sixteenth century. Latin writers transmitted to the Middle ages a system of concentric spheres, one within the other, with the earth at the still centre. Seven of the spheres were occupied by the planets. This system seemed to have been still further strengthened by

219

the recovery, through Arabic texts, of the lost works of the revered Aristotle.

In Classical times the seven known planets (including the moon, and the sun, which, of course, we know not to be a planet) were given the names of the gods. Working out from the earth at the centre, the order ran: moon (Diana), Mercury, Venus, sun (Phoebus Apollo), Mars, Jupiter, Saturn. Each of these dominated his or her sphere. The eighth sphere contained the fixed stars (the constellations), and the whole was contained within the ninth sphere, the Primum Mobile, which was set in motion directly by God himself. The spheres each had their own motion, of varying speeds, and the planets moved independently of each other in orbits inclined at an angle to the celestial equator. As the spheres moved they made a harmonious music, which men in their imperfection were usually unable to hear – though Pericles in Shakespeare's play briefly hears it, and Lorenzo tells Jessica about it in *The Merchant of Venice* (V. i). On this model was grafted the mathematically brilliant (and very complex) system devised by Ptolemy in the second century A.D. to explain the apparent irregularities in the observed planetary motions.

It was discovered that the apparent annual orbit of the sun, the ecliptic, seemed to cut the plane of the celestial equator at an angle of 23.5 degrees. It also appeared, from the earth, that all the planets moved within a narrow belt, 12 degrees wide, along the ecliptic. This belt was divided into twelve equal areas, named after the constellations in the sphere of the fixed stars that seemed to lie within it – i.e. that formed a background to it. This was the Zodiac, so called because of the animal names of most of the signs (from the Greek *zoon*, 'animal'). These signs, each occupying 30 degrees, were further subdivided. Chaucer's *Equatory of the Planets* (if it is indeed his) and *Treatise on the Astrolabe*, and his use of astronomy in various parts of his work (for example, in *The Franklin's Tale*), show clearly that he was very familiar with this complex system.

But the astronomical system is not just a machine. It is alive. It is itself part of a loved Creation, and each part of it has its own purpose, its own autonomy, its own effects. The study of those effects is what we call astrology, and basically the astrologer's task was to ascertain from the balance of the seven great planets and their positions in the heavens the fundamental constraints on human life.

Hebrew writers had developed a theory of angels (the word means servant or messenger) who attended on God's commands and were his intermediaries in the running of Creation; seven great and powerful ones, the Sephiroth, were in later Jewish thought identified with the planets. Early medieval Christian and Moslem writers were much influenced by this idea, and it was quite usual for men to see the planets as the visible signs of the unseen intelligences (a sort of angel) who ruled their specific spheres. (There is a very powerful modern re-use of this idea in C. S. Lewis's science-fiction trilogy – especially at the climax of *That Hideous Strength*.) But, so the argument ran, the pagans in their darkness had mistaken the servants of God for gods themselves; Christians (and Moslems) knew better, and could thus use the Classical pantheon as it should be used, without impropriety or lack of decorum.

The planets, then, are angelic beings who serve the One and execute his purposes for him. In a poem set in a Classical past, like *The Knight's Tale*, they can decorously be 'gods' for the persons in the tale, but will mean something more for the poet and his audience. The planets execute God's purposes by 'influencing' the earth and all that is in it – that is, they literally pour down on it 'influence' (any inexplicable and sudden malady could thus be attributed to 'influenza') which controls some of the events on earth, and, according to one's horoscope, provides a baseline for one's temperament. What they do not do is determine man's response to his data – what he makes of it. They do not remove his free will to respond to a given set of circumstances. Health or disease, weather, trends in society, the occurrence of metals in the earth – all these, ultimately in the control of God, are administered and executed by his planetary agents. Thus by the fourteenth century a physician had to be conversant with astrology, the properties of the planets, the diseases they controlled, and the parts of the body and the times of the days and year over which they ruled (cf. *The Knight's Tale*, 1351ff.) before he could do anything for his patient. Chaucer makes this point in his description of the Doctor in the *General Prologue* (A 414–16); and Arcite's wound and its effects are precisely those influenced by the Saturn who sent a Fury to cause his horse to stumble and who knows that both Mars' and Venus's promises will be kept. Arcite and Palamon speak truer than they know when they refer to the gods; Arcite (230ff.) attributes his adversity to the god Saturn, while the medieval Christian would know that the planet Saturn controlled both the fall of cities (which put Arcite where he is) and imprisonment.

Bartholomaeus Anglicus, in his *De Proprietatibus Rerum* (translated by John of Trevisa in 1398), explains some of the myths surrounding the planets, and the way they are portrayed, by reference to their astrological natures. Saturn, the most malign of all (the Greater Infortune), is pictured as an old man, often linked with wintry cold. But Jupiter, the Greater Fortune, is the best of all planets and is often depicted as a summery figure – Jovial. His warmth and generosity, when in opposition (a term of astrology) to Saturn, cancel Saturn's malignity. Thus the poets' fable of

Jupiter deposing Saturn contains a hint of a scientific truth. Each planet, too, produced its specific type of personality and was patron of particular professions (cf. the description of the temples in *The Knight's Tale*).

Chaucer's use of the gods, then, is perfectly consistent with the best scientific understanding of his day. He cleverly uses them both as gods that his pagan characters could decorously have worshipped, and as agents whose operation a Christian poet or reader may properly seek to understand. Their conflict not only echoes similar literary conflicts among the gods about the fortunes of men – as, for example in the *Aeneid* – but also underlines the fact that the parameters of human fortune are provided by a complex balance of planetary forces who are themselves subject to constraints upon their actions. He is careful to emphasize (in lines 1580ff. and 1805–6) that, though they may *seem* all-powerful to Arcite and Palamon, their knowledge and power is in fact limited: beyond them lies a purpose they cannot modify. It is a neat point that it is Theseus, the mortal, who explicitly points to this loving purpose at the end of the poem.

Appendix 3   Boethius

Summary of *The Consolation of Philosophy*

The Consolation of Philosophy is cast in a dramatic mould: that is, though a work of academic philosophy, it proceeds through dialogue and an imagined situation exactly as do the dialogues of Plato. (The influence of Plato on Boethius is huge.) Its actual literary form is what is called Menippean satire – that is, an alternation of prose and verse passages. Boethius often uses the *metra* to express more memorably what has been discussed in the *prosae*; or explores in the *prosae* what has been powerfully hinted at in the excellent poetry of the *metra*.

Book I

Boethius (that is, the figure of himself the author projects into the poem) is introduced. He has been imprisoned unjustly* and is bewailing his lot, for he has fallen from great power and happiness. He seeks consolation from the Muses (the arts). A mysterious lady, Philosophy, appears to him, who sends the Muses away, and then upbraids him for having forgotten to reflect on the fount of all art and all knowledge. The cloud lifts somewhat from Boethius's mind. Philosophy tells him that as a lover of wisdom he ought to accept that he should stand firm in the convulsions of life and against the cruelty of tyrants. Boethius complains to her that he is suffering unjustly, having done only good yet now receiving evil in return. Why does an omnipotent God allow evil and the suffering of the innocent? (This last is the key question of the whole discussion, and Chaucer was clearly more interested in this section of Book I than any other.) Philosophy offers to bring Boethius back to what she calls his 'true country', where tyrants like Theodoric have no power, and to cure him by administering two remedies, a light one and a strong one.

As a preliminary she asks Boethius whether he believes the world is governed by chance or divine reason; Boethius replies that he believes in divine reason, but questions its justice. Philosophy offers to blow this 'little spark of belief' into a healing fire.

---

* The Ostrogothic emperor Theodoric imprisoned him, possibly to placate certain religious parties in the Eastern Empire.

Book II

The book's main concern is stoic philosophy. On the one hand, the tumult and emptiness of the world is shown through the allegory of Fortune; on the other, the necessity of fortitude and self-reliance for the wise man is demonstrated. Fortune's fickleness is part of her very nature, and if she were not so, she would not be Fortune. She defends herself: however much she gave men, they would never be satisfied, and she gives only of her own and has a perfect right to take back what is her own. Change is necessary to life itself. Philosophy, thus having shown that happiness cannot be dependent on fortune, states the first prerequisite of happiness: to possess peace of soul and to be master of oneself amid the changes of Fortune; to recognize true and false 'felicity'. She then discusses the specific gifts of Fortune – riches, fame, dignity are all useless. But Fortune, says Philosophy, can teach men through adversity and show them who their true friends are. At the end of the book Philosophy states that there is something far greater than Fortune and her gifts, and in the last metrum first speaks of the 'bond of love'.

Book III

The crucial and possibly the finest book of the whole work, Book III deals with the nature of the good and the desirable. After discussing Fortune and suggesting a stoic response in Book II, Philosophy now proceeds to her 'stronger remedy': a Platonic conception of the ideal good.

Boethius says that he has now learnt fortitude. Philosophy points out to him that suffering, and recognizing false felicity, allows one to perceive true good. All men, she says, strive for felicity, though they may be seriously mistaken or deceived about its nature and their methods. Riches, dignity, fame, power and glory do not bring happiness; nobility itself is not something that can be inherited, but comes from virtue and is the gift of God himself (cf. the ballade *Gentilesse*). Pleasures of the body bring only sorrow. Yet men constantly search in the wrong places for happiness. True felicity, which is what all ultimately seek, she shows to be in God, who is the sovereign good. Anything less than God is, by definition, imperfect and changeable, and therefore can never permanently satisfy the longings of men. The nature of the world is such that none can escape from the web of good, yet men do not realize where the real satisfaction of their desires must lie. Boethius is impressed by this argument (as well he might be); but now Philosophy raises again his own question (Book I, metrum 5): the question of evil. How can a good God permit evil?

Book IV

Book IV consists of a discussion of evil. Boethius asks why the evil flourish and the good suffer. Philosophy explains that the wicked never obtain the good they instinctively desire (cf. III, prose 11); they destroy what they seek, and become slaves to their mistaken desires. The wicked really deserve pity, because they can never achieve true felicity. Boethius agrees, but he is still unable to see why the good suffer. Philosophy now shows that providence works in the world through destiny and other agencies, and that there is a web of causality which men cannot escape. Everything is done for the best; and providence may train men through fortune to their fulfilment in the highest good. All is bound by God's chain of love, and ruled so that all turns ultimately to good. Many men have triumphed over fortune.

Book V

The central issues of this book concern providence and chance, and it gives an explanation of how men can possess free will while God, at the same time, uses destiny and providence.

Philosophy explains that fortune and chance are ruled over by the divine ordinance; God sees all things – past, present and future – in a single moment of eternal consciousness. Boethius argues against free will, but Philosophy shows him that, because there is and must be a huge difference between God's knowledge and man's, it may well be possible to reconcile God's prescience and man's free will. Man, despite having the principles of truth implanted in him, can only see imperfectly those things that are beyond his comprehension, just as the idea of a man held by an oyster would be ludicrous to man himself. God's eternal present, in which he sees all, no more constrains man than a spectator watching a chariot race controls the actions of the charioteer. But there are certain laws men cannot escape: death, for instance.

The Use of Boethius* in *The Knight's Tale*

Chaucer worked hard on his translation of Boethius. It was probably written around 1380 – about the same date, perhaps, as *The Knight's Tale* – but it can be taken as certain that Chaucer knew Boethius's work long

---

* The reader who wishes to look at Boethius properly would be well advised to use the excellent study of the man and his work by Henry Chadwick, *Boethius: the Consolations of Music, Logic, Theology and Philosophy* (Oxford, 1981).

before he began to translate it. When he did set to work, it is quite clear that he used not only a Latin text but also a French translation, which may well be by Jean de Meung, the second author of the *Roman de la Rose*. He went to enormous trouble to collate the two, and his own English version shows the marks of both texts. He also used concurrently the standard commentary on the *Consolation*, that of Nicholas Trivet, and incorporated some of its illustrative material in his own version. He also used it to clarify the sense where the Latin or the French version was obscure – Boethius's Latin, very beautiful and almost baroquely rhetorical as it is, is not the easiest Latin to read. In the English text he produced, Chaucer seems to have made a real effort to catch some of the dignity of the original, even to the extent of trying to imitate some of its alliterative patterns.

When we think about the use of the *Consolation* in *The Knight's Tale* (or in any poem), we must avoid the impression that every so often Chaucer ran across to his Boethius and grabbed a good bit that would just fit nicely at the point he had reached in his poem. Though some passages are so closely dependent to Boethius that the text must have been in front of him, what is striking is that Chaucer is particularly interested in what are structurally the turning-points in Boethius's argument. It is clear he was steeped in the book as a whole, and that he obviously read it with intelligence and seriousness. Its ideas became integral to his own thought.

The following is a list of the most important parallels in *The Knight's Tale* (there are others, of less significance);

The Knight's Tale	Consolation
lines 393–409	II, p5; III, p2
445–57	I, m5; IV, p1
805–15	IV, p6
2129–57; 2176–82 (Theseus's speech):	
The First Mover and the Chain:	III, m9; IV, m6
This Mover causes death, birth, progressions;	
Arcite's death is not to be bewailed:	IV, p6
Everything is derived from God:	III, p10
God converts all things back to good:	IV, m6

Chaucer's own translation is readily available in *The Works of Geoffrey Chaucer*, edited by F. N. Robinson (Oxford, 1957), and a straightforward translation of the *Consolation* is available as a Penguin Classic. The relationship of the *Consolation* to Chaucer's work has been exhaustively studied by B. L. Jefferson in *Chaucer and 'The Consolation of Philosophy' of Boethius* (1917), which was reissued in 1965 by Haskel House, Inc., New York. This book is an indispensable guide to further study.

Further Reading

This is not a bibliography of works consulted, nor is it an attempt to provide a full bibliography of recent scholarship for *The Knight's Tale*. It aims to suggest some help for readers who want to take further the issues raised above, and therefore I have included only books which are in print (and therefore readily available) at the time of going to press.

GENERAL

The Works of Geoffrey Chaucer, edited by F. N. Robinson (second edition, Oxford, 1957). The standard edition, with copious and helpful notes and references.

GENERAL BACKGROUND

D. S. Brewer, *Chaucer and his World* (London, 1978). A clear and readable account, well illustrated.

P. Boitani, *English Mediaeval Narrative* (Cambridge, 1982). Provides a clear and incisive account of the literary context.

J. A. Burrow, *Mediaeval Writers and Their Work* (Oxford, 1982). An admirable introductory book, which usefully places writers in their historical context.

E. R. Curtius, *European Literature and the Latin Middle Ages* (paperback edition, London, 1979). Quite indispensable for the serious student, though sometimes heavy going.

M. Keen, *Chivalry* (London, 1984). A thorough discussion of the concept in theory and practice.

R. P. Miller, *Chaucer, Sources and Backgrounds* (Oxford, 1978). An anthology of key texts, which provides a most convenient way of grasping what the actual materials of medieval poetry were like.

F. X. Newman (ed.), *The Meaning of Courtly Love* (New York, 1972). A useful (and occasionally witty) survey of the problems. It does not replace, but modifies, C. S. Lewis, *The Allegory of Love* (Oxford, 1936).

F. Oakley, *The Crucial Centuries* (London, 1979). A systematic look at the main cultural concerns of the period. A stimulating book, which does not shirk the issue of philosophical history. Useful for the way in which it emphasizes links with the Arabs.

B. O'Donoghue, *The Courtly Love Tradition* (Manchester, 1982). An invaluable anthology of key texts on this topic.

J.E. Stevens, *Mediaeval Romance* (Cambridge, 1973). A very helpful and lucid broad survey.

ICONOGRAPHY AND SYMBOL
G. Ferguson, *Sign and Symbol in Christian Art* (Oxford, 1961).

E. H. Gombrich, *Symbolic Images* (paperback edition, London, 1978); *Norm and Form* (third edition, London, 1978).

J. Hall, *Dictionary of Subjects and Symbols in Art* (London, 1974).

E. Mâle, *The Gothic Image* (English translation, London, 1961).

E. Panofsky, *Gothic Architecture and Scholasticism* (New York, 1957); *Meaning in the Visual Arts* (London, 1983).

CHAUCER
P. Boitani, *Chaucer and Boccaccio*, Medium Aevum Monographs, New Series VIII (Oxford, 1977). A fascinating and detailed acount of (among other things) exactly what Chaucer made of Boccaccio's *Teseida* (and occasionally of Boccaccio's own glosses on his poem) in *The Knight's Tale*. One can almost overhear the poet's mind working.

Helen Cooper, *The Structure of 'The Canterbury Tales'* (Oxford, 1983). A very persuasive discussion of the incomplete collection as an artistic project.

W. C. Curry, *Chaucer and the Mediaeval Sciences* (second edition, London, 1960).

E. T. Donaldson, *Speaking of Chaucer* (London, 1977). A collection of short essays and addresses, often penetrating as well as amusing.

D. R. Howard, *The Idea of the Canterbury Tales* (Berkeley, 1976). Stimulating.

B. L. Jefferson, *Chaucer and 'The Consolation of Philosophy' of Boethius* (New York, reprinted 1965). Very detailed survey of Chaucer's use of the book.

V. A. Kolve, *Chaucer and the Imagery of Narrative: the First Five Canterbury Tales* (London, 1984). A most original and stimulating discussion, exhaustively documented.

C. Wood, *Chaucer and the Country of the Stars: Poetic Uses of Astrological Imagery* (Princeton, 1970). Too detailed for the casual student, but a major contribution to this area of study.

Glossary

This glossary is not a concordance: it does not record every word in the Tale, but only those where a modern reader might find difficulty. Line references are given where the same word has two or more distinct meanings. Forms of verbs are indexed as they appear in the text. If not in the infinitive, this has been given in brackets where useful.

abiden await, wait
abo(u)ght (abyen) suffered (1445); paid for (2242)
abood delay
aboute in turn
abregge (abreggen) cut short
accused blamed
acorded (acorden) agreed
adoun below
afered afraid
affeccioun emotion
affermed decided
after according to
after oon alike
agast (was) afraid
ago gone
agoon gone by, passed over
agreved displeased, aggrieved
aiel grandfather
al even though
al and som the sum total of it
al be even if ...
al be it that although
al were they ... even though they
alauntz massively-built, tall hunting dogs
alighte (alighten) arrived
alle and some all together
allegge (alleggen) adduce, cite

amende (amenden) reform, make better
and if, and
anon forthwith
anoon at once
apayd contented, satisfied
appalled faded, weakened
apparaillynge preparation
appetites desires, pleasures
areste detention, confinement, imprisonment (452); rest (for lance) (1744)
aretted imputed, considered
arm greet as thick as an arm
armypotente powerful in arms
array condition (76); splendid display (1074)
arrayed arranged
ars metrik arithmetic
artow are you?
arwes arrows
as as if
as he that as a man who ...
as now for now
as out of that contree with regard to that country
ashamed humiliated, dishonoured
aslaked calmed

asp aspen poplar

assaut assault, storm

assayed tried out, experienced

asseged (*assegen*) besieged; possibly 'courted', using the love/warfare metaphor

assent opinion (2217); *by noon a.* on any terms (87)

asshen ashes

asshy sprinkled with ashes (a sign of mourning)

assureth (*assuren*) guarantees, makes secure

astert escape

astoned amazed

atones at the same time

atrede outwit

atrenne out-run

atthamaunt adamant

auter altar

avauntage advantage

aventure accident (216); *his a* what happens to him (328)

avow vow

avys opinion (1010); advice, consent, opinion (2219)

axe (*axen*) ask (489); ask for (881)

axing request

ay always

baar, beren carried (1961); *b. hym best* performed best (2104)

bad (*bidden*) told, ordered

balled bald

bane ruin, death (239); destroyer (823)

bar (*beren*) *him* conducted himself

bareyne barren

bataille battle

baudrye gaiety

been are

been aboute prepare

beere bier

beete kindle

bente slope

bibled bleeding

biforn before

bihote promise

biknowe (*Biknowen*) have (it) known

biraft (*bireven*) [his appetite for ...] is taken away (503)

biseken beseech

biset established, set up

bisynesse care, diligence

bitwixe between; from between (322)

bitynge sharp

biwreye reveal

bleynte (*blenchen*) started back

blythe happy

blyve quickly

boket bucket

boles bulls

boon bone

boone boon, request

borwe: lay to b. pledge

bouk trunk, body

brak (*breken*) broke out of

brawnes muscles

brede breadth

breme furiously

brend refined

brendest used to burn

brenne burn

brennyng, brennynge burning

brennyngly fierily

brente (*brennen*) burnt

breres bramble patch

brest burst

breste, to breste   smash, smashed
bresten   break
briddes   birds
broghte (bringen)   brought
brondes   logs
browding   embroidery
broyded   braided
burned   burnished
busk   bush
but   only
but if   unless
byde   wait, stay

caas   state of affairs, situation, eventuality, happening
cage   prison, cell, cage
cantel   portion
careful   full of cares
caroles   round-dances, with singing
caroyne   corpse, carrion
cas   chance (216); situation (553); quiver (1222)
caste   cast about (1314); considered (1996)
caste his eye aside   glanced to one side
cause, by the c.   because
caytif   wretched
caytyve   wretched, pitiful wretch
certes   to be sure, certainly
chaar   chariot
champartie   equality
charge: yevest litel c.   take little heed, care little about
charitee   act of kindness
charitee   (see 765n.); *seynte c.* holy charity
charmes   love potions (1069); spells, incantations (1854)
chasteyn   chestnut

chaunce   eventuality
cheere   countenance
chirkyng   groaning
chivalrye   chivalry (see Introduction, p. 27); band of knights
citole   cithara (instrument played by plucking the strings)
citryn   greenish yellow
cladde   clothed
clamour   crying
clariounes   clarions, bugles
clene   pure
clepe   call
clothered   clotted
cokkow   cuckoo
cole   coal
colers   collars
colpons   logs, bits, pieces
comaunde: leet c.   gave directions
communes   common people
compas: in maner of c.   in the fashion of a circle
compassing   putting it into action
compleyne (compleynen)   lament
compleynyng (compleynen)   lamenting
composicioun   agreement
comune: in c.   in general
conclusioun   decision
confus   perplexed, bewildered, confused
constellacioun   planetary conjunction at time of a man's birth
contek   strife
contrarie   opponent
contree   dominion
converting   returning
corrumpable   corruptible
corven   cut

233

cote armures surcoats with armorial charges

couched laid (2075); studded (1303)

counseil confidant (289); confidence (725); council (2238)

counseil: of my c. in my confidence

cours: han a c. pursue (with hunting hounds)

courser charger

covenant agreement

cracching scratching

cridestow: why c. why did you cry out?

crispe curly

croppe top of the tree

cry outcry

cry (cryen) cry out

cryden weep

crye: leet c. had it proclaimed

cryynge wailing

dampned condemned

darreyne decide a claim by battle (751); settle (773)

daweth dawns

deduyt pleasure

deedly deathly pale (55); *d. on to see* deathly pale to look at (224)

degree row of seats (1032); *in this d.* in this position (983); rank (*Knight's Portrait*, 13)

demeth (demen) judge

depeynted depicted

dere trouble, harm

despense expense

despit malice (83); *in d.* in contempt (89)

despitous scornful (738); contemptuous, hard-boiled (919)

despitously angrily

destreyneth (distreynen) afflicts, grasps

devoir duty

devyse (devysen) tell, describe (136); plan, imagine (396); tell him to do, order (567); plan, decide (932); ordain, direct (986); decide (1519); imagine (1284)

devysioun company; those under the influence of Mars

devysynge fashions

deys dais

diden bisynesse and cure took great care and pains

dight prepared, dressed (183); provided (772)

digne worthy of honour

disconfiture defeat

disconfitynge defeat

disconfort grief, annoyance

disconforten grieve

disherited evicted, disinherited

disjoynt: in no d. without difficulties

dispence expense

disposicioun position of planet (229); at your disposal (1506)

distreyne afflict, grasp

divisioun distinction

divynis theologians

don make had had made

don wroght had had made

dongeoun keep

doon his might do all in his power

doon mescheef harmed, injured

dooth hem ... to reste   makes them take a rest

doute   doubt

dowves   doves

drede   fear

dreedful   fearful

drenchyng   drowning

dresse   drawn up, formed up

drugge (druggen) and drawe (drawen)   fetch and carry

duetee   reverence

duracioun   duration

dure   last

dusked   dimmed

dyapred   having patterns worked on it

dys   dice

dyvynynge   guessing, forecasting the result

echon   every one

eek   also

emforth my myght   as far as in me lies

emprise   undertaking

encens   incens

encombred   burdened with

encrees   increase

ende   outcome, result

endelong   lengthways

endite   describe

engendred   produced, born

enhauncen   promote, upgrade

enhorten   hearten

enoynt   anointed

ensaumples   examples

entente   intention

envye: have e.   resent

er   before

ere (eren)   plough

eschue   avoid, reject

espye (espyen), koude e.   was able to find out

estaat   condition of life, rank

estres   inner rooms

eterne   eternal

evene   steadily; *bere hym e.* (665) conduct himself in a balanced way; fair, unbiased (1006)

everich   each

everichon   every one

everydel   completely

ew   yew

eyleth (eylen)   ails

fader   father

fadme   fathom (6 feet)

faille   fall silent, fail

falle   happen (894); felled (2072)

falow   grey

fare (faren)   travel (537); go on, proceed, get on (403, 407, 1577); gone (1578)

fare   goings-on

faste ther bisyde   close by

fayn   happy, glad

fel   fierce, cruel

felawe   companion, member of the company (32); friends (334); partner, sharer (766); opponent (1690)

felicitee   happiness, blessedness

felle   cruel

ferde (faren)   went on

ferden (faren)   behaved, acted

ferforthly   completely

ferre   further

feste   festivities

fet (fecchen)   fetched

figure picture, possibly a horoscope diagram

fil (fallen) happened (176); fell (245)

fil in office got a job

fille: if ther f. if there happened to be ...

fillen fell

fledden (fleen) fled

fleen run away from, escape

fleete swim, float

fletyng swimming, floating

flikerynge fluttering

floryn a fairly high-value coin (originally issued in Florence)

flotry dishevelled, disordered

flour flower

foom foam

for because (1226); despite (1887); so that (2021)

fordo (fordon) destroyed

forpyned wasted away

forthren support, help

forward agreement

foryeve forgive

fother load

foundred stumbled

fowel bird

foyne let him thrust

foynen thrust (796); *foyneth* thrusts (1757)

fraknes freckles

fredom bountifulness, generosity, nobleness

freten devour

fulfild brimful of

fulfille (fulfillen) satisfy

fynde provide

gan, gonne (ginnen) begin (frequently an auxiliary, often indicating past tense)

game match (1250); an enjoyable thing (1428)

gastly frightful

gaude verdant, bright

gayneth (gaynen) helps, avails (318); *g. none* obstacles no obstacles avail or get in the way

gentil, gentilesse nobility

gere equipment (158); behaviour, (possibly) clothing (514)

gerful changeable

grey changeable, fickle

gesse (gessen) suppose, guess

giltelees guiltlessly, without having done anything to deserve it

gladen cheer up

gladere giver of happiness

glede firebrand, burning coal

gon sithen many yeres over many a long year

gooldes marigolds

goost spirit

grace favour, mercy (262, 734); luck (387)

graunt will, grant

gree excellence

grene greenery (654); green

gretter greater

greveth (greven) disturbs, vexes

grisly horrible

groynying discontent, grumbling

gruccheth (grucchen) complains, murmurs against

gruf flat on their faces

gye guide, rule
gyle trickery
gypoun surcoat
gyse fashion, manner (135, 350, 1681; *in many a g.* in many ways (395); *at his owene g.* having things his own way (931)

hakke cut down
han have
happed happened
hardy brave, bold (24, 1728); rash (853)
hardynesse daring
harnays, harneys armour
haryed dragged forcibly
hastily quickly
haubergeoun harberk
hauberke mail-shirt
heed resistance
heed, upon his h. on pain of his head
heelp (*helpen*) helped
heep heap
heer agayns against this
heer biforn before this
heete (*hoten*) promise
heigh great (2055); serious, noble (2131)
held kept to
helden ... with favoured, backed
hele well-being
helmes helmets
helpeth: ther h. noght there is no help for it
hem them
hent caught
hente (*henten*) seized hold of (46); lifted, caught (99); grabbed (442); took, captured (1780)

heren hear
heres hair
herkne hear, listen to
herknen listen, overhear
herkneth listen (imperative)
herte spoon hollow in sternum
heste command
hewe colour, complexion
hewes colouring materials
hidouse hideous
hight (*hoten*) promised (1614)
highte (*hoten*) was called
highte: on h. aloud
hir liste it pleased her
hir their
honestly honourably
holde (*holden*) considered as
holm holm oak
holwe sunken, hollow
honge hang up
hoolly wholly
hoost army, host
hostelryes lodgings
hunte hunter
hunten hunt
hurtleth knocks
hust hushed, silent
hye haste
hye: wonder h. to a great height
hye weye highway
hyndre (*hyndren*) get in each other's way

ire anger

jalous jealous
japed (*japen*) tricked, made a fool of
journee day's journey
joynant, evene j. closely adjacent

juels jewels
juge judge
justen joust
juwise sentence, judgement

kan (konnen) know
keene sharp
keep: as he took k. so he noticed
kembed combed
kempe shaggy
kepe (kepen) care
kepe noght take no account of
kerver sculptor, carver
knarry gnarled
knaves servingmen
knowe recognize
koude ... espye was soon able to find out ...
kynrede kindred

laas net, snare
lacerte muscle
lad led away
ladde led
large: at his l. at liberty
lasse and moore those of both higher and lower rank
launde lawn, glade, clearing
laurer laurel
leep leapt
leet (leten) released
leet forth ... brynge arranged to have brought forth
leet senden had sent for
lene (lenen) give
lene lean
lesinges lies
leste: as hym l. as it pleased him
lesyng losing
lete (leten) leave

letten control, hinder, get in the way of
leve permission
leeve dear, beloved
leveth believe (imperative)
leyde (leyen) lay
leyser leisure
lief willing
liggen lie
liggynge (liggen) lying
lightly joyfully
ligne line of descent
lind lime
listes tilting-ground; *for l.* for a tournament
lite little
liketh: if that yow l. if it pleases you
list: me l. pleases me
lode load
lodesterre pole star
longeth appertains to
looth unwilling
lowe: bar him l. conducted himself discreetly, kept a low profile
lust pleasure, enjoyment (392); joy, pleasure, desire (1074); desire (1620); *as hir l.* according to her pleasure (1092)
lustes desires
lusty joyful
lychewake watch over a dead body
lyfly to the life
lymes limbs
lynage lineage, race
lyth to wedde is at stake, is pledged
lyve: on l. alive

maat sorrowful, cast down

maistow one can see

make opposite number

manasynge threatening

maner kind of

manly courageously

mantelet mantle

manye mania

mapul maple

maugree in spite of (749); *m. his heed* in spite of his resistance (311, 1760)

mayntene stand by, uphold (920); *m. his degree* support the obligations of his rank (583)

maystow might one

me list it pleases me

meeste and leste the greatest and the least (in rank)

meeth mead

memorie: yet in m. conscious

mencioun: maken m. to be talking about

meschaunce bad luck

mescheef: doon m. harmed, injured

meschief: at m. at a disadvantage

mete suitable (773); meat (1042)

meynee household

ministre general chief executor

mirre myrrh

mo more

moerdre murder

mone complaint, lament

moore: lasse and m. those of both higher and lower rank

moot must

mooste greatest

mordryng murdering

more: the m. part for the greater part

morwe morning

morweninge morning

mosel muzzle

mountaunce value

mowe may

muchel great, much, a lot

murye merry, happy

mysbōden ill-treated

myshappe: if that me m. if it goes badly for me

myster lot, deal, situation

myte mite, small coin

na moore no more

nakers kettle-drums

name reputation

nam (ne + am) I am not; *n. but* I am simply ...

namoore no more

nas (ne + was) was not

nath (ne + hath) has not

navele navel

ne ... ne ... neither ... nor

nedes: moot n. must needs, can't avoid

nedes cost of necessity

nedeth (impersonal verb) it is necessary

neer nearer

nere: if it n. (ne + were) if it were not

nere it were it not ...

nexte nearest

nis is not

nolde (ne + willen) did not want to, would not

nones: for the n. particularly (often a tag or metrical make-weight)

noone none

noot (ne + wot) knows not

norisshynge period of growing up

observaunce rite (187); observance of laws, obedience (458); due rites and ceremonies (642)

office rite, duty

ones once

ook cerial holm-oak

oon: in o. without ceasing

oratorie chapel, oratory

ordeyned fixed, allotted

ordinaunce in due order of rank and precedence

orisoun prayer

othes oaths

outhees alarm

outher either

outrage violence

overal everywhere

overthwart crossways

paas: a paas at walking pace

pace go (744); stretch, go beyond (2140)

palfreys riding-horses

pan: by my p. by my head (skull)

par amour as a lover

paramentz robes worn over armour

parfit perfect

parlement decree (448); parliament (2112)

part share

parte party

partie partial, biased (1799); part (2150)

party mixed

passant name reputation above all others

passyng (passen) surpassing

payen heathen, pagan

perrye jewellery

perturben disturb

peyne torture (275); torment (439); punishment (461); *up p.* on pain of (849)

pighte pitched

pikepurs pickpocket

pilours plunderers

pipen whistle

pitous full of pity, compassion (95); pitiful (97, 1520)

plat plain

plesaunce: in thy p. to please you (1551); pleasure (1627)

pley jest

pleye funeral games

pleye (pleyen) amuse himself

pleyn full, fully

pleynly plainly, openly, fully

point part

polax pole-axe

pomel top of head

pose (posen) suggest for the sake of argument

positif (see 309n.)

pourely in humble fashion

poynt end, conclusion, aim

preeseth throngs

prescience foreknowledge

preved (preven) proved

preye (preyen) beseech

priketh (priken) stirs, stimulates

prikyng riding about, darting about

prively secretly

privetee private affairs

proces: by p. in the course of time

progressiouns actions proceeding from a source

propre own

prykyng darting
pryme 9 a.m., or early
prys reputation, renown, prize
pryvee secret
pryvely secretly
pure very
purtreyour painter
purveiaunce providence
pyne pain, suffering (466);
  torture (888)

qualm disease
queynt extinguish, go out
queynte odd, strange
quike alive
quitly completely, at liberty
quook shook, quivered
quyte (*quyten*) ransom

rage blast of wind (1127); fury
  (1153)
ransake (*ransaken*) search
rasour razor
raughte (*rechen*) reached
raunsoun ransom
recche care
reccheth cares
recorde confirm, endorse
rede (*reden*) advise
redoutynge reverence
reed help for it
regne kingdom, state (8, 19, 780);
  dominion (766)
rehersynge going over the terms
  of the agreement
rekke care
rekne relate, itemize
remedye way out
remenant remainder, rest
rending tearing
renges ranks

renoun reputation
rente (*renden*) tore down
rente income
replicacioun right of reply
rescus rescue
rese shake
respit delay
rewe take pity on, have mercy on
  (1005, 1375); row (2009)
reynes reins
richesse riches
right anoon forthwith,
  straightaway
right as just as
righte direct
rightes: at alle r. in every respect
rightful righteous
rit (*riden*) rides
romed (*romen*) wander about
roreth resounds, echoes with
route company
routhe pitiful, a pity
rowketh (*rowken*) huddles
rufulleste most sorrowful
ruggy rough
rynges ringlets
ryte religious rituals (1044);
  ceremonial washing (1426)

sad serious, grave
sadly firmly, seriously, gravely
salueth (*saluen*) greets
saluynge greeting
saugh (*seen*) saw
save medicine (see 1855n.)
savyng except
sawe saying (305); what he said
  (668)
scape (*scapen*) escape
scriptures writings, books
seen see

sege   siege

seigh (seen)   saw

selde   seldom

selve   very same, same

sepulture   burial place

servage   slavery

servant   servant in love, lover

servyse   love-service

serye   argument

set (sitten)   sitting

seten (sitten)   sat

seuretee   formal pledge, guarantee

seyn   seen

shaft   arrow shaft

shaltow   shall you

shamfast   modest

shape: is me s.   it is destined that I ...

shape (shapen)   fixed, planned

shapen   destined, determined (534, 608, 708); ensure, make it certain (1683)

shene   beautiful

shepne   shippon, cowshed

shere   scissors

shet   shut

shode   temple (of head)

shot   missile

shrede: to s.   hack to pieces

shrighte (shryken)   shrieked

shul   shall

shuldres   shoulders

siker   sure, secure

sikerly   certainly

sithen that   since

slakke   slow

slawe   slain

sleen   slay

sleere   slayer

sleeth (sleen)   slays, kills

sleighly   discreetly

sleighte   tricks, cunning

slider   slippery

slogardye   laziness, sluggardliness

slough (sleen)   slew

slow   slew

smerte   pain

smoot (smiten)   struck

socour   help

softe   gently (163); quietly, under his breath (915)

solempnitee   due ceremony

sone   soon

soothly   truly

soper   supper

spak (speken)   spoke

sparre   beam

sparth   battle-axe

speces   species

special: in s.   clearly, distinctly

spedde (speden)   hastened

spore   spur

sprad (spreden)   spread with

spronge (springen)   got about

sprynge   break of day

sprynge (spryngen)   grow

spycerye   spices

stabliced   established

starf (sterven)   died

startlynge   leaping, mettlesome

staves   staffs

stedes   chargers

steer   bullock

stent (stinten)   stopped

stente   bring to an end

stenten   stop, cease

sterne   grim (1583); flowing strongly (1752)

stert: at a s.   at one bound

sterte   leap up (186); *s. hym up*

burst out of (721); started, quivered (904)

sterte (*sterten*) sprang off

sterve (*sterven*) die

stevene sound, voice (1704); *at unset s.* unexpectedly (666)

stille quietly

stith anvil

stok royal blood royal

stoke stab

stokkes stumps, block of wood

stonden so be the case

stonden in hir grace win her favour, be accepted by her (as suitor)

stongen stung

stounde hour, time

stoute strong

straunge foreign

stree straw

streighte direct

strepe (*strepen*) strip, despoil

strouf (*striven*) vied with

stryve struggle

stubbes stumps

studie fit of musing

stynt cease, stop

stynte stopped

stynte (*stynten*) leave, cease talking of

stynteth (imperative) stop, be quiet

subtil fine (196, 1172); clever (191)

suffisaunt sufficient

suffren allow

sustene support

suster sister

sustren sisters

suyte: of the same s. of the same material or cloth

swelte (*swelten*) was overcome by emotion

swich such

swoote sweet

swowned (*swownen*) fainted, swooned

swowninge swooning, fainting

syk sick

syke (*syken*) sigh

sykes sighs

syn since

sythe: ofte s. very often, many times

taak (*taken*) *at herte* consider favourably

take captured

taken hym so ner accepted him (as servant) much nearer (to himself)

tare seed of vetch (i.e. thing of very little weight or value, jot)

targe small shield

tarien forth spend

tas heap

telleth (*tellen*) tell (plural imperative)

tene annoyance

terme duration

testeres helmets

that what

ther where

thider thither

thikke herd with a good head of hair

thilke that

thirled pierced

tho then

thoghte (*thinken*) thought, intended

thoughte: hym t. it seemed to him

thral in bondage

threste thrusts, forces his way

thridde third
thryes thrice
thurgh through
thurghfare thoroughfare, highway
thurghgirt pierced
to toe
tobrosten shattered
togydre together
tonne greet as big as a cask
tour tower
touret turret
tourneyinge tournament
transfigure manifest yourself
transmutacioun the changes and chances of this mortal life
trapped accoutred, caparisoned
trappures trappings or caparisons of horses
trays traces
tretee agreement, treaty
trompe trumpet
tronchoun broken shaft of spear
trone throne
trowe believe
trowed (*trowen*) believed
tweye and tweye in pairs
twynes thread strand of twine
tyrannye lack of the proper kingly qualities; tyrannousness

unkonnyng ignorant
unkouth strange
unwist of him it being unknown to him …
unyolden unyielded
up haf lifted
up peyne of on pain of
up yaf gave up
upsterte (*upsterten*) flared up
usedest (*usen*) enjoyed

vasselage prowess, exploits as a knight
venerye the chase
verray true
vertu power
vestimentz clothes, robes
veze rush of wind
vileynye something shameful, disgraceful, wrong
visage face

waiteth (*waiten*) looks for an opportunity
wan gloomy
wan (*winnen*) won
wane (*wanen*) decline
wanhope despair
wantyng: for w. of because she could not have her way
wanye wane
war: was w. noticed, was aware of
waste devastated
wawes waves
wayke weak
waymentynge lamenting
wedde: lyth to w. is at stake, is pledged
wede clothing
wele success (37); *in hir w.* at their happiest (1815)
welle source, beginning, origin, well
wende (*wenden*) thought
wenden go
wene think, suppose
wenen think
wepne weapon
were defend (1692)
were (*weren*) wore
werre attack

werreye (werreyen) make an
attack on, make war on
wessh washed
wex (waxen) grew
wexeth (waxen) becomes
wey, weye way, route
weye: atte leeste w. at least
weyeth weighs
weylaway alas
wheither whichever (of two)
whelp cub
wher that hym liste wherever it
pleased him
whilom formerly, once upon a
time
whippultree dogwood; possibly
cornel
widwe widow
wight person, man
wighte weight
wikke malign, wicked
wille desire, will
wilnen desire
wilneth (wilnen) desires
wirche work
wise: double w. twofold
wiste (witen) knew
witen to know
withseyn deny
wo lament
wodebynde honeysuckle
wol (wilnen) desired, wished,
wanted
woldestow (see 1977n.)
wolt noght do not wish
woltow will you?
wonder extremely (796);
wondrous (1215)
wone custom
woneden (wonen) had dwelt
wonne (winnen) conquered, won

wood madly angry (471);
distracted (598); mad,
maddened (720)
woodly madly
woost (witen) know
woot (witen) knows
worshipful honourable
wostow (witen) do you know?
wot (witen) knows
wrecche unfortunate, wretched,
miserable
wreke (wreken) avenge
wroght (werchen) fashioned
wrothe angry

yaf gave
ybete embroidered (121);
stamped (i.e. with gold tooling)
(1304)
ybounden pledged, bound
ybrent (brennen) burnt
yburyed buried
yclenched riveted, nailed,
studded
ycleped (clepen) called, named
ycorve cut
ydon: hath of his helm y. took off
his helmet (1818)
ydrawe dragged together
ydropped sprinkled
yelle (yellen) cried, shouted
yelpe boast
yerde yard
yeve (yiven) give
yeve (yeven) give, given
yfetered fettered
yholde held as, considered as
yif give
yiftes gifts
ylaft left
yliche alike

ymeynd mixed, mingled

ynough enough

yolden yielded, surrendered

yow you

yowling howling

yraft snatched

yronne (*rennen*) was arranged (1307)

yronnen rushed

yserved (*serven*) dealt with

yspreynd sprinkled

ystiked pierced, thrust in

ystorve dead

yturned cast

yvele ill

ywrye covered

Glossary of Rhetorical Terms

adnominatio – repetition of a word root with different endings; when similar-sounding words refer to different things (cf. pun).

amplificatio – elaborating an idea by saying it several times in different ways.

anacoluthon – passing to a new grammatical construction before the first is complete.

asyndeton – words heaped up without conjunction.

chiasmus – two words, phrases or syntactical units repeated in reversed order.

commutatio – reversal of the order of the first half of the sentence in the second – 'eat to live, not live to eat'. Often used with *contentio*; cf. *chiasmus*.

compar – rhythmical, syllabic and syntactical balance of halves of lines or of sentences against each other.

complexio – a sequence of clauses or sentences where the same word or words begin them and similar words end them.

conduplicatio – emphatic repetition of a word or phrase under stress of emotion or to create feeling in the audience.

contentio – strong, often patterned contrast.

conversio – ending clauses with the same word.

correctio – cancelling what has just been said in description and replacing it with something more suitable.

descriptio – systematic enumeration of the appearance or qualities of a person or thing.

diminutio – the modesty convention; winning the audience's sympathy, or whatever, by disclaiming competence or excellence.

diversio – a short turning aside from the main line of the narrative.

effictio – the expression in words of someone's bodily appearance.

exclamatio – apostrophe; elaborate exclamatory address, sudden stopping of discourse to address some person or thing, present or absent, personified or not.

exemplum – a short story or reference used to illustrate a point.

expolitio – repetition under a different guise; speaking of the same thing but not in the same way.

frequentatio – drawing together for climactic purposes of all the different ideas in the passage.

gradatio – anadiplosis; beginning the succeeding clause or line with the last word of the previous one.

hypallage – transferred epithet.

interpretatio – repeating an idea by using not the same word but a near-synonym: 'parent' replacing 'father', for example.

occupatio – a refusal to describe or go into details, for whatever reason.

parataxis – literally 'laying side by side'; the use of a series of coordinate clauses rather than subordinating one to the other (which is hypotaxis).

parison – similar structure in a sequence of clauses.

ratiocinatio – elaborate way of structuring the argument in speech or soliloquy by arguing with oneself, posing objections and ideas and meeting them.

repetitio – beginning clauses or lines with the same word.

sententia – a proverb or quotation or citation of another author to support argument.

significacio – the 'deep' or hidden meaning of a symbol, thing, or story.

similiter cadens – balancing of words with similar endings at ends of phrases.

traductio – repetition of key words in different places for emphasis.

transitio – when one shows briefly what one has said, and outlines what one is going on to next.

zeugma – making a single word refer to two or more in the sentence, e.g. 'She came in a pink carriage and a flood of tears'.

Further Reading

Pseudo-Cicero, *Rhetorica ad Herennium* book IV.
Aristotle, *Rhetoric* III.
Geoffroi de Vinsauf, *Poetria Nova*, trans. Margaret F. Nims.

Index